RUNNING
BLIND

ROB MATTHEWS
RUNNING BLIND

HarperCollins*Publishers*

National Library of New Zealand Cataloguing-in-Publication Data

Matthews, Rob, 1961-
Running blind : the inspiring story of one man's
journey into the night / Rob Matthews.
ISBN 978-1-86950-801-2
1. Matthews, Rob, 1961- 2. Blind athletes—Biography.
3. Long-distance runners—Biography. I. Title.
796.42092—dc 22

First published 2009
Reprinted 2009
HarperCollins*Publishers (New Zealand) Limited*
PO Box 1, Shortland Street, Auckland 1140

ISBN 978 1 86950 801 2

Cover design by Nada Backovic Designs
Cover image by Filo/Stockphoto.com
Typesetting by Springfield West

Printed by Griffin Press, Australia

70gsm Classic used by HarperCollinsPublishers is a natural, recyclable product
made from wood grown in sustainable forests. The manufacturing processes
conform to the environmental regulations in the country of origin, Finland.

Dedication

To my beautiful son, Thomas Aubrey Bruce Matthews.
You've made such a profound impact on my life.
Watching you grow and develop is a constant
source of wonder and joy to me.
I could never have imagined how incredibly
rewarding being your dad would be.
I hope you enjoy reading your dad's story, my boy.

Contents

Acknowledgements

I'm so grateful to those who have played a part in my story and helped shape my life.

To Mum and Dad for providing a happy and supportive home, together with Ange and Sue, my loving sisters, who have all given me some of my inspiration.

To Cara for introducing me to her daughter and to Kath for those precious 12 years we were together and making me so happy for the nine years we were married.

To Sarah, my beautiful wife, for coming into my life, my soulmate who I met at the Soul Bar at the Viaduct in Auckland. Thank you for being such a fantastic wife and mother of our son and still having the time to help edit *Running Blind*.

To my New Zealand family, Bruce and Sharron, Veronica and William, Damian and Tessa, thank you for making me feel so loved and for your unconditional support.

To Robert Tighe, freelance journalist, thank you for giving me the vision to write more fluently and for the time you spent editing much of my book.

To my 115 guide runners, many of whom became close friends and some who are like brothers to me, who went that extra mile. I can't thank them enough for helping to make it possible for me to become the person I am today and, of course, to excel at athletics.

I am so fortunate for the wonderful things that have happened in my life so far. I have thoroughly enjoyed remembering and writing about them in this autobiography and I hope you enjoy reading about them.

Chapter 1 – Fade to black

In my mind's eye I can still see everything. I remember clearly defined images, spectrums of colour, light and shade, but most of all I remember the face of a frightened 15-year-old staring back at me in the mirror. This is the last image I have of myself, stored away as my sight disintegrated. Like most teenagers I was scared of what lay ahead. Unlike most teenagers I had reason to be scared. I was losing my sight. Five years later, at the age of 20, I was blind.

Still, I consider myself fortunate because I have so many vivid memories from those first 20 years of my life. I can picture my sister's blonde hair and her green eyes, and my dad sitting in his armchair smoking his pipe. I remember the colours of family holidays: the brown and orange canvas of the family tent that screamed the 1970s, and the beige Austin 1100 that took the Matthews brigade to the seaside. I can recall the waves crashing against the rocks and the incoming tide gradually changing the dry, golden sand into a damp, brown mass. I can see white marshmallow clouds against a mid-blue sky, and I remember the colours of the houses and the hotels on the Monopoly board, a game we played for hours on end as the rain made a mockery of another English summer. I can still see my grey school uniform and the red, yellow and green school crest on the breast pocket, and for the most part I remember living a normal, happy childhood.

I got into lots of adventures with my mates, like most young boys do, and I was your typical gormless, gawky teenager. But try as I might to fit in, my failing sight made me different, and it was something I resented at the time. I just wanted to be normal. It is ironic really, because since I lost my sight I've rebelled against the norms of what's expected when you're blind. If someone says 'that's not something a blind man can do,' then I set out to prove them wrong.

I made it my goal to be the fastest blind man in the world, and I've achieved more than I ever dreamed of on the track. I've won eight gold medals at seven Paralympic Games, set 22 world records, and been awarded an MBE for Services to Sport for the Disabled. Away from running I've driven a race car around Brands Hatch at 80 miles per hour. I've cycled across the UK and Europe. I've played golf and football. I've skied and scuba dived. And in 2006, at the age of 45, I left behind my family and friends in England and moved to the other side of the world to New Zealand to marry the woman I love and start a family.

So what's next? Well, I want to run a 250 km ultra-marathon through the Sahara Desert, and I have set my sights on completing a 650 km ski/run to the North Pole in temperatures which reach minus 50 degrees. I truly believe that anything is possible if you set your mind to it, and we can all strive to be extraordinary. But as a child and as a young man growing up, all I wanted to be was ordinary. All I wanted was to be the same shade of vanilla as the rest and not stand out from the crowd.

I was born in May 1961 in the single bedroom at the rear of our family home in Strood, near Rochester, in Kent. My father, Aubrey, and my mother, Patricia, had bought one of the first houses in a new development on Poplar Road. Strood was much more affordable than London yet still only 35 miles (55 km) from the city. I was the second of three children, the middle child between my older sister, Angela, and my baby sister, Susan. You could say I was the rose between two thorns.

My dad, Aubrey Thomas Matthews, was also one of three children, but was the only one of his siblings to be born with very little useful vision due to the condition now called retinitis pigmentosa (RP). He was the third generation in the family to lose his sight as a result of a degenerative eye condition, after his mother and her father. It was too coincidental for it not to be considered hereditary. He was just three years old when he was taken away from his parents and sent to the Sunshine Home for Blind Babies. When he was seven he was transferred to another boarding school for blind children, Lyndon Lodge in North London. Conditions were tough and the children slept in 12-bed dormitories, but Dad had one advantage over many of the other kids. He'd learned to read Braille from a very young age, so when the lights went out he could read in the dark under the bed covers.

Dad learned quickly how to stand on his own two feet and stick up for himself. I'm certain he underplayed it, but I can't help thinking how hard it must have been for him to be separated from his parents and siblings. I am so grateful that it was no longer standard practice for blind children to be sent to boarding school by the time I started to lose my sight as a young boy. At least attitudes to children with poor eyesight had improved from when my father was a baby.

With the advent of the Second World War, Dad's school was evacuated to Dymchurch on the Kent coast, which is where this story could have ended as this was a direct route for German bombers on their way to attack London. When he was 16, Dad and a friend were fired at by a German fighter plane returning home. They probably saved their skins by diving into a roadside ditch. This is the closest he would get to the action, as his blindness made him ineligible to be drafted into the forces. Still, it was a scary time for him, and when we were youngsters Dad regaled us with stories about the nights he spent sheltering in Tube stations in London during the air raids. He described the experience as a mixture of dread tinged with nervous excitement and anticipation, as he sat and waited for the bombs to whistle out of the sky, hoping and praying they exploded somewhere in the distance.

Mum has also talked about her experiences during the war; of being bombed by the Germans in her home town of Scarborough, East Yorkshire. Her side of the family were no strangers to war. Her grandfather, Patrick Crow, was from Clones, Ireland, and he served in the Scots Guards, fighting in the Boer War; he was one of the founder members of the Irish Guards in 1900. Mum's father (my grandpa) Jon Crow served in the Black Watch in the trenches in the First World War. He suffered the horrors of hand-to-hand fighting and being sent 'over the top'; after one occasion in 1917, he was found two days later, wandering around no-man's land, suffering the effects of mustard gas, and was demobilised. He was just 18 years old.

My parents first met after the war when they worked in the same office in the Treasury in London. Mum told me that she noticed my dad immediately, as he was a tall, dark and handsome fellow. She didn't hesitate when he asked her out for a drink, and things progressed quickly from there. Dad's blindness was never a problem for Mum, although it took her parents some time to adjust to their daughter's choice of partner. They obviously learned to adjust, because Mum and Dad were married on 21 May 1955.

By this time Dad was working as a shorthand typist for the Ministry of Defence at Chatham Dockyard, and he commuted from Strood every day by bus. He had to walk 400 m from the bus stop to his office, and he made the journey using a symbol cane, a short, white folding cane to indicate the carrier was blind. His cane was just over a metre long, and Dad used it to follow walls or grass verges. His cane worked reasonably well, apart from the occasional collision with a lamp post.

Lamp posts are the bane of the blind and those with poor or fading sight, as I was to discover as a teenager. The council always seems to place them a foot or so from the edge of the pavement to deliberately catch out unsuspecting 'blindies'. Dad often came home from work with an assortment of cuts and bruises, and it was a huge relief for him and for us when he organised a lift to work with a colleague and gave up his daily battle with lamp posts and late buses. Why Dad was only taught to use the symbol cane — which was clearly inadequate for any totally blind person navigating journeys alone — we'll never know. He should have been given a long cane, or better still offered a guide dog. They were different times, I guess.

My older sister, Ange, was born in 1959 and then our baby sister, Sue, in 1964. While we were aware of our father's battle with blindness, Ange, Sue and I never considered him anything but normal. He was just someone who happened to be blind, which was fine by us — we loved him for what he was, cuts and bruises and all. While we may not have worried about Dad's blindness, it must have been a source of concern for him and Mum, particularly when they first decided to have children, given that RP is hereditary. As soon as Ange and I were born, Dad asked the doctors to check our eyes for signs of anything out of the ordinary. Mum says they turned our eyes 'inside out' to see if there was any retinal damage. Ange and I screamed our lungs out, but to our parents' relief the doctors found nothing wrong with our eyesight. When Sue was born, Mum refused to put her newborn daughter through the same ordeal.

Although given the all-clear when I was born, by the time I was two Mum had begun to notice that my movements around the house were less confident and precise in poor light than they should have been. She took me to see our local GP, Dr Pritchard, who saw no reason for concern at that stage. By the time I was eight, it appeared my sight hadn't improved, nor for that matter noticeably worsened, and Dr Pritchard referred me to Maidstone Eye Hospital for tests. The specialist at the eye hospital confirmed my sight wasn't perfect, but he predicted it would improve and I would have normal sight by the time I was 13 years old. I guess he didn't really know what he was dealing with because we would soon find out how wrong his initial diagnosis was.

Maidstone is only ten miles (16 km) from Strood, but we needed to catch two buses, and the trip would take an hour on a good day. The journey started out as an exciting adventure, but over several years of travelling there — and later to Moorfields Eye Hospital in London, the leading eye hospital in the UK — the excitement and expectation were replaced by the hope that the pain and discomfort I was to be put through would mean I would have improved vision. Only this outcome would make the whole experience worthwhile.

Once Mum and I arrived at Maidstone Eye Hospital, the doctor would shine his torch into my eyes, which wasn't too bad until he applied the drops to dilate the pupils. This gave him a much better view of the retina and the back of my eye, but with the pupils enlarged more light was let in. Considering my eyes were already sensitive to bright light, it made it incredibly uncomfortable. Try as I might, it was impossible to keep from screwing them shut, so the doctor would use his thumb to hold my eyelids open, making my eyes water. Next up, the doctor would take a photograph of the back of my eye, which entailed placing the camera right up against my iris. The pressure was severe, and even with the drops my eyes felt numb and sore.

My visits to Maidstone Eye Hospital became more and more frequent, with the ophthalmology department finding my condition extremely fascinating and unusual. I was invited in for 'guinea pig' sessions on Saturday mornings when anyone — or so it seemed — with a passing interest could drop in to have a look into my troublesome eyes. Sometimes up to 30 ophthalmologists and their students would be there, shining their little torches into my eyes.

This was tantamount to torture. I was ordered to 'look up . . . look down . . . look left . . . look right' without a please or a thank you, and little more than an occasional grunt or a worrying sigh in the way of feedback. Some of them got quite irritated if I complained about how painful it was to keep my eyes open for so long. Most of the eye doctors walked away without even the courtesy of a goodbye, and the first I knew of the changing of the guard was when I heard a different voice telling me to 'look up' or 'look down'. I put up with this in the hope that somehow, some day, they would find what was wrong and fix it.

It took ten years before I was eventually diagnosed with RP, the same condition as Dad's. It's hereditary, gets progressively worse with age, and there is currently no cure for it, although there is some promising research into gene therapy being carried out at the moment.

There are approximately one million people in the UK who are registered blind (less than one per cent are totally blind) and approximately 33 per cent of those have some form of RP. People with RP are not born blind; their sight slowly deteriorates until most useful vision has gone, typically during middle age. Night blindness is usually the first symptom, followed by a gradual loss of peripheral vision. This leads to tunnel vision, which means people with RP can often read a sign 20 m away, but fall over a chair under their nose or — like Dad — walk straight into a lamp post.

Most people with RP don't go totally blind until their 40s or 50s, but the rare strain of RP I inherited meant I went blind much earlier in life. I remember lying in bed as a young boy with the lights off, looking in the direction of the bedside table, willing myself to see it. I used to hold my hand up in front of my face, convincing myself that I could see it — surely that was a shadow, an outline . . . something . . . anything? But soon I realised it was just my imagination. I couldn't see anything in the dark. I knew exactly where the bedside table and my hand were, but the rods, the light-sensitive cells in my retinas, were next to useless.

I couldn't see in the dark and I was dazzled by bright sunshine, but when the light was somewhere in between I was able to get around confidently enough. I had some peripheral as well as central vision, enabling me to see colours and quite a bit of detail. I could read normal-sized print in a book if the light was good, but ironically I struggled to read large print as I couldn't see all of each letter at the same time. I could watch our black-and-white television, read a car number plate from 25 m away, and played football fairly well, although it was difficult to focus on the moving ball.

As I got older, scar tissue formed on my retinas, creating ever-increasing gaps in my vision. A very interesting piece of equipment used to test my peripheral vision looked like a big mixing bowl on its edge. I had to put my chin on a rest, look into the 'bowl' and focus, one eye at a time, on the lens directly ahead, then press a button each time I saw a pinpoint of light. Later the eye specialist described my sight as 'like looking through a net curtain at a jigsaw with pieces missing'.

By the time I was 13 I had accepted that my sight was not improving. In fact it was fading relatively quickly, with my central vision seeming to disintegrate faster than the peripheral vision. I found it more difficult and uncomfortable to see in bright light. Like Dad, I started suffering more and more physical injuries as a result of my failing sight, many of them caused by those damned lamp posts.

Walking into a lamp post at high speed results in a curious mixture of sensations. First there is the sickening sound of bone hitting concrete, followed by a jarring jolt as you come to a sudden stop, and a nauseating feeling as though you are falling from a great height. Then there is the pain, which I desperately tried to ignore, figuring that if I acted as if nothing had happened, nobody would even notice that I had walked into a lamp post.

Once, on my way home from school, I learned a valuable lesson: that I needed to concentrate on where I was going at all times and not allow myself to be distracted, however briefly. I was walking along Lilac Road, kicking my football in my bag, and daydreaming of playing for Chelsea one day. It was a dark, dingy evening, but I noticed a bloke on the other side of the road who was walking quite quickly and I decided to race him. I was doing well and had him in my sights until a lamp post leapt into my path from nowhere, and bang! I bounced off it and stumbled backwards before finding my feet. I wondered what the hell had hit me. I was still a mile from home, and the last thing I wanted was the prying eyes of nosy neighbours wondering 'what happened to young Matthews then?' I tried to hide my battered face behind my bag and hurried home as fast as I could, never stopping to think that maybe a kid walking home with a bloody face wouldn't look half as strange as I did carrying my bag in front of my face.

When Ange got home from school she was more horrified than usual at the state of me. I had done a really good job on myself. My right eye was closed for a week, and the bruising was bad enough to keep me off school. I worried about what the other school kids would say when they found out, but they just assumed I'd been in a fight. They were more impressed than anything, and wanted to know how badly I'd hurt the other kid. Naturally I kept quiet about what had really happened.

You'd think I would have learned my lesson, but a few years later I was running to get an ice-cream for my girlfriend. I saw the ice-cream van, but didn't see the lamp post. This time I chipped a couple of teeth and bruised my knee. I wouldn't have minded so much if she'd been worth it, but she wasn't.

My failing sight did nothing to help my shyness and lack of self-confidence. I was reluctant to draw attention to myself, and it took a lot of courage to put my hand up in school and ask a question or volunteer an answer; I didn't want to feel foolish or look stupid. Whenever I opened my mouth in front of the class, I felt my cheeks burn as the blush spread across my face.

My efforts to blend in weren't helped by some of my teachers. At the beginning of my first summer term at Rede Court Comprehensive, Mr Shoot, the physical education teacher, told me I wasn't allowed to do summer sports. I guess he felt my bad eyesight and my resultant clumsiness would make me a major liability when putting the shot, not to mention throwing the javelin. I couldn't have agreed more, and I was relieved to hear this good news. I wasn't so happy that Mr Shoot decided to deliver the news to me in front of the whole class. It was as good as advertising the fact that there was something wrong with me, and I remember wishing the ground would open up and swallow me.

My time at Rede Court was difficult because the classes were so big, and the teachers just didn't have the time to give special attention to a child who was losing his sight. The fact that I couldn't see a thing that was written on the blackboards didn't help. It was a traumatic couple of years as I slowly came to the realisation that I wasn't a normal kid.

Ange noticed how difficult things were for me at school, and told Mum and Dad who decided it was time to move me to a school that would help, rather than hinder, my development. Leaving Rede Court for the Nansen School for the Partially Sighted at the age of 13 was the best thing that could have happened to me, and was one of the major turning points in my life. Nansen was a small, friendly and intimate school, with 60 pupils ranging in age from four to 17. It shared its facilities with a school for children with learning disabilities and one for 'delicate' children — those with disabilities such as brittle bone syndrome, pulmonary or cardiac problems and dwarfism. This was the first time I had come into contact with other children with sight problems, let alone children with disabilities and some who had a terminal illness. It was the beginning of an important learning curve for me — I learned to see the person, not the disability.

My first day at Nansen was a terrific eye-opener. It was completely different to anything I'd experienced. The classroom seemed practically deserted with only eight children. I felt almost exposed, but soon learned that there was now no need to hide, and I settled into my new way of life quickly, despite it being so different to anything I'd yet experienced. It was at Nansen that I learned to accept my fate. I was going blind.

When I was 15, the specialists examined Dad and me together for the first and last time. I don't know why it took so long, but the doctors were able to confirm that our loss of sight was caused by the same condition and that it was hereditary. It was another 10 years or so before the doctors at Moorfields Eye Hospital confirmed that the condition we shared was RP.

At that time, there was very little known about the causes and effects of RP, but over the years of seeing countless specialists and genealogists, I've learned that my family has a dominant form of RP in its genes — dominant in that there is a 50/50 chance of the affected parent passing it on.

I inherited RP from Dad, who inherited it from his mother, who probably inherited it from her father. This means that by deciding to have children, my wife, Sarah, and I have taken a gamble. There was a 50/50 chance our baby could have had RP, but indications to date show that our son Thomas's eyesight is normal, and I fervently hope that he doesn't inherit the rogue gene that causes RP. If he does have RP, I will be there to help Thomas through it, just like my father did for me, and show him there is no reason he cannot do whatever he wants in life.

As a father, I now realise that Dad must have felt guilty about passing his condition on to me, but we never discussed it. I must admit, I probably didn't make it easy for him to broach the subject. It was something I didn't want to talk about, and for a long time I refused to acknowledge it. I convinced myself that if I didn't talk about going blind, it wouldn't happen. I recall Mum telling someone that I was 'partially blind', and I corrected her that I was in fact 'partially sighted' — a small but very significant difference, to my mind.

But as my sight deteriorated, I began to feel increasingly sorry for myself. I am also embarrassed to admit that I felt bitter towards Dad for passing the rogue gene on to me, for condemning me to a life of blindness. Why me? Why should I have been cursed with losing my sight when Sue and Ange both had 20/20 vision? But the truth is, I'm glad that it was me and not them who inherited RP. I truly believe that I never would have been so focused on becoming an elite athlete and would never have gone on to set 22 world running records, win 29 international gold medals, or be presented with the MBE by Her Majesty the Queen, had I not lost my eyesight.

Going blind forced me to focus. It forced me to take a good hard look at myself and challenge my own and others' preconceived notions about what a blind man could do. When I started coming to terms with my sight loss, I realised self-sympathy is no sympathy at all. Dad enjoyed a full life, helping to produce and bring up three fit, happy and healthy children. Where would we have been without him? Selfish feelings were forgotten. There was no reason I couldn't live my life to the fullest, too.

And I soon realised that life can be funny, compensatory and unpredictable, all at the same time. As I learned to cope with my blindness I stumbled upon an escape, more by accident than by design. Blind people can feel isolated and alone, trapped in a world of darkness. I can't say that I've never felt isolated, but I was lucky enough to find something to fill the void. I found running.

Chapter 2 – Blind panic

It took me 20 years to discover my gift, my aptitude and my talent for running, but since then it has been the one constant in my life, apart of course from being blind. One of the reasons I run is that it is something I am good at. I feel alive when I run. When I was growing up, my failing sight just made me feel clumsy and awkward, but when I run I feel tall and graceful and confident.

I was lucky I had Dad to remind me that blindness is a long way from being the worst thing that can happen to anyone. He used to say: 'Life is a challenge, and sometimes it's more challenging than at other times.' My father enjoyed few of the advantages I did, because there was less support for the blind when he was growing up. When he was courting my mother, being ever the gentleman he would walk her home and then catch the Tube back to Fulham. Once he became disoriented on the platform at Leicester Square station and fell onto the track. Thankfully there were no trains coming at the time.

By the time they began dating, Dad was able to see very little, but he did his best with the limited sight he had by focusing intently on what was around him. Mum used to tell the story about them catching a train to go on their honeymoon; when the train pulled into a station, Dad leaned forward to look out of the window and eyeballed a chap who was minding his own business on the platform. She says she wasn't sure who got the biggest fright.

Despite the occasional gaffe, at no stage during our childhood did Ange, Sue or I consider Dad to be anything other than normal. We couldn't take advantage of his blindness by creeping around the place in an effort to avoid jobs or punishment, as he would nearly always hear us. If we were about to be punished, we knew he would find us quickly; even running outside to avoid him only delayed the inevitable. Giving ourselves up was usually the smarter option. I was stupid enough to answer him back once too often, and Ange and Sue told me later, laughing their heads off, how my white bottom turned bright pink with just two or three of Dad's smacks.

As a family we would go blackberry picking on hot summer afternoons. We'd been to this one place a few times before we discovered it had been the garden of what must have been a large house. Once we'd picked enough blackberries for a crumble, we'd go exploring, with Sue, being the daredevil she is, usually leading the way. We found a bomb shelter in the garden, and reckoned the house must have been hit by a stray bomb meant for Chatham Dockyard. We imagined there must be bodies in the shelter and scared ourselves silly talking about ghosts.

We loved the ghost stories on the radio and television, particularly *The Signalman* by Charles Dickens. Sue would often read ghost stories to me, even when we were grown up. I remember one family Christmas we spent in a village just outside Maidstone, staying in a converted 400-year-old oast house. The building was incredibly old and creaky. Every evening we'd relax in front of a roaring log fire after eating far too much, and would head off to bed with full stomachs. Lying in bed I could hear every creak and groan as the old house settled down for the night. I managed to subdue my imagination about ghosts coming to visit, and usually fell asleep quickly, but one night I was startled awake by the rattle of the door latch, my heart hitting race pace in milliseconds — it was only Sue, coming to sleep in the other bed. She didn't want to sleep in her bedroom alone, she said, as she could imagine waking up to see an old lady in the rocking chair. For the next couple of hours we chatted, and Sue read me stories from a ghost book she'd just received as a Christmas present. She really made the stories come alive, and we both jumped at every sound the house made.

Something I was able to enjoy as well as the girls was mucking about pillow-fighting — being the boy, I was the main target. Growing up, I did lots of things with my sisters, but especially with Sue. Despite being my baby sister, she easily led me astray. Sue and I have always been very close, and when she wasn't playing with her friends, we generally hung out together.

Ange, being the eldest, was forced to take on added responsibilities. With Dad at work and Mum working part-time, it was her job to try to keep her two younger siblings in line. If we didn't do what she told us, when she told us, she threatened to let Mum or Dad know, but most of the time we got on really well. One of my chores was to sweep the stairs with a dustpan and brush. If Ange found a speck of dirt after my efforts, she made me do those stairs again and again. I was struggling just to see in front of me, so seeing a speck of dirt was a big ask, but I remember once she made me do those stairs 11 times. When I think back on it, I realise now that Ange was following Mum and Dad's lead of not treating me differently just because of my failing vision.

Although Sue was my younger sister, she was very protective of me; she looked out for me and defended me whenever she could. On a visit to Swanley Swimming Pool when I was 14 and Sue was 11, we were playing on the water slide, waiting our turn with the other kids. Initially I was a little apprehensive about the slide. I wasn't confident about climbing to the top of the ladder and launching myself into the pool, because I couldn't see if there was anyone waiting at the bottom, but Sue walked me through it, described what I'd find, assured me it was easy, and told me she would tell me when the pool was clear. It was obvious I was a bit nervous, though, and one boy asked Sue what my problem was: 'Is he blind or something?' He soon regretted his comment, because Sue wasn't shy about using her fists.

Sue and Ange weren't always around to look out for me, and I could have been bullied for being different because of my poor eyesight. I was lucky, though. A boy at my school called Darren was my only tormentor, but he wasn't a very good bully. His efforts were pretty half-hearted and he never really hurt me, although he threatened to on quite a few occasions. One time he caught me after school, wrestled me to the ground, placed a stick on the back of my neck, and karate-chopped it — hard core or what! I played dead, and when he realised I wasn't going to fight back, he got bored and walked away; I didn't pose enough of a challenge for him. Another time I left school early to go to the dentist, and he intercepted me and offered to do the dentist's work himself.

Darren was just a pussy cat, however, compared with Mr Sharp, the head of maths at Rede Court Comprehensive. He was a much more experienced bully. On the same day I went to the dentist, George, my best friend at school, came with me to the staff room at lunchtime so I could let my teacher know I needed to take the afternoon off. We knocked on the door, and the next thing we knew our heads were being knocked together by Mr Sharp. Before we could get a word out, he pointed at a piece of paper on the door and asked us to read what it said. George wasn't a good reader and he stared dumbly at the sign. I was able to see red writing on a white background, but it was a poor colour contrast for me, and blurred. Mr Sharp shook his head and spelled it out for us: 'Do not disturb, it says,' and he shut the door in our faces.

I ran my first race at Rede Court, a cross-country race over 3 miles (5 km). Things went quite well while there was someone running in front of me, but when I took the lead and had no one to follow, I didn't know which way to go and I was afraid of running into unseen hazards. It was terribly frustrating. Once back in the school grounds, though, I picked up the pace fairly confidently, using the trees and goal posts as landmarks. I came 11th out of 20 runners, and the teacher was quite impressed, but I knew I was capable of doing better.

Even though I enjoyed my first race, I was more interested in soccer (or football as it's known in the UK) at the time. Chelsea was my team, and the 1971 FA Cup final between Chelsea and Leeds United is the first game I remember watching on television. My team won 2–1 after extra time. The next year they beat the mighty Real Madrid to win the European Cup Winners' Cup. I remember the royal-blue shirts and the white socks, and the white numbers on the players' shorts and backs. It really contrasted well against the lush green grass of the pitch. Those games started my lifelong love of football and Chelsea.

One of my favourite footballing memories is going to the recreation ground on Saturday afternoons for a kickabout with Dad and Valiant, his first guide dog and the family pet. I'd like to think we looked like any other father and son, and we did until we lost the ball. One of the first balls we lost was my treasured England World Cup football, a beautiful white leather ball with black pentagons and the official logo for the 1970 Mexico World Cup. We reckoned it would be difficult to lose, despite my failing sight and my dad's total lack of it, but somehow we did. I don't recall who kicked it last, but I do remember spending what seemed like hours stumbling in the undergrowth around the perimeter of the park. To passers-by, our stomping and foraging in the grass must have looked like some weird tribal dance. It was exasperating for both of us, knowing that we must have been so close to my prized football. Having no one with better vision there to help us, we just had to head for home, leaving it for some other lucky bugger to find.

Next time, we took no chances and bought a 'bell ball' from the Royal National Institute for the Blind (RNIB). The ball had a thick skin of bright red rubber with holes pierced through it, so that players could clearly hear the bells inside. As long as the ball was moving we had no trouble hearing it, but if neither of us was close enough to it when it stopped rolling, our old dance routine would commence. However, the red of the ball against the green grass usually provided enough of a contrast for me to see it with the small amount of residual vision I had left, and this broadened our horizons tremendously for playing games, particularly cricket.

Although Dad enjoyed outdoor pursuits, he was equally happy with his nose stuck in a book. The RNIB had a very extensive Braille library which Dad made good use of. Our local postman had recently upgraded his bicycle to a van, which was lucky for him because the Braille books were bulky. Some novels exceeded 12 volumes, and sometimes two or three novels would be delivered on the same day.

On the day I left Rede Court for the Nansen School for the Partially Sighted, the headmaster, Mr Pope, invited me into his office and asked me to read a newspaper to him. As I read, Mr Pope measured from my nose to the newsprint. I had to hold the paper 8 inches (20 cm) from my face, which Mr Pope felt was acceptable. My speed was fair, and he advised me to practise reading print as much as possible and to forget about Braille. But a year or so later, it became obvious that reading print wasn't an option for me any more. My eyesight was deteriorating, and so I started Braille lessons.

Initially I wanted to keep what I was doing from my friends. Having to leave print behind and focus on Braille really made me feel blind. But as it turned out, my friends were really supportive. They were interested and a little envious that I was learning something different and exciting. English and history course notes were converted to Braille for me. I would do my best to read them, but I was so slow initially that by the end of each line I'd forgotten what was at the beginning. It was incredibly challenging, learning what was effectively a new language while simultaneously learning new subjects for the exams.

I got a great deal of help from Dad who often read the notes to me. With Dad's help I got an O level in history, and CSEs in English and art. One of the other subjects I really enjoyed at

Nansen was woodwork. It was wonderful to turn wood on the lathe and use a variety of planes and saws to see pieces of wood gradually become something identifiable. The most satisfying work I did in woodwork was when I made a fish mobile from pine. Having drawn the outlines in thick pencil, I was then able to follow the lines with saw and chisel. I loved the feel of the grain, the smell of fresh-cut wood, and watching the pieces of wood gradually become recognisable as fish. I was very proud of my twin candlestick holder, jewellery box and even a musical instrument that I carved out of pine. My crowning glory was a mahogany coffee table.

My worst day at Nansen was when I flattened Mrs Wickham in a head-on collision. She was an old lady, and although she was a formidable presence in the classroom she was obviously quite frail. Mrs Wickham was our music teacher, and one morning after she had played the piano at morning assembly, I nipped back to the classroom to retrieve a book for the first lesson. I came racing out of the classroom into the hall where I collided with Mrs Wickham and knocked her flat on her back. She lay there, repeating 'stupid boy,' while I was too stunned to ask if she was all right.

A few minutes into my next class, the deputy headmaster, Mr Smith, knocked on the classroom door and asked to see me in the hallway. I was still in shock and was worried about what I had done to the poor woman, and as soon as Mr Smith closed the door behind us I burst into tears. Poor Mrs Wickham — she would be out of action for six weeks. I did have the sympathy of my friends, who thought she should have looked where she was going. After all, she was a fully sighted teacher at a partially sighted school. Nevertheless, I felt uncomfortable and self-conscious in her classes from then on.

Running into things was beginning to become a habit. The Nansen school sports day was the first sports event that I did any training for, and I took it very seriously. I dragged myself out of bed at 6 a.m., wolfed down some breakfast, then stopped off at the recreation park, on my way to catch the train to school, to do some 100 m sprints, using my school bag as the finishing line. I did all right, considering I couldn't see my school bag until I was about 30 m away from it! There were a few times when I thought someone had nicked it, but I'd just strayed off course a little. One morning I was feeling particularly brave and ran around the park to warm up. I ran straight into a rope that marked off the cricket pitch and landed flat on my back. I hurriedly picked myself up and retrieved my school bag, hoping no one had seen me making a fool of myself.

Despite the odd mishap, my training for the school sports day paid off and I won the 1500 m, nearly lapping my buddy, Hugh, in the process. I felt on top of the world! I was even more excited when I was picked to run at the London inter-school championships. Right before the 1500 m final I was asked to run in the 400 m as well, because the school didn't have anyone entered in the event. The gun went, and within a couple of metres the rest of the field had sprinted away from me. I was a middle-distance runner after all, not a sprinter. I did my best to keep up with them, but I was running so hard I failed to see the water-jump barrier until the last second, and I narrowly avoided an early bath. It was an incredibly humiliating experience and I hated the sympathetic applause I heard as I trotted over the finishing line.

My confidence was shot, and I pulled out of the 1500 m, feigning sickness. I wasn't lying either — I felt sick with embarrassment, and I took the easy way out to avoid the prospect of further humiliation. Hugh took my place, finishing fourth, less than 200 m behind the winner. That made me feel even worse, because I knew that if I'd run the race, I could have won it. That was the end of my short-lived school running career.

My sight was fading relatively quickly at this stage, with the central vision disintegrating faster than the peripheral vision. I was finding it more difficult and uncomfortable to see in bright light, and I had no useful vision at night at all. I struggled to read print, even with a strong light. I could see my watch, but by then it was a Braille watch with a hinged glass face. I could still see desks or trees from a distance, but as I drew closer they dissolved and then disappeared.

I found getting home from school on dark winter evenings a real struggle. I tried walking home from the station using an enormous torch — more of a lantern really — in the hope that I could manage without advertising the fact that I had poor sight, although in hindsight it must have struck passers-by as peculiar: a young boy shining a lamp along a fairly well-lit street. Unfortunately it didn't work due to the peculiar nature of my sight problem. Even with the torch I could still only see a small square of pavement and nothing else around me. I had to walk at snail's pace and accept that it would take me ages to get home. It's difficult to explain to anyone with good night vision just how mentally taxing it was to avoid walking into anything.

This deception was fuelled by another incident on my way home from school one very warm, bright, summer's afternoon. I was about 15 years old and I made a miraculous discovery. By turning my head slightly and looking out of the corner of either eye, what had been a bright blur resolved into distinct, although dazzlingly bright, features. Pavement slabs appeared, along with maybe a hedge or wall at the side. This gave me some clarity, and although it was only a small field of vision, while it lasted it was very important and precious to me. When I discovered this trick I was quite excited, thinking I had found the key to improving my sight. It was a temporary reprieve, however. As my sight continued to deteriorate, I was able to rely upon it less and less, and I gradually made the transition into accepting that I was going blind.

The most difficult part of losing my sight was first of all admitting it to myself, and then admitting it to the world. Advertising the fact that I was blind was something I was reluctant to do. I had seen Dad cope with being blind and all the symbols that came with blindness, such as walking with a cane and reading Braille. I just couldn't get my head around the fact that I was really going to be like him. So when the optician at Moorfields Eye Hospital insisted that I needed glasses, I was so upset at the prospect that I was unable to focus on the eye chart through my tears. I was finding life difficult enough, without having to draw attention to myself in school by wearing glasses. It wasn't until I moved to a partially sighted school that I didn't mind wearing glasses. In fact you tended to look out of place without them.

The next step in accepting the fact that I was going blind was agreeing to start using the white cane. When I left Nansen I bowed to the inevitable and had long-cane training from Social Services, but I refused to have the lessons in my home town of Strood. This was because I felt people who had known me all my life as a sighted person would see me using the white cane and realise that I was blind. I didn't want them staring at me, I didn't want them sniggering at me, and most of all I didn't want their sympathy.

Although I knew by now that I needed to use a cane, I loathed what the thing represented. I felt I might as well have worn a sign saying, 'Look at me, I'm blind!' I wanted to manage my situation in my own way. I hated it when Mum would get all upset about me losing my sight; she'd try to comfort me, saying 'I understand, darling'. I knew she was being loving and supportive, but I just didn't want her sympathy. I thought I was fine.

Dad's attempts at talking to me about my failing sight were met with a brick wall. I felt that if I talked about it, the inevitable would happen, and I really would have to accept the unimaginable — that I would become blind. In truth, I felt sorry for myself, because I clearly couldn't be a normal kid at school, and this made me shy and lacking in confidence. I couldn't see in the dark, I couldn't play team sports, and I was in the lowest-grade class until I was 13, when I was transferred to Nansen, because I couldn't see the blackboard nor read print very well.

Things definitely improved with my move to Nansen and I could do a lot more, but even then, although I was learning to accept and adapt to life with my failing vision, I still wasn't able to think about a future with no vision at all.

Chapter 3 – Finding my feet

I was 16 years old when I left home to start my new life at the Royal National College for the Blind (known less formally as the RNC). I had survived fully sighted school, and my time at a partially sighted school had helped me start to come to terms with my blindness. A year after commencing my studies at the RNC, the college relocated from Rowton Castle, just outside Shrewsbury in Shropshire, to Hereford in the west of England, 16 miles (26 km) from the border with Wales. This would be my home for the next four years.

Sue, Mum and Dad came with me to the open day before I started at the RNC. I was following in my father's footsteps as he had also attended the college many years ago. Dad was pleased to see the college had improved dramatically since his time there. Where he had slept in a cramped dormitory, I shared a dorm with three other students. The rules had been significantly relaxed, too. During my dad's days there, the college had been run with a draconian regime, where girls and boys were forbidden to fraternise outside the classroom unless they were strictly supervised, such as at the monthly dance.

That didn't stop Dad. He often got into trouble for climbing the fence around the girls' boarding house to meet his latest flame, or to flirt with his next sweetheart. As we walked around the college on the open day, Dad revealed that he had been considered something of a rogue at school, and was threatened with expulsion on a number of occasions.

Moving away from my family and the familiar surroundings of home was a huge wrench. It only really dawned on me as the open day came to an end and it was time to say goodbye. I found it particularly difficult to cope with the feelings of loneliness and loss, feelings that were exacerbated as I came downstairs to see off my family. I heard Sue getting upset as she wanted to say goodbye to me one last time, but Mum and Dad told her it would be easier if they just left. I stayed inside and listened to them leave. I only just managed to hold back the tears.

I knew no one. I had no friends, and the family home I grew up in was 200 long and lonely miles (320 km) away. I walked along the driveway and assured myself there was probably nothing to bump into. I chanced breaking into a short jog, and even then I was aware of how running made me feel better.

I returned to my room, feeling slightly better, and met one of my room-mates, a guy called Mark Rochford. He went by the name of 'Roch' which made things difficult for me as I struggled to pronounce my R's at the time. So instead of embarrassing myself by calling him 'Woch' I called him Mark instead. So that we were both on first-name terms, I introduced myself as 'Bob' rather than 'Robert', a name I am known by in the UK (I reverted to Rob when I moved to New Zealand, nearly 30 years later).

Mark and I became close friends at the RNC. Although we have gradually lost touch over the years since, he was a good friend to me in those difficult early days. He was a year older, much more mature, and he seemed to take everything in his stride. I volunteered for the job of locking up the swimming pool every night, a job I took on during the long, bright evenings in late summer. It was a nice job initially, but when the cold, dark winter nights set in, it wasn't such a cushy number. Mark used to come with me on those winter evenings, knowing how scared I was of what might be lying in wait for me in the dark corners. Fortunately this fear of the dark was something I learned to conquer.

I started at the RNC in 1977. *Star Wars* was the biggest movie that year, and in the US a computer wiz by the name of Bill Gates was just getting a company called Microsoft off the ground. Personal computers have made life so much easier for blind people, but back then I learned to type and became proficient on an Olympia manual typewriter.

The Olympia was a tough taskmaster. Any mistake meant a complete retype, but I still managed to leave college with an accurate typing speed of 40 words per minute. I also took spelling lessons which I found particularly challenging because my spelling was rubbish. I had trouble visualising words, and had only finished one adult reading book before I started at the RNC. The other subjects I studied were English, commerce and geography.

Towards the end of my second year at college, Prince Charles came to officially open the new site of the RNC in Hereford. We all awaited the arrival of the royal helicopter in front of the main building, decked out in our finest. One lady, wearing a very glamorous hat, got a bit of a surprise — the wash from the rotors blew her hat clean off, and it was last seen sailing over the rooftops. I was lucky enough to be chosen as one of the students to meet His Royal Highness during his tour of the college, as my geography teacher had asked me to demonstrate a tactile map of England. We didn't speak for long, but I have always remembered this first meeting.

While my studies were an important part of my time at the RNC, the biggest lesson I learned was to appreciate what I had. Because of my failing sight I had spent much of my early teenage years wallowing in self-pity. I was angry, and wondered why everyone had better sight than me and why the little I had left was fading fast. At college I soon discovered that I had better sight than many of my fellow students, and it helped me realise I wasn't so badly off after all. With Mark's help I found my feet in my new surroundings quite quickly, and was in a position to help some of the totally blind students get around.

It took me a bit longer to get used to the 'rockers'. Congenitally blind children, especially those educated in institutions such as boarding schools, often tend to pick up odd mannerisms and habits such as rocking backwards and forwards. I couldn't understand why they rocked, but learned that the motion was comforting to them, and some of the 'rockers' told me it also helped their concentration. The rocking gets more vigorous as the person becomes more animated or agitated, so I quickly learned to keep out of range of the more excitable 'rockers' — I didn't fancy the idea of suffering concussion from a collision with a head-butting 'rocker'.

Mark Campbell, who introduced himself to me as 'The Fonz', was one of the 'rockers'. We'd often find him sitting on his bed in his underpants (if we were lucky) with his thumb pressed firmly in his eye, rocking himself back and forth. When he wasn't rocking he was a great mimic. When he first introduced himself to me he spoke with a strong American accent. The next time we met he had a broad Black Country accent (the Black Country is an area of the West Midlands in the UK) and told me he was from Wolverhampton and to call him 'Cams'. I remember drinking with him one evening at the college bar where one minute he was an Everton fan with a broad Liverpudlian accent and the next he was a Spurs fan with a strong London accent. I often wondered whether Cams had an identity crisis.

As well as Cams' array of accents, I also had to get used to the other brogues and dialects spoken at college. Before I started boarding at the RNC, I had only been outside Kent on our annual family holiday and on a canal trip to Wales with the Nansen school. The only accents I was familiar with were from London and the Home Counties. At the RNC my classmates included natives of Scotland, Northern Ireland, Liverpool, Newcastle, the Black Country and the West Country. Despite listening closely I sometimes struggled to understand what some of them were saying.

I hope they understood me a bit better because I made my radio debut in my first year at the RNC, as a DJ on Radio Severn, the college radio station. I was a big fan of BBC Radio One. I listened to UK radio icons Noel Edmonds and Tony Blackburn in the morning, Ed 'Stewpot' Stewart who presented 'Junior Choice' at the weekend, and 'Pick of the Pops' with Jimmy Saville on Sunday afternoons, so to be a DJ myself was a huge thrill. Despite my nerves I got through my first show and it was well received. I even got requests to read excerpts from Braille books, but I was more interested in playing the music that I loved.

Before college my taste in music wasn't exactly what you'd call cool. The first single I ever bought was 'I'd Like to Teach the World to Sing' by the New Seekers. Sweet, Slade, Wizard, the Collective Consciousness Society (or CCS as they were known), the 'Ying Tong Song' by The Goons and Dad's favourite, 'Monster Mash' by Bobby 'Boris' Picket and the Crypt-Kickers, were others on heavy rotation in the Matthews household. We were also forced to listen to Ange's music, which she inflicted on us over and over again while she was plastering on her make-up, from bands like the Stylistics, Donny Osmond and T-Rex.

At college I started listening to Blue Oyster Cult, the Eagles, Lindisfarne, Status Quo and Queen. The best thing Cams did was to introduce me to the music of Queen when he loaned me their LP, 'A Night at the Opera'. I played the album on my portable record player and as soon as I heard 'Bohemian Rhapsody', a song I still think is one of the best ever, I was hooked. Late one night, three of us decided to have a Queen extravaganza and we played their first six albums back to back. We couldn't understand why the lads in the bedroom above were not so impressed. It was sunrise before we finally called it a day and fell asleep to the 'Test Match Special' radio cricket commentary from India. I slept through lectures the next day and got several 'don't do that again' warnings from the teachers.

Music has remained an important part of my life. It has helped me to maintain my sanity whilst running well over 10,000 miles (16,000 km) on my treadmill. The sound and vision of Freddie Mercury strutting his stuff at a Queen concert I went to in Birmingham in 1979 have often helped me run through the pain barrier. I can still see the spotlight washing over the audience as the concert began with a crash of thunder. Then the spotlight turned to Brian May as he played the guitar intro to the heavy version of 'We Will Rock You' before Freddie emerged in glorious technicolour and started singing in that inimitable voice of his.

While I took to rock music with great gusto, my early experiments with smoking and drinking at college weren't nearly as successful. I soon realised I was rubbish at both. Thankfully I had the good sense to give up smoking, but I did persevere with drinking. Actually it was Dad who took me for my first drink on my 16th birthday. We went to his local pub for a couple of halves of bitter, and soon after I started at the RNC, Mark and I found the Windmill pub. Dad and his cronies at school had been regular visitors there many years before, so once again I was following in my father's footsteps.

The Windmill was a mile or so from the college and it was on a busy main road, a pretty hazardous walk for a couple of boys with poor sight, with or without drink inside them. I have great memories of staggering back to college with my blind mates. Being the one with the most vision, I was usually at the head of the crocodile, with two or three mates hanging off each other behind. Talk about the blind leading the blind! There was no pavement, so I walked as far inside the white line as possible on the grass verge, and usually I got us to the pub and back without a hitch.

I say usually; one Sunday lunchtime, Cams, his girlfriend and I were walking to the Windmill. Cams' girlfriend was holding my arm, and he was holding hers. He should have been walking much closer to her than he was, but tended to weave over and back across the white line on the side of the road. His weaving was suddenly interrupted when he was clipped by a van. It took a moment to realise what the 'thunk' sound was. Turning around, I saw him on all fours, picking himself up. The driver helped us to the pub, and we hoped that was an end to it. However, he contacted the police, and the next thing we knew a policeman was asking us questions and filling in an accident report. We thought we were cornered when he asked our ages. None of us was 18, and legally we were not allowed to drink. He assured us that he was more concerned about three blind youngsters walking on a busy road, rather than what age we were, and let us off with a caution.

The incident didn't put Cams or me off our experiments with alcohol. We had never tasted whisky, so one Sunday afternoon we bought half a litre of cheap Scotch whisky and drank it that evening. I have never been so ill for so long. It took me two days to recover. Just the thought of Scotch whisky used to turn my stomach. However, since my trips to Ireland, I have enjoyed the much smoother taste of Irish whiskey. I was in a hotel bar, telling a friend why I couldn't touch Scotch whisky, and they insisted on buying me a Laphroaig, one of the great Scotch single-malt whiskys, which changed my mind. The aroma was amazing; it reminded me of a tin of pipe tobacco Dad once smoked, called 'Balkan Sobranie' — it had a lovely smooth and peaty taste.

Although I loved the smell of Dad's tobacco, I was a miserable smoker myself. Despite my best efforts to get better at it, no matter how much I huffed and puffed it still made me sick. Again it was Dad who introduced me to smoking. Every Christmas my baby sister, Sue, and I used to badger Dad for a puff of one of his Manikin cigars which we'd given him as a present. He would usually let us, but insisted we only have one puff. From there Sue and I graduated to cigarettes. I had my first cigarette with her when she was only 12 and I was 15.

The thrill of smoking was more to do with the excitement and anticipation of lighting up and the risk of being caught, rather than the experience itself. I was never a heavy smoker, and the most I smoked was five cigarettes in a day; any more made me feel ill. Once after school I lit my second cigarette from the first, and by halfway through I was nearly sick. I also experimented with smoking a pipe when I was 17. I made plenty of smoke, just like my dad who enjoyed his pipe, but it just made me feel ill so I decided to leave it to the expert. I was 19 when I finally stopped the disgusting habit of smoking cigarettes. I hated the smell of tobacco on my fingers and the taste in my mouth. I found myself puffing and panting after running up the stairs, and I could also feel the effects now that I was doing the occasional run.

As well as experimenting with drinking and smoking, my fortunes with the fairer sex were improving at college. At least they did until the night I paid a surprise visit to my girlfriend. Pauline was the nearest I'd come to a proper girlfriend, and the first girl I'd really kissed. We got along famously, even if her best friend was always present as a chaperone, until one night when I got blind drunk. I had just turned 18 and I was getting used to the novelty of being able to order a pint legally. My 18th birthday coincided with my O level exams, and after my English exam, which I was convinced I'd failed, wrongly as it turned out, I retired to the college bar to drown my sorrows. One-and-a-half hours and eight pints later, I staggered outside in a stupor.

Pauline had said to me before how funny it would be to see me a little tipsy, so I set sail for Gardiner, the women's hostel. I stumbled around in the dark, trying to find it, until a kind lady and her guide dog escorted me there. How I wish she hadn't. Somehow I found Pauline's room and she quickly realised I was in a bad way and was trying to show me the door. Before she could get rid of me, however, my stomach decided to get rid of some of the beer I had poured into it earlier. Poor Pauline bore the brunt of my stomach-heaving ugliness. Fortunately for me, my mate Mark was also visiting a young lady in the hostel, and he heard the commotion and came to rescue me. He helped me clear up some of my mess and took me back to our room. The next morning, the warden of the women's hostel gave me a letter, banning me from Gardiner for two weeks and billing me for the clean-up. I learned my lesson well, but alas Pauline and I had reached the end of the road.

Life at college was pretty routine. Our home in Kent was too far away for me to consider going home, except at half-term and school holidays, so most weekends I'd catch the bus into Shrewsbury town centre. I'd wander around the shops, mainly with Mark, buy a record or two, and while away the time enjoying a companionable pint while we waited for the bus back to the college. I quickly realised there was only so much to do and see in Shrewsbury, so I set about finding a hobby. Cams introduced me to train-spotting. This might not be the most obvious pastime for a blind and a partially blind teenager, but we loved it. It helped when we hooked up with train-spotters who could actually see the trains, but even so, we still had lots of fun ticking off the serial numbers of the different-class diesel engines in our train-spotting books. Occasionally we found a friendly driver who let us ride in the locomotive with him; it was a real treat to hear and feel the power of the engine.

If train-spotting was fun and exciting, train stations were often cold, boring and sometimes dangerous places. Dealing with train stations I tried to walk carefully and confidently along the platforms, assuring myself with wide sweeps of the cane that I wasn't straying too close to the edge. One scary time I did stray too far: one moment I was safely walking along the platform, the next I found myself sprawling across the track. Man, I've never moved so quickly as when I vaulted back onto safe ground!

Arriving at Shrewsbury station one time, Cams and I stepped off the train and walked boldly across the platform towards an area of darkness which I took to be the ticket hall. He held my arm while I guided us, using the white cane, trying not to hit anything on our way. Sometimes things happen which you just don't expect: instead of stepping into the ticket hall and onto a firm surface, there was nothing but a brief falling sensation and a horrible moment of wondering 'what the . . . ' before we landed in a heap on what I realised was another track. Shrewsbury station has four platforms, and two of them are dead ends. Fortunately it was one of these dead ends we'd stepped off and were in no danger of being hit by a train, but it certainly put the wind up me.

While train-spotting was an enjoyable hobby, sport became my passion. Like most English teenagers, I was obsessed with football, but playing it was another story. All my life I had used my eyes to find the ball, or waited to hear it bounce to give me a clue, but now the world of blind football was open to me. We used a normal ball inserted with lead shot that made it rattle and helped us track the ball. The five-a-side football pitch at the RNC was surrounded by chain-link fencing, which helped us work out where we were on the pitch.

I didn't see eye to eye with the football captain, and was rarely picked to play for the college team. However, I did get to play with another club, the National Sports Club for the Visually Handicapped, which came to play against the RNC one Saturday. I hadn't been picked to play for the RNC, so I played for the opposition and was delighted to score a hat-trick in our 4–1 win.

I also joined the cricket team. The rules of 'blind cricket' state that there has to be a minimum of four 'totals' (as in totally blind) per side, that a 'total' on the fielding side can catch a batsman out on the bounce, and when batting, the ball has to bounce twice before reaching the batsman's crease. Oh, and the ball we used was the football with ball bearings inside of it which made it audible. In 1981, I was a member of the college team which won the national blind cricket knockout competition. I'll never forget the catch I took at 'silly short leg', a diving, leaping effort that somehow stuck to my hands. It was one of the proudest moments of my life.

But it was goalball, a game I had started by my 18th birthday, where I was to enjoy the most success at college. Goalball is a game specifically designed for the blind, with three players a side, each having to wear blindfolds to eliminate any sight advantage. The ball has bells in it, weighs nearly 3 kg (7 lb) and is bowled with an underarm throwing action. The aim is to get the ball past the opposition at the other end of a badminton-sized court into their goal. I found I was good at goalball and I played for a team called the Eagles. We played competitions up and down the country. Eamon, one of my best buddies through college, played on the left for the Eagles, and another good mate, Bill, played on the right. I played in the centre. We had trained together regularly for months and had done really well as a team. That was until the big competition when Bill was promoted to the Falcons and Derek replaced him.

In February 1980 we travelled to Nottingham where the team to represent Great Britain in that year's Paralympic Games in the Netherlands would be selected. The method of selection was unusual, to say the least. Rather than picking the best players at the tournament, the team winning the competition would be selected en bloc. We played the Falcons in the final and we came out on top. I was on my way to my first Paralympics.

As part of our preparations for the 1980 Paralympic Games, we travelled to the European club championships in Copenhagen, Denmark. We caught the boat to Scandinavia. The crossing took 24 hours and there were discos, bars and restaurants on board.

The Great Britain coach, Steve Dewhurst, and I went to one of the discos, the others having thrown in the towel for the evening. Steve spotted two attractive ladies around our age sitting on their own, and persuaded me that we should join them. What follows is one of the most embarrassing experiences of my life. Steve was chatting away to his girl and discovered they were sisters and came from Hertfordshire. Feeling self-conscious I tried to think of something, anything, to say to mine, wondering how I would start the ball rolling. As Steve and his friend were chirping away to each other, I couldn't be totally sure, in the noise of the disco, that my friend wasn't joining in with nods or other gestures. Eventually I plucked up my courage during a lull, looked towards where she should have been sitting, and asked, 'What are you planning to do when we arrive in Denmark?' There was no reply — she'd gone to the loo. I was mortified — where was that hole to swallow me up? I'm squirming as I write this and recall the details.

Next morning we were bussed to the competition venue with the other teams from around Europe. It was really strange sitting there and not being able to understand anything anyone else was saying. The competition went really well for us, and we learned a great deal. None of the teams was a pushover, but we came third, winning the bronze medal.

Back at college, it was a proud moment for me when Mr Marshall, the principal, proudly informed the whole college at assembly of our success at the European championships. I enjoyed the applause and cheering of the other students, but there was hard work ahead. For the next three months we prepared for the Paralympics, improving our fitness and devising tactics. Despite being absorbed by my sport, I managed to remember why I was at college and found time to practise for, and take, shorthand and audio typewriting exams as well as O levels in geography and commerce.

Just prior to the Paralympics we joined the other members of the Great Britain team for a training weekend at Stoke Mandeville, Buckinghamshire. We were given our track suits with 'Great Britain' embroidered across the back. These may not have been the trendiest, but I felt very proud every time I put mine on. After all, I was joining a select club: very few people are good enough, or lucky enough, to represent their country. For the first time in my life I felt that I was an achiever, and that I was part of something big.

The next time I met the other members of the team was to catch the plane to Amsterdam. We should have been on our way to Moscow, of course. The 1980 Olympics were held in Russia, but at that time Russia refused to recognise the fact that they had any physically disabled people, and so refused to host the Paralympic Games as well as the Olympic Games. This was never allowed to happen again. Today every country bidding to host the Olympic Games has to make equal provision for the Paralympic Games.

I didn't mind too much where we were flying. It was my first time on a plane, and that was exciting enough for me. Dad had often talked about his first experience of flying, 15 years earlier, when he likened the sound of the aeroplane to 50 spin dryers going at the same time. I experienced such an adrenalin rush as the volume of the engines grew and the plane accelerated down the runway, and once we were airborne I felt like my cup really was overflowing. I was on my way to becoming a Paralympian, and even if I was never good enough to be picked for the Great Britain team again, that status could never be taken away from me.

From Schipol airport the team was bussed to the Paralympic athletes' village in Arnhem, a town that became well known during the Second World War when allied paratroopers were dropped there behind enemy lines. Ironically the Paralympic village turned out to be a converted army barracks just outside the town. I was used to mass catering at college, but the Paralympic village food hall seemed massive. There were lots of really nice food smells, but when the Dutch helpers described the dishes, I was none the wiser.

As the Paralympic village had previously been an army barracks, it wasn't a surprise to find our accommodation was a dormitory. The Great Britain goalball team shared its dorm with some Canadians, and it was difficult initially to understand why they spoke French but little English. One of their guides explained they were from Quebec where 80 per cent of the population speak French as their first language. One of my Canadian room-mates, a guy called Jacques Pilon, changed my life without knowing it. Jacques was totally blind and won the 1500 m running with a guide who gave him verbal instructions, along with tapping or pulling his elbow, to navigate him around the running track.

Talking to Jacques and his guide made me realise for the first time that it was possible for me to run again, despite losing the remainder of my vision. Excited by the thought that perhaps I could be a 1500 m runner, I asked the late Ron Murray, one of the Great Britain team coaches, whether this was feasible. He told me I had a good build for middle-distance running.

There were 13 teams in the Paralympic goalball competition, with each team playing 12 matches on a round-robin basis. In truth the Eagles team, masquerading as Great Britain, did not have enough in the way of fire power to compete with the other nations, and we only scored one goal in the tournament. Our defence saved us as we never conceded more than two goals, but we had to settle for 12th place. It wasn't a very auspicious start to my Paralympic career, but there would be better days in the future — not on the goalball court, but on the running track.

I was 19 years old and in my final year at RNC when I started running with Steve Timmins, one of the sighted volunteers at college. Not having a clue about training or the level of discipline required, we would cover up to 6 miles (10 km) twice in one week, but then not put our running shoes on again for a fortnight. Not surprisingly we didn't break any records. I was keen to get serious about running, and realised that I would have to take my training to another level to do it properly.

During that summer, Mum came with me one time to a sports shop and, not being shy like me, got talking to the owner, Lyn Hughes. As soon as Lyn mentioned he was an ultra-distance runner, before he knew what had happened Mum had cajoled him into running with me whenever he was able. After he had trained with me a few times, he introduced me to a small running club in Rainham where I did some training with Colin Lemmis. Mum even came running with us a few times, but unfortunately she got a little overzealous and hurt her knee, putting an end to her brief running career. It was just the start of mine.

During the next year I ran 5 miles (8 km) in 33 minutes in Southend, the Rainham 10 mile (16 km) road race in 70 minutes, and the Rochester half-marathon in 96 minutes. I also lowered my personal best for 1500 m, clocking my first sub-five-minute time, 4:59, in a blind race. Despite being well beaten by Patrick Kelly from Ireland, who ran 4:37, I was really chuffed — I felt like raising my arms and celebrating. I kept thinking, 'I'm a sub-five runner', which spurred me on during my weekly runs with Colin. I now started feeling as though I could be a good 1500 m runner.

While running was starting to take over from goalball as my sporting passion, I still played and enjoyed the team game. We won a tournament in Nottingham in 1981, and afterwards we went to a local pub to celebrate. Discrimination is something I've encountered as a blind person — on just a few occasions, thankfully — and that evening in Nottingham is one that I remember well. Unfortunately, the manager of the pub, instead of seeing us as a bunch of happy, slightly noisy blind lads who had something to celebrate, threw us out on the grounds that he didn't want us to upset his clientele. He interpreted our show of jubilation as a sign that not only were we blind, but mentally disabled as well. Obviously this put a dampener on our celebrations, but we found another pub and enjoyed a good night regardless. The next day we wrote to a couple of newspapers, telling them what had happened. The story was published and the manager of the pub lost his job.

My final international goalball tournament was the world championships in Indianapolis, USA, in 1982. There was a much more sensible method of selection this time around: the best players were picked, rather than the most successful team. As it turned out, three of the five players came from our team, and I was the only survivor from the 1980 Paralympic team. I moved to the right wing, as my shot was more effective from there; Martin Brown, with a terrific shot, played on the left, and Andy Apsey played in the centre. Ivan Mortimer and John Wells were the substitutes. We were the most successful team ever to represent Great Britain; we had a very good defence and scored regularly — my highlight was scoring three goals in a match against Yugoslavia. In the end we placed fifth overall, narrowly failing to make the semi-finals.

I really enjoyed my first experience of the USA. Being English, I have to say that at first I was taken aback to meet such enthusiastic people who would welcome you into their homes at the drop of a hat. I couldn't believe how different this was from home. It was here that I had my first taste of pumpkin pie — what an incredible dish that is. It's always on my 'must have' list whenever I return to the USA.

The Rotary Club raised most of the money for the goalball team to compete in the USA on the understanding that we would 'sing for our supper' and talk about our experiences at one of their dinners. 'Singing for my supper' at my local Rotary Club proved to be much more important than I could ever have imagined. I spoke about the goalball world championships, our success, and how close we'd been to reaching the semis. I also talked of my ambition to run the 1500 m, how I knew it was possible for a blind man to run, and how I'd met a Canadian who'd triumphed during the last Paralympic Games. After dinner, a chap approached me, offering to mention my ambition to a friend of his at the Medway Athletic Club. One thing led to another and within a month, Chris Newman, my first regular guide runner and coach, picked me up from home to go training.

I had been on quite a journey. I had by now lost all my useful vision and was coming to terms with this. I had qualified as a shorthand audio typist and was ready to make my way in the world. I had also been to my first Paralympic Games. With new friends and a new sense of self-confidence, I was living my life to the fullest, but knew there was more to come. I had found running, and life would never be the same again.

Chapter 4 – My life in his paws

My four years at the RNC ended in July 1981. I had learned some valuable life lessons, I'd been in some scrapes and adventures, and I'd passed the typewriting and shorthand exams which would have stood me in good stead for a lifetime of employment in dull and boring jobs. I soon discovered, though, that I wasn't cut out for a lifetime of dull and boring jobs.

I had to start somewhere, however, and within a few months of leaving the RNC — and with a lot of help from the employment officer at the Royal National Institute for the Blind — I started my first job with Lloyds Bank and took my first, tentative steps into the real world.

I flunked my first interview, which Dad set up with the Home Office, part of the Ministry of Defence. I was getting along famously with the interviewer and felt relaxed and confident, until she asked for a demonstration of my typing skills. The interviewer sat slightly behind me with her feet resting on the drawer of the desk, and dictated while I typed. What very little sight I had left was peripheral, and I was able to catch a glimpse of her leg where her skirt finished just above her knee. I could try to blame her for distracting me from the job at hand, but in reality my poor typing skills let me down. At that time, employers were required to have three per cent of their workforce registered as disabled. But despite my disability, my transcription was peppered with mistakes which no employer, whether they were short of their quota of disabled employees or not, could tolerate, and so my search continued.

My next opportunity came at the head office of Lloyds Bank. Again I thought the interview went well, and again I was getting on just fine with the attractive-sounding female interviewer, until she asked me to type as she dictated. I was determined not to be distracted this time, but I still made plenty of mistakes. Imagine my surprise then, not to mention how pleased I was, when I learned the bank was prepared to offer me a job at its branch at 263 Tottenham Court Road.

When I heard later that the position I'd been given at the bank was described as 'supernumerary', I certainly felt as though I were an extra. I didn't feel great getting a job purely because the bank had a quota to fill, but how else was I going to get my foot in the door? In those days I just didn't have the skills to compete with qualified sighted typists, and even after four years of training, I wasn't convinced I was cut out for office work. However, I had few other options at the time. The main thing was that I had a job and was earning a wage.

Fortunately for me, Dad left home for his job in London at a similar time so I was able to tag along with him and Valiant, his guide dog. Having a dog guiding two people was frowned upon by the Guide Dog for the Blind Association, as it can confuse the dog. It didn't seem to worry Valiant, though, and he charged ahead with the additional hanger-on. However, I couldn't always rely on Dad and Valiant going to work when I needed to, and I often had to resort to making my way using a long cane.

Just three months after finishing college I started my first day as a working man. It was Monday, 26 October 1981, and I was 20 years old. I left the house with Dad just after 7 a.m. and walked to the station to catch the 7.30 train to Charing Cross. The train took 80 minutes to reach the city, and it was a fairly boring journey. Dad, along with many other early risers, went back to sleep, whilst I read Braille novels and tried to ignore the grunts and snorts of many sleeping passengers.

Braille books are bulky, and as we drew closer to London the train became more crowded, leaving me with less and less elbow room to move my hands across the page. By the time we reached London Bridge, there were people virtually sitting on my lap, so

I had to put the book away. Although you read Braille books by touch, my eyes get tired after reading for a while, as I tend to visualise the words as I go along, which is probably why I'm not such a fast reader. Things are so much easier now, with audio books you can load directly onto your mobile phone or MP3 player.

Having been swept through Charing Cross on the tide of commuters, Dad and I would part ways, him heading to his job on Fleet Street while I went underground to get the Tube. Tottenham Court Road is one of the deepest Tube stations — the escalator takes around two minutes to reach fresh air. Once I reached the top of the escalator it was simply a case of finding the correct flight of stairs to street level, and then it was just a stone's throw past the Dominion Theatre to the bank. Later, when I had my own guide dog, I found it was safer to carry him up the escalators because of the fear of his paws getting caught in the revolving steps. But considering he weighed in at 80 lb (36 kg) it was a serious workout for me and a test of endurance.

Since leaving secondary school for Nansen when I was 13, this was the first time I had been with fully sighted people exclusively, and I found it pretty daunting. The knowledge that everyone could see whatever I did really concerned me; they could be in the same room as me and I wouldn't even know it. But I would get over that. It was an exciting prospect to be paid, however, especially what was for me a king's ransom for the skills learned over four years at college, most of which I had spent mucking about. A man from accounts, Mr Fillingham, came to see me on my first afternoon in the job, and asked how much of my first month's salary of £200 I'd like forwarded to my account to cover travel and living expenses. He was astounded when I asked for just £60. 'Surely that won't be sufficient?' he said, but to me it was a fortune. I'd been used to surviving on £37 a week from my supplementary benefit.

My desk was at the back of the office, facing four girls with whom I had nothing in common. They were pleasant enough, but we were poles apart. I couldn't get excited about the topics of their chit-chat, and whenever we made polite conversation I could tell the feeling was mutual. It wasn't as though they were hostile or rude to me. I was so shy and I hoped they would forget about me; I'm sure they did a few times, judging by some of the more intimate tit-bits I overheard.

I was very immature, very self-conscious and very quiet, and kept myself to myself as I learned to cope with my by now total sight loss. My poor typing skills didn't help my feelings of inadequacy either. Mixing with people in a similar position at college had helped my social skills, but working with and being surrounded by fully sighted people all day, every day, was a different matter altogether. I couldn't help but feel somewhat inferior.

My confidence soared briefly at my first office Christmas party. I accidentally found myself a girlfriend — for an evening at least. One minute I was minding my own business, trying to hear what was happening over the loud music, visualising people dancing and cavorting, the next minute the girl I'd been chatting to was playing 'tonsil hockey' with me. Alas, she'd changed her mind by the next morning, or hadn't even remembered our brief encounter, because she never made herself known to me again, and because the party had been so loud, I hadn't been able to identify her voice.

My job involved taking shorthand dictation using a Braille shorthand machine. The Braille was stamped onto a paper roll which came out of the machine, much like ticker tape, and gathered into a pile on the floor. When the dictation was finished, I wound the 'ticker tape' back on the spool which I transferred to the guide in front of my typewriter, and then the slow, laborious process of decoding the Braille into a finished document began.

Every few words I had to raise my hands from the Braille to the typewriter and back again. It wasn't unusual after pondering a mysterious sequence of Braille for me to have forgotten the last word I'd typed. My work was painfully slow, and frequently came back from my boss needing to be retyped. Often one of the girls would have to do it, which didn't do anything for my popularity. Try as I might, my efforts were returned with spelling as well as typing errors. Most of the skills I'd acquired during my four years at college seemed to have deserted me. I was rubbish.

It was difficult and frustrating to work in a job where I didn't feel in any way equal to my colleagues in the same role. Access to a dictionary would have helped my accuracy, but I was too shy to communicate to my boss that I needed the Braille *Little Oxford Dictionary* (the word 'Little' is misleading as the Braille version runs to 16 volumes and weighs over 10 kg). From time to time, overcoming my embarrassment, I would ask the girls, 'How do you spell . . . ?' but I couldn't keep asking them every five minutes. Instead I just kept my head down and counted the seconds until it was time to go home.

Making matters worse, my commute to and from work with just a white cane was a hell of a strain. I'd get to the end of the journey mentally exhausted, not to mention bruised and battered. I really had to concentrate on where I was walking to avoid lamp posts, bollards or benches, not to mention illegally parked cars on the pavement. When I found these obstacles with my cane, I'd stop dead in my tracks, but I was not necessarily fast enough, and would often arrive at work looking as though I'd fought a round with Mike Tyson.

Dad put off training with a guide dog until he was 53, when he was posted to the Ministry of Defence on Fleet Street, London and he found the daily commute a trial. After training with Valiant, a 90-pound (41 kg) black labrador, he never looked back. Seeing the degree of independence and confidence Valiant brought Dad, not to mention a much faster walking pace, I wanted to apply for a guide dog there and then. Aged only 15 at the time, I was too young by law, and I probably wasn't mature enough to care for a dog 24 hours a day.

However, I was now 20 years of age, and believed I was at last mature, knowledgeable and capable enough of being responsible for my own guide dog. Even more importantly, the Guide Dogs for the Blind Association agreed. As you can imagine, I was relieved but also incredibly excited to receive that phone call, telling me they had a dog they believed would match my needs. After commuting to London for three months with my long cane, I was more than ready to get my new set of eyes, knowing I would be able to walk faster, more confidently and without the mental strain and anxiety with which I'd had to cope until now. I would actually be free to go anywhere, any time. If I fancied a walk, then my dog and I would go for a walk. The independence he'd give me would help me establish my self-worth, proving that I could be as good as anyone, only needing to ask for directions and not guidance.

I'd had a walk with Valiant once and found the experience liberating, feeling much less 'blind' — certainly less self-conscious — than I did with the cane when I could often feel people watching me. I'd walked into a post one day, probably hurrying and not using the cane properly, and someone standing there had said: 'I wondered whether you'd hit that post.' Now I could go wherever I pleased, carefree.

Back then it was compulsory for every trainee guide dog owner to live in the Guide Dog Training centre for four weeks, the better to allow them to bond with their dog and get away from external distractions. There were six of us in the class, aged between 20 and 50, and I was the youngest.

None of us was allowed to know anything about our prospective dogs, not even their breed, sex or size, for another 24 hours. The trainers spent much of this time assessing our speed, balance, reactions and spatial awareness whilst guiding us around the outside of the centre where there were pavements, curbs and an artificial obstacle course. The trainers played the part of our guide dog at the business end of the harness, while the student held the handle through which we could feel the 'dog's' movements and learn how to react. We learned how the dog sat to indicate a step down, and stopped with his front paws resting on a step to indicate a step up.

One of the trainers, a guy called Andy who had a dry sense of humour, showed me what I should do if my dog were to brush me against an obstacle, which in this instance happened to be a stack of tin foil. 'You should show the dog this by tapping it, attracting his attention and letting him know he has made a mistake,' Andy said. 'Ask him: "What's this?" If the dog tells you it's a pile of tin foil, you say "Good lad" and carry on.' This tickled me — I guess simple things please simple minds.

We were instructed how to feed our dogs: to make them wait for our command to 'take it' which would help establish who the top dog was. Another golden rule was not to give the dog treats or tit-bits outside meal times, other than as a reward for maybe coming back after being called on a free run, or finding a door or pedestrian crossing. If the guide dog learned to associate the rustle of a potato crisp packet with food, it was possible he wouldn't be 'switched on' to his work when someone passed on the street eating potato crisps. The next thing you'd know would be a collision with a lamp post. The trainers reiterated that we needed to be consistent at all times, as the dog would try to push the boundaries to see how far he could go.

We were also shown how to groom our dogs and clean their teeth properly. It was interesting to learn that there were many flavours of toothpaste for dogs — chicken liver was particularly popular in the kennels.

On our second morning at the training centre we were told we'd meet our dogs for the first time. It was all becoming more real and exciting, especially when the trainers gave out the equipment we'd need for our dogs. Firstly, we received the four parts of the white leather harness, which buckled together, with a fluorescent sleeve fitting over the breast plate; the leather lead and the chain came next. I counted 24 links on the chain which I realised meant my dog must be reasonably large. Lastly the trainers handed us the leather collar with bells attached, the better for hearing our dogs on free runs.

At last the interminable wait was over, and we were told to go back to our rooms where the dogs would be brought to us. We would only be together for an introductory period of 30 minutes, and the trainers told us to be very positive and to make a big fuss of the dog. We were advised to get down on the floor with our dog, encourage and play with him, and above all not to impose our will on him. The aim was to leave the dog with no negative impressions so he would consider us fun to be with, making it easier for him to accept us more willingly the next time we met.

I was nervous sitting in my room, waiting to meet the dog who would open so many doors for me. He would be such an incredibly important part of my future. And then he was there — I met, or rather was taken out by, Henley, a yellow labrador. Aged only 16 months, he was an energetic, playful bundle of fun, fur and muscle, with a tail that swept coffee tables clean. During those first few minutes I learned he enjoyed playing tug-of-war with anything that was within his reach, and he wasn't terribly fussy what it was. My sweatshirt was good for starters; it didn't seem to matter that I was still wearing it (the bruising on my forearms went down after a couple of days, but my sweatshirt was a write-off). He also brought tears to my eyes when his iron-hard skull whacked my chin.

Having taken refuge on my bed for a minute to recover, I realised that maybe I'd taken the 'play' thing a little far and had allowed things to get out of hand. Although I was excited about knowing that this bundle of energy was going to be my guide dog, I have to be honest and say I was faintly relieved when the trainer came to take Henley back to the kennels. It had been like being in a boxing ring with my hands tied behind my back, and he was most certainly ahead on points after round one.

If our first meeting had surprised and slightly disconcerted me, I quickly learned how obedient and controllable Henley was, switching from excitable to his 'don't mess with me, I'm working' persona as soon as I picked up his harness, and it didn't take long for us to bond and become mutually dependent upon each other.

Before being let loose on the streets with an extremely valuable and well-trained guide dog, it is essential to learn how to follow him, allowing him to do what he's trained to do. It sounds easy enough, but to place your life in a dog's paws initially requires a lot of courage — it really is blind faith until you relax, safe in the knowledge that, as long as standards and control are maintained, no harm will befall either of you. Commands and the gestures accompanying them have to become second nature. Your dog's obedience and respect are vitally important, such as when he's running free. We were instructed that our dog should have returned to us by our third call. Initially Henley was pretty good at this, but he developed selective deafness in his middle age.

One of the most vivid memories I have of training with Henley was our first few steps together. It was thrilling to tell him 'forward' and suddenly we were away. It was as though we were a hot-air balloon and our moorings had been cut. I was moving freely, almost gliding. I felt an immediate trust that this superbly trained dog wouldn't bump me into anything, which I was quite capable of doing when walking with my cane. I could have shouted with glee during that first walk. I was free! For the first time, I was safe on the pavements, and I could travel so much faster and easier than I had thought possible.

I was familiar with the route Henley and I were on, having already walked it using my cane. When Henley stopped and sat, I couldn't believe we had arrived at the first curb so quickly. I felt like going down on my knees to hug him, to share my euphoria with him at how my life had changed forever. However, I contented myself by patting his head and telling him that he was 'the best ever boy', knowing he was concentrating and needed to remain focused while he was working. No longer would I need to struggle through crowds, attempting to use my cane and needing to ask for assistance if I became disoriented. With Henley, I could walk almost anywhere, knowing he would guide me through crowds, past bus shelters, pot holes, pillars and posts. I would never again feel disabled. I told Henley to 'do a right turn' and he smoothly guided me around the corner. This first walk set the scene for a successful 11-year partnership.

Soon enough I had proved myself capable of following and being guided by what many blind people refer to as 'the elite mobility aid'. The next step was learning to walk with Henley along a busy street. Sighted people naturally take this for granted, but I was intoxicated by my new-found ability to swerve in and out of pedestrians and other obstacles without bumping into them. I felt like a slalom skier — it was so tremendously exhilarating and exciting, and I gained so much confidence and satisfaction from this one experience. Only running at speed along a path, swerving in and out of trees, have I known this sense of freedom and motion. It seemed so natural.

It really is quite something to put blind faith in a dog, to trust that your next step won't be your last before piling into a bollard or hapless pedestrian. When walking with a cane, I sweep it from side to side which should locate obstacles as well as bus shelters, post boxes or doorways. I also use pedestrians' voices or their footsteps to judge how close they are, and whether I might trip them accidentally. I find noisy environments can be disorienting and make me suspect a numbing collision, causing me to close my eyes and hope for the best.

However, with Henley I learnt that he couldn't guide properly if I was afraid and hesitant, and this was when collisions could happen. Crossing a road with a guide dog, even when there is a pedestrian crossing, can be hair-raising. No matter how hard I listen to the traffic and how good the dog is at watching out for moving vehicles, there's a nagging suspicion that someone behind the wheel of a vehicle won't be paying enough attention.

Henley and I came to understand each other during the hard work we put in at the training centre. Gradually we gelled, and finally became a unit. Things like the correct body positioning, from the starting point to approaching curbs and doing turns, became second nature during four weeks of intensive and mentally exhausting training. However, training had just begun, and the rest of our working life together would be an ongoing learning curve. I understood that I shouldn't take for granted the responsibility of this magnificent dog's health and welfare, and that when crossing roads, it wouldn't just be my life at stake. It was heavy stuff, but so important. Since that very first time, I have always tried to maintain consistency with my guide dogs, and not to compromise the standard of their training.

The day came for Henley and me to be set free into the big wide world, and I was exultant and awed by the realisation that freedom and independence were now mine, much like taking ownership of your first car. All I needed to do was buckle on Henley's harness and we could go anywhere I chose — even if returning to work wasn't top of my list. Maybe I wasn't sure if I was ready to go back to the bank, but it had to be done. Over the next few days I taught Henley the routes to the station and to work, with his trainer shadowing us. Going back to the office was nerve-wracking but I couldn't have imagined the difference that Henley would make to my life. Our first solo journey into work was incredible. All of a sudden, people were talking to me. They'd probably been there every day when I was using my cane — I guess there's nothing like a cute dog for pulling the girls.

Three weeks later the trainer came to see how things were progressing. By now Henley and I had settled into a routine and were confident with the route to work, and although I hadn't been allowed to let him off for a free run, we were familiar with the route to the park. Being satisfied with how well we'd bonded and worked together, the trainer felt it was now time I let Henley run free. I had been to the park regularly throughout my childhood and thought I knew it really well. I certainly didn't know it had four exits.

It was the end of the day and starting to get dark, and maybe that was why Henley became confused, even though visibility was still pretty good when I let him off. I called him back the first time and heard his bells as he came straight back to me, giving him a little treat as a reward for doing so. I confidently let him stretch his legs again. He went farther away this time, and when I called him back he ran in the opposite direction towards another exit, where a lady he must have mistaken for his trainer was entering the park. To my horror he kept going — the exit led out onto the busy A2 Rochester road. And then the inevitable — there was a terrible 'thump'.

The trainer and I ran as fast as possible to the road, but there was no sign of Henley. The motorist who'd hit him had stopped and was very shaken — he told us he'd feared the worst as Henley had been pushed on the bumper for 30 m, but then he'd run off. We found him a few minutes later, cowering on the grass verge, but seeming to be in reasonable shape. The vet was able to confirm that Henley only had a bruise to the cheek and a couple of abrasions — he was an extremely lucky dog.

I had never been so scared in my life. Incredibly, Henley's work wasn't impaired by his experience, and he didn't suffer from traffic shyness, despite his scare.

While my daily commute improved, my job at Lloyds Bank wasn't getting any better. I can't say I look back on the 22 months I spent at the Tottenham Court Road branch with any great fondness. However, away from work my life was changing significantly, and for now I was chuffed just to have a paying job — proof that not all of the four years I had spent at the RNC had been wasted — plus the money I earned allowed me to broaden my horizons. I was eager to try new experiences.

One spring I grabbed the opportunity to join a group of blind and partially sighted travelling to Norway for a week's cross-country skiing in Beitostolen, 200 km north of Oslo. The five-star hotel had its own 25 m swimming pool, but more exciting for me, it had a sauna — another first. Thankfully, someone explained that the idea wasn't to sit in the sauna as long as possible, otherwise I could have fried my brain, but I quickly took to it and enjoyed the invigorating feeling of a cold shower followed by a few minutes in the piping hot sauna.

My guide for the cross-country skiing trip was a fellow called Tom from Boston in the USA. Tom had skied before, and although he wasn't fit, his superior technique and experience allowed him to keep up. We had four days to learn how to cross-country ski. By the end of the third day the muscles on the insides of my legs were really stiff, but with some stretching, swimming and probably a few too many sauna sessions, I was ready for the first of three races on consecutive days.

The first was over 10 km through the beautiful Norwegian countryside. The starting area was a hive of activity. I heard skiers whooshing past as they warmed up for the race. Skiers were sent off at one-minute intervals, like the time trials at the Tour de France. We had to negotiate two laps of 5 km, and the tracks were getting pretty chewed up by the time I started my second lap, which made matters even more challenging for a novice like me, but I survived the race.

The next day was even more challenging as we tackled the biathlon, an event which combines skiing and rifle shooting. We actually used a .22 calibre rifle to fire pellets at the targets. The event was supervised by the Norwegian army and we were shown how to handle the rifles. We skied up to the rifle range, lay down behind the rifle and put on a pair of headphones. Targets were located using an ultra-sonic sounder wired into the headphones. We waved the muzzle of the rifle around until we heard the highest pitch which was the centre of the target. If you fired as the pitch descended by only a fraction, you missed the target, which meant skiing a penalty loop of 100 m.

The Riderran was the main race on the final day of competition and was a 21 km trek through the countryside. I loved it! I really enjoyed the sound of my skis on the snow, the peace and tranquillity, but I remember getting quite irritated at Tom who kept stopping to take photographs. This was a skiing holiday for us all, but Tom's costs were subsidised as he was acting as a guide, and I was annoyed that he kept stopping to admire the view. This was a race after all and I wanted to do my best. I have always been competitive in everything I do. Even if I know I am not good enough to win, I'll still try my hardest. I didn't like waiting for Tom to stop and smell the roses. I wanted to keep moving.

Chapter 5 – Doing the second lap

By the time I celebrated my 21st birthday I was learning to cope with being totally blind. Despite my future looking like a long dark tunnel, I felt as though I could definitely see light at the end. My life wasn't half bad. I had a job, albeit one I didn't enjoy that much, which afforded me a great deal of independence. My goalball career was progressing nicely and had opened a lot of doors for me. Henley, my guide dog and new best friend, had changed my life significantly, making it easier and faster for me to get around, as well as helping me become more independent and less self-conscious about being blind. And I had found athletics.

Athletics gave me confidence, self-belief, friends, freedom and success, and very quickly became the most important thing in my life. The evening of Tuesday, 28 September 1982 was one of the most significant landmarks in my life. It was my first training session with my first guide runner and coach, Chris Newman, who accepted the challenge of moulding me into an elite athlete.

Before our first training run together we talked about the practicalities of running with a blind person. Chris hadn't even met a blind person before, let alone one who wanted to run, so we were both coming into this unusual situation totally blind. The limited experience I had of running blind had always been done with a guide who ran side by side with me, elbows touching, and gave me verbal instructions along with the occasional nudge in the right direction, similar to the method used by Jacques Pilon, the Canadian Paralympian.

Chris and I agreed this was a pretty inadequate way of doing things, as it gave me little time to react, or for the guide to grab me if I veered off the footpath or was heading for a lamp post. We needed some kind of tether to help prevent this, but one that wouldn't restrict our arm movement. With no one to ask for

advice, we were breaking new ground, so much so that
and I helped develop a new way of guide running that was l
adopted by the International Blind Sports Association (IBSA) a
the international standard.

Our first guide rope — very much a prototype — was a metre
length of catapult elastic with a loop tied at either end. The elastic
gave Chris a degree of control over where I ran, and gave me some
assurance that I wasn't drifting too far from him and in danger
of colliding with someone or something. But because the elastic
stretched so far, Chris had to reel me back in before I even realised
he was trying to communicate something to me. We learned that
costly lesson at a track session one night when a 13-year-old boy
stepped onto the track in front of me. My guide tried to warn
me, but by the time he had reeled in the elastic, we had collided.
Thankfully we were both unharmed. It was a rare accident, but
it convinced us we needed to improve our system.

One night at training, Glenn Piper, one of my key early guide
runners, brought along the Mark II version — a rope which he'd
knotted with a hand-sized loop at either end for us to hold. It was
a huge improvement, being long enough to provide freedom of
arm movement as well as preventing me from drifting far. I still
use a similar guide rope made from 80 cm of ship chandler's very
light rope, with 20 cm between each loop. That gives both runners
enough slack to move their arms freely, and it also allows me to
respond instantly to the slightest pull.

As I experimented with guide ropes and running styles I quickly
learned that synchronisation is the key to running relaxed, which
is the key to running fast. Using a rope made synchronising our
strides a lot easier, and made for a much more efficient and safer
running action than the elastic allowed. But synchronisation
and speed were all in the future. On our first run together I was
focused on survival.

Chris picked me up from home and we drove to the nearby
motorway bridge across the River Medway. This was an ideal spot
because we could run a 3 km loop along the cycle lanes on either

...torway without having to worry about traffic or ...her obstacles. Initially there was a little bumping ...hythm. I had to trust that Chris wasn't going to ...ng, and he had to trust that I would respond as ...e made any adjustments, or gave me any instructions. ...k a while, but we soon got the hang of it.

After one loop of the circuit I was absolutely stuffed, and I hoped and presumed Chris would call it a night. But he had other ideas, convincing me that I could manage another round. I thought I would die, but didn't have the breath to argue, so I kept going and finished the second lap in much better shape than I thought possible. I learned a few important lessons on that first run: focus on one step at a time, and don't worry about how it might feel further down the road — it never hurts quite as much as you think it will. I also learned that if I wanted it enough, anything was achievable.

Someone once said that running is only 20 per cent physical; the rest is psychological. I firmly believe that this is true as I've always been mentally strong, and it has helped me to dig deep and find another gear in the big races. From the start I believed that I could be somebody, that my dreams could come true, that I could be a world-class athlete. That belief and a great deal of hard work have led to a successful running career spanning 24 years.

But it all started in the more mundane surroundings of the Medway Athletic Club on Dock Road in Chatham. During that first winter I got to know and became friends with many of the club members who met for training at the RAFA (Royal Air Force Association) hut. I remember how proud I was when Chris handed me my first-ever club vest. I felt as though I truly belonged. I felt accepted and part of something, and I was chuffed to bits to put it on.

Many people assume that because I'm blind, I have only

competed against other blind athletes. Given that there has never been a blind runner in the UK to challenge me at the 800 m or any other distance right up to the marathon, my racing has always been against sighted athletes, with the exception of international competitions.

After some weeks of regular training it was time to see how far my fitness had progressed, and the only way to assess this was in a race. As it was winter, and therefore the cross-country season, we ran in a 5 mile (8 km) race in Moat Park in Maidstone through mud, rough ground and one stream. It was quite a challenge, and as usual I was running against fully-sighted athletes. Chris and I had trained at Moat Park regularly on Sunday mornings without any major mishaps, but the race didn't go as smoothly. By the time I'd picked myself up off the ground for the fifth time, I was seriously frustrated.

We were still learning and developing the best method of communication when running at speed. We found shouting 'curb up' or 'slope down' to be much more helpful than just shouting 'curb' or 'slope' — many of my beginner guides often forget the important 'up' or 'down' bits. Running cross-country, the terrain is forever changing, most often subtly, which a guide certainly cannot communicate. Just a slight ridge or divot can throw my stride pattern or, worse, buckle a knee or turn an ankle. I developed very strong ankles and good reflexes due to the constant adjustments I needed to make. But my stumbling first race only served to make me more, not less, determined to be a runner. It wasn't a setback and it didn't put me off; rather, it was just the beginning — the start line if you like.

On Saturdays we trained at the Deangate track at the wonderfully named village of Hoo (an old-English name meaning 'spur of land'), just outside Rochester. It was so exciting — I felt like a proper runner as I had bought my first pair of 'running spikes'. These are shoes with six holes in the forefoot of the sole into which spikes are screwed. Different-length spikes are used for different surfaces; for example, for all-weather (rubber-like surface) tracks you use 5 mm spikes, for cinders 7–9 mm spikes, and for cross-country 12–15 mm spikes. These running shoes with their spikes provide excellent grip.

Back then Deangate was a cinder running track, which is a type of compacted grit surface. It was my first experience of running on a cinder track, and I took to it straight away, enjoying the sound and feel of the grit crunching beneath my spikes, assuring me that even if it didn't feel as though I were moving, progress was being made. The only downside was after a training session or race, when you'd be pretty dirty from the flying grit, especially if the track was wet. The great advantage for me, however, of running on a cinder track, as opposed to an all-weather track, was that I could hear other athletes around me and tell how close they were in a race. This kept me focused and helped me be more competitive. On all-weather tracks I might only hear some grunting, breathing and the guides talking to their athletes.

Running blind around a 400 m oval running track, especially as it has two bends and two straights, takes a little time to learn and master. If the guide runner says nothing else, there are two essential words he needs to utter — 'bend' and 'straight' — after which it is down to timing and confidence, learning to change direction as and when instructed, leaning into the bend, and straightening up out of it. Reacting to the call and change of direction quickly enough is critical. Should I react late, I shoulder-charge my guide or hit the curb on the inside of the track.

Following only a few training sessions, I became so confident with each of my guides that they'd be able to say 'bend' or 'straight' and we'd rarely touch; even if we did, it would only be a light touch. With experience we learned these calls were most effective one stride before we reached the bend or straight, giving me enough time to adjust.

In race situations, guide runners need to tell me where my rivals are, how far they are behind, or if they're in front, in which case offer encouragement such as 'he's really struggling, you're in better shape'.

When I started running there were many athletes fast enough to guide me, but six months after that first run with Chris Newman my fitness had improved to the extent that, for an athlete to work me and still be able to guide and talk to me, he'd need to be able to run the 1500 m in 4:10. This was when Chris concentrated on coaching me, while Colin White and Glenn Piper became my main guide runners as well as great friends, and were chiefly responsible for the next stage of my development and early success. I'd seen Colin clock just over two minutes in an 800 m race. 'What an amazing time,' I thought to myself. I could only dream about running that fast, but within three years I became the first and only blind athlete to break the two-minute barrier for the 800 m.

I'd been training consistently for four months when in January 1983 I improved my 1500 m personal best (PB) by 12 seconds to 4:47. My improvement didn't go unnoticed by those involved with British Blind Sport (BBS) athletics. The late Graham Salmon, who was the outstanding blind athlete of the late 1970s and early 1980s, gave me a call, asking whether I'd be keen to join the BBS squad at a training weekend in Nuneaton, near Coventry. What an incredible moment! I had been recognised as a runner. I couldn't believe that my dream might well come true — that I was going to get an opportunity to run for the Great Britain team if I could impress the selectors enough.

My first BBS squad training weekend was exciting, great fun and bloody hard work all at the same time. I became friends with many athletes who over the years competed with me on the international stage. Amongst my new mates were James Brown and Neil Peerson, who were also running in the middle-distance events (800 m up to 5000 m); but, having partial sight, they were in a different race category to me. The one major difference between able-bodied and disabled athletes is the concept of classifications, and they are quite confusing. Simply put, the classifications are designed to enable athletes to compete against other athletes of a similar disability. T11, T12 and T13 are the 'blind' categories: athletes classified as T11 are either totally blind or, at most, have limited light perception; T12 athletes have some useful vision, being able to see the lines of the running track, which is a huge advantage; whereas T13 athletes can train by themselves unaided. Other categories exist for athletes with cerebral palsy, those confined to wheelchairs and with amputations.

John Anderson was the manager of the BBS athletics team that travelled to Bulgaria for the European championships in October 1983. He was unique: a wonderfully upbeat, friendly, larger-than-life guy who was fun to be around, although not if you crossed him — he was a Glaswegian, after all. Later he became much better known as the referee in the television series *Gladiators* with his famous catchphrase, 'Gladiators, ready.' John made sure Neil, James and I finished all three of the track sessions that were set that weekend without any slacking. No matter where we were on the track, we could hear John's shouted commands and instructions. I don't think it's an exaggeration to say that John's support was worth a second per lap.

I was delighted with how well I handled the training, and surprised when John assured me that after what he'd seen, I would be in the British team for the European championships for the blind in Bulgaria in seven months' time. John told me I'd be running in the 800 m and 1500 m, my two specialist events, but when he told me I'd also be running in the 5000 m, my jaw scraped the floor. I'd never seen myself as a long-distance runner. 'But that's 12-and-a-half laps,' I gasped. 'I'll get dizzy.'

'You can do it — you have bags of ability,' John told me, and he wasn't someone I was brave enough to argue with.

On 29 April 1983, running with Glenn Piper at the Deangate track in the Medway club championships, I set my first world

record for the 1500 m. I ran 4:29 to smash my personal best by 18 seconds, and improved on Jacques Pilon's record by two seconds. It was only three years since Pilon had convinced me that I could be a runner when I was playing goalball for Great Britain at the Paralympics, so it was extra special to break his record. Only a fortnight later Glenn was once again my guide when I improved my 1500 m world record in Ireland by a further five seconds. Guinness never tasted so good.

I didn't stop there. Two weeks later, this time with Colin White by my side, I took another five seconds off my 1500 m world record in the Kent championships, coming home in 4:19.40. In most of these races I was running against fully-sighted athletes. And I was starting to beat many of them. There is a level of chauvinism in sport. Men don't like being beaten by women, and similarly, fully-sighted athletes don't like being beaten by a blind runner. I've raced against runners who have stepped off the track in the final 100 m rather than have me pass them. With 200 m to go in the Kent champs race I heard someone shout to the guy I was closing in on: 'Don't let the blind man beat you!' It spurred us both on, and although the effort nearly killed him, he just hung on to beat me.

Sometimes even the people involved in blind sport underestimate how fit and capable their own athletes are. Before the European championships, BBS (which is a charity) wanted to see whether they could get away with taking only one guide runner to Bulgaria to guide the two totally blind athletes on the team, Graham Salmon and myself. Neither of us was particularly happy with the idea, but the guys in the suits saw it as a way of cutting costs, and so they held a series of time trials at one of our training weekends to see if it was possible. John Anderson brought along one of his athletes, Dave Hislop, a Scottish international 400 m hurdler, to see if he was capable of running everything from the 400 m to 5000 m in Bulgaria. It was obvious from the first time trial for the 1500 m that Dave would not be up to the task.

We ran 4:31 which for me was fairly comfortable, but poor

Dave started struggling and slowing on the third lap. As we crossed the finish line, he fell flat on his back, utterly exhausted, muttering something in his strong Scottish brogue that I couldn't quite understand. When he got his breath back he said, 'Well done, you're too fast.' It wasn't his fault. He was a 400 m hurdler, and running the 1500 m and 5000 m was alien territory to him. Graham and I took our own guides to Bulgaria. I think Dave was quietly relieved.

By the time I was 20 I was totally blind. By 21, I had my first running coach and was training hard with guide runners, experiencing enough success to be recognised and selected to run for Great Britain at my first international event. By the age of 22 I had set my first world record for 1500 m. What an amazing feeling! I couldn't believe it — I was actually the fastest blind person in the world.

I couldn't wait to run on the world stage. Running had become the most important thing in my life. I finally had a sense of purpose, and had found the determination to succeed.

Chapter 6 – The joy of running

It was only four months out from the European championships in Bulgaria. These would be my first major international championships which left me feeling both nervous and excited. I was on fire, though. I'd just set my first world records, in the 1500 m, and a British record in the 800 m of 2:15, beating my personal best by 22 seconds.

I was exhilarated with the success and wanted to keep training hard, but Chris, my coach, decided I needed to put the brakes on, and he suggested I take a holiday to ensure I didn't sustain an injury. I had one last opportunity to race before leaving on holiday: I ran 2:07.9, improving my personal best by 7 seconds — it was the first world record I would set over 800 m. All the hard work I had been introduced to over the winter and the 'no mercy' training I'd done with Colin and Glenn were worth it. I was growing in confidence, becoming ambitious, and coming to realise that just possibly I could become someone.

Reluctantly I took the opportunity to go to Greece for ten days with Mum, Dad and Nan. It was brilliant to get away from the daily grind of my London commute, not to mention the office. Ange and Sue met up with us, having spent the past three months travelling by bus around Europe. The only thing they hadn't enjoyed was having their bottoms pinched continually, especially in Italy. In our hotel, it was interesting to see how much more attentive the restaurant waiters became once we were joined by two attractive girls.

After ten days of swimming, eating and sun-bathing, I felt much more relaxed than I'd been for a long time, which helped me realise just how unhappy I had been working for Lloyds Bank at the Tottenham Court Road branch. I was so glad I'd put in a request for a transfer in April, and there was some good news waiting for me when I returned to work. My request had been accepted. Two months later I was on my way to the personnel division in Lloyds Bank's head office on Lombard Street, in the City of London. This move improved my work life no end as well as reducing my travel time by an hour a day.

I was given my own desk and telephone in the centre of a large open-plan office with my guide dog, Henley, in his bed beside my desk. I worked with 15 other people, most of them girls again, but this time everyone was very friendly and included me in the office chit-chat, which was such a contrast to my previous experience. Things were so much better that I often went to lunch with some of them. My time there was so much happier — it was a relief to be able to ask what the last thing I'd typed was, or to check a spelling mistake without feeling as though I were an inconvenience.

I was introduced to an ingenious electronic device called an Optacon, an acronym for Optical into Tactile Converter, which helped me become even more independent. An Optacon converts individual printed letters on a page into a tactile form under the left index finger via thousands of tiny pins stimulated by electrical impulses. Using the Optacon I was slowly able to read Sebastian Coe's biography by sweeping the device across the printed page. The beauty of the Optacon at work was that by inserting it into a fitting on the typewriter, I was able to check whether I had indeed made a mistake in that last word, thereby reducing the help I required from others tremendously.

But to be honest, work came a distant second behind my athletics. I was thriving on the hard work I was putting in for the European championships, and there were some nice perks. At one of our training sessions I was chuffed to meet Dave Moorcroft, who had recently broken the world record for the 5000 m in Oslo. He gave me two tickets for the athletes' enclosure at a Grand Prix meeting at Crystal Palace. I took Steve Agolini, one of my guides, and we had a fantastic time meeting athletes such as Steve Cram after their races. I felt as though I belonged, I was one of them, I was someone.

October finally arrived and I was all set for the European championships in Bulgaria. The flight from London to Sofia, the capital of Bulgaria, was uneventful, but we had to change planes in Sofia, and our flight on to Varna, our base for the games, was in a 40-seat, noisy, rattling, twin-propelled 'cigar tube'. I've never been on anything like it since. Not surprisingly, the atmosphere on the plane was pretty subdued. Most of us were suffering some nerves because, for most of us, it was our first big international meet, but I think all of us were just hoping and praying we would get off the plane alive as it swerved and plunged, dipped and dived, in a rather alarming fashion.

Varna in those days wasn't considered the glamorous and popular holiday destination it has since become, but this was my first international athletics competition, I was 22, and I was going places! I certainly wouldn't have swapped it for anywhere else. I've been extremely fortunate that running has enabled me to travel all over the world and sample many different cultures, but suffice it to say that Bulgaria wasn't one of the highlights. One of my lasting impressions was that Bulgarians ate only lukewarm, greasy sausages and cheese on toasted French bread for breakfast — and for most other meals, come to think. The best thing I can say about our accommodation is that it was functional. It was an army barracks; the bedrooms had twin beds with two tin cupboards. There was no such thing as an ensuite back then — not in Bulgaria anyway.

I was just excited to be there, however, and was looking forward to checking out the first international stadium in which I would compete. The next morning the whole team visited the stadium and made a couple of unpleasant discoveries. The toilets were nothing but a hole in the middle of the floor. It was the first time I'd seen anything like it, so I had to take lessons from Colin on how to enter, where to stand, and where to find the toilet paper. It certainly wasn't the nicest way to spend those crucial last moments before a competition. To make it worse, when you can't see, your imagination takes over. As I lined myself up on the footplates and crouched over what I envisioned to be the 'black hole of Calcutta', I prayed that my feet wouldn't slip and land me in the shit. Apart from anything else, it was a strain on the legs.

The other unpleasant discovery was that the track was in dire condition. It appeared to have been imported from another stadium and laid in strips by some dodgy carpet layer who obviously wasn't up to the task. I was actually able to walk around the track on my own using the ridges between each lane as a tactile guide. Six-inch nails had been used to tamp down parts of the track. Mark Whiteley, one of the sprinters in our team, felt the track slip from beneath him at the start of the 100 m.

Despite the dodgy accommodation and the less-than-pristine track I was still extremely proud as I pulled on my Great Britain vest before my first-ever international race, the T11 1500 m final. By the time Colin and I were into our second lap, all of my nerves were forgotten and I couldn't hear anyone behind. With 300 m to go (and bearing in mind that we had three races still to run), John Anderson, standing on the track edge, shouted that we were well clear and to ease off. I was tempted to push on and go for a fast time, but Colin was more sensible and told me to ease off. We crossed the line 50 m ahead of the second-placed athlete. I'd done it! I'd actually won my first gold medal for Great Britain, in a time of 4:27, a time much slower than my personal best. I couldn't believe how straightforward my victory had been.

We were surrounded by team-mates at the finish, and one of them lifted me off the ground in a big bear-hug. When he dropped me, however, he dropped me on Colin's foot, and I was still in my spikes — ouch! We had the 800 m semi-final to race that afternoon, but with Colin in no fit state to run, I was faced with having to withdraw from the race — but then Graham Salmon's guide, Roger Rae, offered to take over the guide rope. Normally it takes at least three training sessions to get synchronised with a new guide runner, but Roger had had plenty of experience running with Graham over 400 m, and we gelled instantly, and I ran the semi to be the fastest qualifier in 2:11.

Although still sore, Colin's foot was much better the next day and he was able to run with me in the 800 m final, much to Roger's relief. We won in 2:06, lowering my own world record by nearly two seconds, and that was even after easing down towards the finish line. We'd eased down because there was still the 5000 m to run in a couple of hours. That's 12-and-a-half times around the running track, and I'd never run that amount in one go. I didn't know what to expect, other than pain, but Neil Peerson gave me some good advice: 'Don't think about how far you have left to go, just think about how far you've run.'

Whatever way I looked at it, it felt like a marathon to me. It was hot, and I thought I would pass out before we got to the finish line, but Colin had things under control, running a perfectly paced race and keeping an eye on my competition. We won in a new world record of 17:13, winning by 55 seconds and beating the 37-year-old Norwegian Toffiri Kibuka, who had previously been the dominant force in T11 middle-distance running. Toffiri admitted to me after the race that he had become complacent, but having just been beaten in three races, he was now going to take a serious look at his training. Toffiri and I had some great battles over the next few years, and we became firm friends.

Our very young GB team celebrated long and hard on the final night of competition. A few of the youngest members of the team got very drunk before dinner on slivovitz, the local moonshine which tasted like paint stripper. Colin and I thought we'd steer away from the hard stuff, opting instead for what we mistakenly took to be dodgy-tasting beer that came in big brown bottles. By the time we realised it was the local wine that was even more potent than the moonshine, it was too late. Soon we were knocking back the slivovitz with gusto. By the end of the evening we crawled up the stairs on our hands and knees; our excuse was that our feet were sore from all the running. Boy, did we suffer the next day with the mother of all hangovers.

Our delicate heads weren't helped by the massive explosions that started shaking the hotel at regular intervals. The windows were literally rattling in their frames and the whole room shook. We thought it was Armageddon, but it turned out to be the local quarry doing some blasting work. How insensitive could they be?

Following my success at the European championships, I found myself in big demand and started receiving invitations to a lot of sporting events. One of the more interesting ones was an invitation from Maidstone Prison: I was asked (me?) to present prizes for their annual 10,000 m race. It was a fascinating afternoon being shown around the prison, seeing the gym, meeting some of the prisoners and walking the racing circuit. Instead of the usual 25 laps around a 400 m track, the prisoners had to run 46 laps of the prison yard. I presented the winner's trophy to an inmate called Dave, who I had just learned was in for murder.

I was also invited to the ITV World of Sport Awards where I was nominated for the Courage Award. ITV wanted some footage of me at work so they brought their cameras into the office. Just before the winner of the Courage Award was announced, Colin nudged me and told me I was on the big screen, shown banging away on my shorthand machine while my boss dictated a letter to me. Jimmy Hill, a well-known football pundit at that time, shouted at me from across the table, 'Take this down, would you, Bob?'

'Very funny, Jimmy,' I thought. I was just disappointed they didn't use footage of me running — after all, I didn't deserve any awards for my typing skills.

However, I was delighted to pick up the silver award. After the ceremony, Colin and I posed with the MC for the evening, Dickie Davies, who was the presenter of ITV's *World of Sport*. I watched him regularly on television, so it was a bit surreal to be standing beside him, having our photo taken. He was the first celebrity I'd met, but it was an experience I would learn to get used to.

I couldn't wait to see what effect the hard work I'd put in over the winter with my guide runners would yield; everything had been focused on preparing for the 1984 Paralympic Games in New York. After my performances in the European championships, the selectors had told me that if I remained fit, then I'd be on the plane to the US. But I didn't just want to prove to them that I was fit; I was determined to run faster than ever and smash my three world records.

My first opportunity to do this came in April, where Colin and I ran in a 1500 m race in Reading. The first race of the season always seems disproportionately tougher than any others, and this one was no exception. I really felt as though I was dragging myself around, but it was worth it — we ran 4:15.9, taking nearly four seconds off the world record. I was ecstatic, especially as I knew this performance would rubber-stamp my place in the British Team that would compete in New York. Only two years ago I had exchanged the confines of the goalball court for the wide open space of the running track, and now I would be going to my second Paralympic Games, but this time as an athlete. Could it really get much better?

It did. A few weeks later, I started running with Vic Smith. Vic had been one of the fastest 1500 m runners in the country, and over the next few years he became my most important guide runner, trusted coach and adviser. He was a huge factor in helping me become even stronger, fitter and faster.

Our first race together was the 1500 m semi-final in the Kent championships. We set another world record and learned a great deal about racing together. Sprinting from the gun to get in a good position, we had to run wide as the others were bunched together, leaving no room to make the inside. Not until we were running along the home straight for the first time did it dawn on me that we were actually leading the race. It was hard for me to believe that I was in front of some of the best, sighted middle-distance athletes in England. As we went through the first lap, the timekeeper called out our time: just 60 seconds. This was the fastest I'd run the first lap in any 800 m race, never mind a 1500 m, and I was so surprised that I slammed on the brakes. We went from first to last within 50 m and lost our synchronisation.

As we crossed the finish line, we had to lean on each other so we didn't collapse in a sweaty, heaving mess. When Vic caught his breath he told me he'd never worked that hard in any other race. Running out of synchronisation is so much harder — we were practically fighting each other. Despite that, I'd still taken a further two seconds off the world record, but at that moment, we were too knackered to care.

The next day was the 5000 m, which we were pretty nervous about as it's far enough to run when things are going smoothly, let alone when you are running out of synchronisation. We needn't have worried — the race went perfectly. We gelled so well that it felt like we were running as one, and we blitzed the world record, finishing in a time of 16:06.8, a full 67 seconds faster than the mark I'd set in Bulgaria the previous year.

By this time I was running six to seven days a week. If a guide runner wasn't available, I couldn't run and suffered withdrawal symptoms. On one such occasion I had the bright idea of going out for a run with my guide dog, Henley. We headed down to the start of the motorway bridge and I took his harness off, realising that it would be extremely unfair to expect him to guide me at speed while he was in his harness. I then just held on to his lead in much the same way as I did the guide rope. By the time we'd done a lap, I'd realised what a stupid idea it had been, having nearly broken my ankle on the curb three times. It was the last time I asked Henley to take the place of my guide runners.

Another regular guide runner was Jim Stelfox, who worked in the same building as me and used to take me out for a lunchtime run. We had a narrow escape just two weeks before I was due to fly to New York for the Paralympics. We were crossing Lower

Thames Street when . . . wallop! The driver of a green Morris Marina, having signalled to turn right, drove straight into us as we crossed the road. The first thing I knew was Jim being launched into my arms. I merely felt the car's bumper brush my knee, whereas Jim took the brunt of the impact on his thigh. Even this didn't prevent him running the next day, though. We'd been very lucky — the driver had at least been alert enough to slam on the brakes before any serious damage was done.

Lloyds Bank was really supportive of my running — I guess they might have seen some benefit from being associated with a successful British Paralympian. They were only too happy to give me time off to compete in international events. Still, it was a struggle to work full-time, with training every lunchtime and from 7–9 p.m. every night. But it would be another 15 years before Paralympic athletes received full-time funding for their training, so I had little choice but to work.

All the difficulties of fitting running in around work were soon forgotten when the British team left London en route for the 7th Paralympiad on 14 June 1984. The Games were to be held on Long Island, New York, and travelling into New York City was a fantastic, unforgettable experience. As we emerged from the subway, the first thing to hit me was the noise. A full, professional-sounding jazz band was playing on a street corner. I would have liked to have stopped and listened to it, but there was shopping to be done.

I bought my first Walkman in New York, one with a built-in radio. It really helped while away the hours whilst I was saving my energy for racing. Now I could switch between Queen's latest album, 'The Works', on cassette, and the local radio. A favourite on the airwaves was 'Time after Time' by Cindy Lauper, a song which will always remind me of those Paralympics. The Games were even more special because Mum and Dad flew out to support me. It was their first major international meet and their first time in the United States, and their presence made me even more determined to win a medal.

In the early evening of 17 June the opening ceremony of the Games began. The teams had spent a large part of the very warm afternoon waiting around whilst the athletes from each country were directed into their correct places for the procession into the stadium. At the previous Games in 1980, most of the athletes had gone straight into the stand while just a select few had represented their countries in the ceremony. From now on, every athlete had the opportunity to take their rightful place in the march around the stadium's running track.

Once again Colin was my guide and we spent the time mingling with the other athletes. I chatted with a 'wheelie' (wheelchair athlete) and, being inquisitive, wondered at the strength he must have in his arms. He let me feel them: his shoulders and arms were nearly as large as my legs! I also learned that, like the 'blind' categories, there were several 'wheelchair disabled' categories and that, just like ours, the lower the number, the greater the disability; the same applied to athletes with varying degrees of cerebral palsy, and amputees.

After a couple of hours spent getting to know our neighbouring athletes, it was finally Great Britain's turn to march in front of the 10,000-strong capacity crowd, which made the noise of four times that number. What an amazing, incredible atmosphere! Finally I understood what being an international athlete felt like. I was so proud, and loved being a part of it.

The 1984 New York Paralympic Games were declared open by none other than President Reagan. I was awed by the occasion, the drama and the spectacle. I felt as if I could see the impressive fireworks display; the sound of explosions and shrieks the fireworks made formed coloured pictures in my mind. This was further heightened by the exuberance of the crowd. The whole experience was amazing.

The competition promised to be tough, and not just because I was running six races in nine days; the standard was much higher than in Bulgaria. In my first race, the heat of the 800 m, we decided to give it everything. It was the ideal opportunity to get rid of some nervous energy, blow away the cobwebs, set a fast time, and send a message to my opposition. I won in 2:05.49, taking just over half a second off the world record. Toffiri, my main opposition in Bulgaria, ran 2:07 so it promised to be a good final. I was delighted, even though my lungs were burning and my hamstrings felt as though they were torn to shreds. The physio soon quieted my whining by throwing ice packs over them, reducing the inflammation and shutting me up for a while.

If I thought I had experienced pain in the 800 m, it was nothing compared with that experienced by a fellow competitor, a sprinter and triple jumper who had a tough time of it in New York. Competing in the triple jump can be a daunting prospect for a blind athlete. Just think of how much courage it must take to sprint full tilt down the track before leaping into the dark. This poor guy became disoriented on one jump, took off too early, and landed well short of the sand pit. He skidded along the track and received nasty wounds to several parts of his body. In the 100 m sprint he lost his bearings and ran off the track, taking the wind gauge with him.

I was having no such problems, thankfully. Having qualified for the 800 m as well as the 1500 m finals, Toffiri and I had our first head-to-head in the 5000 m. There were 16 athletes on the start line, plus their guide runners, so it was pretty crowded. We wanted to avoid trouble so we started fast — perhaps too fast. At the halfway mark I was 80 m clear of Toffiri and cruising. Within the space of a lap, though, I paid for my fast start with a crippling stitch in my right side, which made it difficult to put one foot in front of the other. The Norwegian caught up with us so quickly that with just over three laps to go he ran into the back of Colin, partially pulling off his right shoe. If Toffiri had gone straight past me at that point, I doubt whether I could have responded, but he was just as tired, waiting until 600 m before making his move.

Colin shouted at me: 'Forget the pain. Just shift your arse! We're not here for the silver.'

Hearing the bell, I managed to claw back the few metres the Norwegian had won from me, and with 300 m to go we moved out wide to overtake him. It took the entire back straight for all cylinders to fire, and then I kicked. Toffiri had nothing left. Colin finally kicked his shoe free and my pain was forgotten as we crossed the finish line. I'd won by seven seconds. I was 23 years old and had won my first Paralympic medal.

In the euphoria of winning, the pain was gone. Jogging around my lap of honour and waving was hard, though. The stadium might not have been filled, but I didn't care. Finally we made our way around to my parents. They were very excited; Dad was almost as tired as me, having jumped up and down a fair bit. Toffiri had to be carried off the track and put on an intravenous drip, but he recovered in time for the medal ceremony. The pain in my side had reasserted itself; it was excruciating for the rest of that day, and very uncomfortable for a couple of days after. It felt like a pulled muscle, but I wasn't about to let that stop me.

Two days later Toffiri and I did it all again in the 1500 m final. Again I managed to pull away from him in the closing stages. My team-mate, Pete Young, came in fourth. My last race was the 800 m final and I was determined to do the hat-trick. Our plan was to get away to a fast start, hold onto the lead and then kick when Colin gave the word 300 m from the finish line. Our plan worked perfectly, except that in my eagerness to get away quickly I false-started, so we had to go back to our marks. On the second attempt we got off to a good start, but so did Toffiri. We ran a blistering race and both of us went under the world record I had set in the heat. Toffiri came home in 2:04, but once again I managed to get my nose in front and improved my heat time by three seconds to win gold in 2:02.33.

I had won three gold medals! I couldn't believe it.

I made the news back home, but it was not nearly as big a deal as it would have been if I were a fully-sighted athlete. A BBC camera was at the Paralympics, but the only coverage was a highlights programme which aired five months later. The cameraman seemed to have spent most of his time in the athletes' village rather than recording the action from the stadium. I felt the 45-minute programme couldn't have been more patronising.

It implied that the most important thing to these disabled people wasn't the competition, but rather how well they got on with each other. 'Look at how they are enjoying themselves and how nice it is they are making the best of their lot in life,' was the gist of the highlights package. It was insulting. I was competing against athletes who had devoted years to their sport and committed themselves 100 per cent to training to compete at the Paralympic Games. We deserved better.

In saying that, there wasn't a great deal of political correctness in the Paralympic Village where the disability categories were referred to as 'blindies', 'wheelies' and 'amps'. When the competition was over, I let my hair down a bit — at least I still had some then — and went with Colin to the End of Games party. It was a sight to behold. A group of amputee athletes were doing the 'Hokey Cokey', singing 'You put your left leg in, take your right arm out . . . ' There were prosthetic limbs flying everywhere.

Arriving home was a bit of a shock. Not only did the papers want to talk to me, but the mayor of Rochester called to congratulate me on my achievements and let me know I was to receive an award from the City of Rochester. 'Would Monday be convenient?' he asked. It was my first taste of being a minor celebrity. I had little time to talk to anyone, including my family, and to take it all in. To make things even more hectic, Colin married his long-time girlfriend, Angela, soon after we got back. It was tough for Colin to be away for three weeks in New York just before his wedding, and tougher still for his bride to make the final wedding preparations on her own. I will always be grateful for their support and sacrifice.

Just seven days after I got home from the US, Chris, my coach, and I were on another plane, this time to Norway where I was competing in the Bislet Games, a major Grand Prix athletics meeting. I was running with Steve James, a new guide runner, who had just run his first sub-four-minute mile. Fifty years ago Steve would have been a top international athlete, whereas the top milers now are running over ten seconds faster.

The Bislet Stadium in Oslo has a unique, intimate and electric atmosphere. Filled to capacity, which it was that night, the buzz is unbelievable. Warming up, I was struck by how close the crowd was to the track. In sprint events, the spectators were almost able to touch the athletes in the outside lane. The straights were longer than any other track I had run on, which I guessed would be especially noticeable on the home straight when trying to head for the finish line.

The 1500 m race in the Bislet Grand Prix was a mixed-disability race. I had to battle it out with an arm amputee who didn't want to let me past him, and he held the lead for most of the second lap. Eventually I managed to get around him to win the race in a new world record of 4:10.96. I had followed in the footsteps of Steve Ovett, Seb Coe, Steve Cram and Dave Moorcroft who had all set world records at the famous Bislet track in Oslo. Mine was the 47th world record. The lap of honour was brilliant — it seemed as though everyone wanted to shake my hand.

After the race, even though I was sitting at the same table as him, Andy Norman, the team manager, ignored me and handed Chris the equivalent of US$100 to give to me in recognition of my world record. It was my first financial reward, but it was ironic really because the fully-sighted athletes were being paid thousands of dollars just to put on their shoes. Still, at the post-Games party for the athletes, as Chris and I walked in everyone started applauding. I was astonished to learn that they were applauding me. Here I was, a blind bloke from Strood, getting a standing ovation from some of the best athletes in the world. I was a runner, and at that moment I felt so proud of what I had achieved.

Chapter 7 – World record on a shoestring

I was starting to get used to the limelight, and was about to add mixing with royalty into this heady brew. In November 1984 I was awarded the Disabled Sports Personality of the Year by sporting icon Sebastian Coe. A highlight of the evening was being introduced to the guest of honour, Princess Anne, who was the after-dinner speaker.

In 1986 I met Prince Charles and Princess Diana in the quadrangle outside Buckingham Palace. I was one of several well-known athletes selected to run from Pall Mall to the gates of Buckingham Palace to raise awareness of famine in Africa. The one-mile run was led by Homar Halifer who was 'running for life' in cities around the world. Then a couple of years later at a dinner celebrating the achievements of the Paralympic and Olympic athletes at the Savoy Hotel, I was introduced to Prince Andrew's wife, Sarah Ferguson, better known as Fergie. As she walked away, my friend heard Fergie ask an official from the Paralympic Association how old I was, and on hearing the answer she commented on how impressed she was by what I'd achieved at such a young age. It was nice to know she was genuinely interested.

At the height of my running career, I was running regularly with four very good mates who were at least as fit as me. Vic Smith set the sessions and, as my main guide runner, inflicted the most pain. Jim pushed me hard at lunchtimes. Mick Banfield and Vic's son, Rod, had also become regular guide runners. I was on the verge of running sub-two minutes for the 800 m, under 15-and-a-half minutes for the 5000 m and, most significantly, breaking the four-minute mark for the 1500 m. But all the running was starting to take its toll. I found myself limping occasionally, but like many elite athletes I ignored the warning signs and kept on running.

Finally I went to see the British team physio in East London. Again, work couldn't have been more supportive; they allowed me to use the Lloyds Bank chauffeurs to drive me to appointments. The physio suspected the problem was more than just muscular, and sent me straight to a bone specialist. He took one glance at the X-rays and told me I had a massive lesion on the upper third of my right tibia (the larger of the two bones below the knee) which would take up to three months to mend. There were fewer than four weeks to the European championships in Rome, and it was clear I wouldn't be going.

I was devastated not to go to Rome. I had trained so hard. I was fit and ready to fight it out for the gold medal. Running was such a big part of my life by now. Not only did it feature in my daily routine, but it was also a part of my social life, as my guides had become my friends. To get the sentence from the physio not to run for five months was a real blow, and the months off were a very difficult and frustrating time for me. I managed to maintain a decent level of fitness by getting permission from the chairman of Lloyds Bank to use his exercise bike and shower at lunchtimes. I also went swimming a couple of times a week. Again it was my friends who helped get me through it.

I had learned a very important, if costly, lesson. I was determined to make up for lost time, regain my fitness, and show the world what I was capable of achieving.

The first indication of just how fit I was came in May at the 1986 Kent county championships. Vic and I ran a great race in the heat of the 1500 m on Saturday morning; in the last 300 m I could hear us overtaking athletes who'd been ahead of us the whole race, which gave me even more strength to keep going. I finished fourth in a time of 4:08.8 which was good enough for a place in the final. This was a significant achievement. It was the first and only time I made the final of one of the strongest county championships against sighted runners, and I'd taken two seconds off the world record into the bargain.

Arriving at the stadium the next day to run in the 5000 m race, I had a bit of a scare. You'd think I'd be really well organised, with everything in its place and knowing exactly where to lay my hand on anything, right? Well that's not always the case, especially when I'm nervous. I had actually forgotten to pack my guide rope. Luckily Vic had a spare pair of running shoes in his car, and we used one of the laces with a loop tied at either end as the guide rope. It worked perfectly. I ran 16:01.4, taking five seconds off my own world record. You could say it was my 'world record on a shoestring'.

My training was going extremely well. I was back to full fitness, and getting faster. In July, Vic and I discussed the possibility of setting another world record, this time over 800 m. In my first 800 m race of the season I'd clocked 2:03.5, so I knew I was close. What would it mean to run a sub-two-minute time for 800 m? I can't put that into words — it would be the most significant achievement of my running career. While it certainly seemed within my reach, we thought it would surely take two, probably three, races to get anywhere close to breaking that barrier.

Then I got a big confidence boost on one particular track session with Steve James: I ran two successive 600 m in under 90 seconds, convincing me I was oh so close to becoming the first blind runner to break that magical two-minute barrier. On a high after that training session, I caught the train to Wembley Stadium to see Queen play live. The support acts were The Alarm, INXS and Status Quo. It couldn't get much better really.

But it did when, a week later, Vic and I drove to Brighton for a track meet which was supposed to be a stepping stone to an attempt on a sub-two-minute time. The venue for our record attempt was Withdean Stadium, which was set in a natural bowl. It was surrounded by woods, with a beautiful pub on the outside of the home straight, the veranda of which overlooked the finish line. As soon as we arrived and took a walk around the track, we knew the conditions were ideal for running fast times. There had been rain overnight, leaving the air smelling lovely and fresh, and now it was dead calm. During our strides, the final part of any warm-up before a track race, I felt relaxed on all four of my short acceleration runs — a really good sign that all cylinders were firing.

Assembled behind the start line, the starter called us to our marks. The race won't start until everyone has their toes behind the line. We'd developed a technique to make this easy for me. Vic placed his foot on the line, I moved my foot forward until it touched Vic's, and we were ready.

The starter's gun fired and we were released on the two-lap journey. We tucked in at the back of the field and were pulled along at what seemed a good pace. At the bell to signal the last lap, Vic was shocked and I nearly wet my pants when I heard the timekeeper shout 57 seconds. It hadn't felt that fast. Was it? Although I was hanging on for all I was worth, inevitably the pace slowed a little. Vic said later: 'With 300 m to go, I tried to get you to speed up, but you refused, which I now think was a wise decision, because with 150 m to go you sprinted, and for the first time ever you were dangerously close to dropping me. You pushed so hard all the way through to the finish.'

We had no idea what time I'd run, but we both felt the world record must have gone. We didn't dare hope for more. While the judges conferred, Vic and I passed the time by warming down as Vic kept one eye on the track for a sign. Finally, over the public address system, we heard the result: 'Bob Matthews of Medway AC — 1 minute . . . ' We didn't hear the rest because we were jumping up and down, whooping with joy. I'd done it! I'd broken the magical two-minute mark.

Ten minutes later we were told my official time — 1:59.90. It is a record that still stands to this day — no other blind person has come within three seconds of beating it.

It was one of the proudest moments of my life. Since losing my sight at the age of 20, I had taken up running to discover who I really was. Although I had focused on breaking the two-minute barrier for the 800 m, I still found my success incredible. Now I was really on the same playing field as quality sighted athletes, and hoped I had their respect as well as their admiration. After all, had Seb Coe and I set our world records for 800 m at the same meeting, I'd have finished just 120 m (18 seconds) behind him.

It takes a level of understanding and mutual trust between guide runner and athlete to run as well and successfully as did Vic and I. I went running with one bloke who in the space of 200 m ran me off a curb, bounced me into a fence and finished off by running me into a lamp post. I didn't ask him for another run.

However, when I'm running with a competent and confident guide in whom I have complete faith, I run freely, not worrying if we have to run either side of a bollard or take curbs without slowing. Naturally, running as fast and confidently as I do increases the chance of an accident, from twisting my ankle to banging my knuckle on a post. Branches are sometimes more difficult to gauge — I've often thought that I'm too tall to be blind. It's not always easy for a guide to take in all the obstacles at ground level as well as looking out for low branches. I sometimes come home with scratches and bruises, but it's something I have got used to.

I've run tens of thousands of miles, guided by over 100 athletes with whom I have a great rapport, but have only raced and trained cross-country with the more confident guide runners as it is so much more demanding and technical. One of those guides was Vic. Vic would arrange our long runs to include plenty of ploughed fields which was great fun, even if the heavy, clinging earth made lifting one mud-caked foot after the other so much harder — I felt like I was wearing diving boots.

The training paid off, though. In a Kent league race at Moat Park whilst being guided by Vic, we had to jump over a stream, and I got such a buzz when we landed safely on the other side. Friends watching told me later that I'd jumped it like a sighted athlete. Years later in the Warwickshire cross-country championships, Paul Harwood and I scaled a steep climb, then stormed downhill, with Paul using his shoulder and the rope to guide me in and out of trees. Shouting 'left' and 'right', he pushed and pulled me around two tight turns, then 20 m later he shouted 'stream' and we plunged down a muddy bank into cold, knee-deep water, before clambering back up the muddy bank on the far side and regaining our normal stride. You just don't get this level of exhilaration anywhere else.

I love the challenge of racing over the country where each stride is more than ever a step into the unknown. Naturally, my guide will tell me about hills, streams and hazards such as tree roots, but it's impossible for him to communicate every dip or bump. I just have to adjust. As I'm not able to anticipate how each foot will land, I've naturally developed a slightly higher knee lift to help cope with the uncertain terrain. Inevitably there's the odd stumble which slows me slightly but I'm still able to compete with my sighted peers.

If I'm honest, some days it's just plain hard to get motivated. Like the days when the rain lashes down, soaking you to the bone. Or those winter training sessions when your breath freezes and ice forms on your eyelashes, while your fingers stop working as they are numbed to the core, and it's quite a feat of patience and concentration to untie your shoelaces. It is times like these that you think, 'Is it really worth it?' But then there are few experiences that come close to those fantastic-to-be-alive moments: like running with a good mate where you feel free and are completely unaware of the guide rope; feeling the sun on your face on a clear morning and listening to the sounds of birds singing as you speed by; and, of course, those moments of complete elation when you reach your own personal milestone and you know then that all the hard work was worth it.

I was fitter and faster than ever, and I was ready for the inaugural world championships for the disabled in Gothenburg in Sweden. It was my first time in Scandinavia since the goalball trip to the 1980 European club championships in Copenhagen six years earlier. So much had changed in that time. Again I was competing in the 800 m, 1500 m and 5000 m, with Vic fresh from the European masters' (veterans') championships. The accommodation was the best I'd enjoyed at a major meet, the food was good, and we had Sky television — another first. The racing also went really well.

In the absence of Toffiri who was injured, I won the 800 m and 5000 m. In the 1500 m final I wanted to run hard from the front and try to improve my world record. I set a new mark of 4:08.33. The Gothenburg championships were a total success for me, especially as I proved to myself that my form and fitness were at least as good as they had been before the previous year's stress fracture.

Off the track I had another romantic dalliance. This was becoming a habit on these trips abroad. No wonder I enjoyed international running so much! Matilda was a volunteer for the world championships and was a local girl. Post-competition we had a couple of days to ourselves and it was a great opportunity for me to unwind and have some fun. One night a few of us got quite drunk, and I have a vague memory of being carted back to the hotel in a shopping trolley. The next day a few of us decided it would be a great idea to go windsurfing at a nearby lake. After a quick lesson and demonstration on land from James Brown and his brother, Will, I was let loose on the water. I got a stiff back from continually having to haul the sail out of the water, but it was great fun, especially when everything 'clicked' and I felt the wind fill my sail as I zoomed a full 40 metres across the lake, with the lads shouting directions from their windsurfing boards.

I managed to improve my 1500 m time again a month later, running with Steve James in Birmingham. We were on for a really fast time until the last 600 m when it felt like I was running in treacle. If I hadn't known better, I'd have sworn we were running uphill. But Steve's racing experience shone through, and the record attempt would have been shot to pieces had he not been able to talk me through it and give me the confidence I needed. We clipped just over a second off the world record to set a new mark of 4:07.2. During our lap of honour, I was really pleased to be recognised and congratulated by the late Ron Pickering, the extremely well-respected and knowledgeable coach and BBC commentator.

One of the biggest charity fundraisers in the UK began in 1987 and is called Comic Relief. Its main event is known as Red Nose Day, where people make a donation and receive a red nose. One of my guide runners, Rod Smith, owned Barnet's Hairdressers in Chatham. He asked me to be the guest hairdresser at his salon for Red Nose Day. The victims were given no prior warning that a celebrity, let alone a blind celebrity, would be wielding the clippers, giving them a 'number one' hair cut. I don't think I was the hairdresser they had in mind — I was anxious and they were nervous — but we did manage to raise some money towards Red Nose Day.

With all the training I was doing it was important to include some downtime. My sister, Sue, and I went away together on holiday in 1987, just the two of us, to Spetses, one of the Greek islands. June was the only time we could go; it was in the middle of my running season, and just three months out from another major international, the European championships for the blind, in Moscow, but I was determined to have some quality time with Sue and not put my running first for a change. I was less worried about the mini-international athletics meeting in Paris in which I would be competing the day after flying home from Spetses.

Although I really wanted to go away with her, I explained to Sue how it could affect my preparations, so we worked out a really good compromise: I spent much of the holiday aqua-jogging in the sea under Sue's supervision. I waded out into the sea towing Sue on her lilo airbed so she could sunbathe nearby and time me while I simulated a track session in the water. I can only imagine the looks we got from the other people on the beach, but it didn't matter. As ever, Sue and I had a great time together.

We travelled home overnight and arrived back in London early on the Friday morning. At Victoria station, Sue went to work and I caught the boat train to Paris. It was a crazy travel schedule ahead of an international race meeting, and my preparation wasn't helped by finding sleep impossible. Strangely enough, the races went really well. With Rod as my guide runner, I won a fast 800 m and then I took on Graham Salmon in the 400 m; he had been the fastest blind athlete when I first started running. I edged past him to win in 55.3, equalling his British record.

Next day, before catching the train home, Rod and I did a spot of sightseeing. From the top of the Eiffel Tower, Rod described the city of Paris laid out below as a patchwork quilt with an array of different colours, shades and hues. His description really did paint pictures with words and made me feel as though I was the one with eyes.

For the European championships in Moscow, I was guided by Gavin Burren who was an exceptional athlete. Only 17 years old, he had already proved his ability by having run below 3:48 for the 1500 m when aged just 16. Moscow in 1987 was the capital of the communist empire, and was very different to the Moscow of today. The sight of armed guards wasn't unusual. Similar to Bulgaria, the food was particularly unappetising. At breakfast we were served a kind of cheesy sponge cake that weighed as much as a house brick. I can eat most things and hate to leave food on my plate, but even I couldn't finish that tasteless slab of sponge. As you can imagine, I wasn't too happy when the same sponge was served up for our evening meal.

The weather was dull and dreary for most of the week we were in Russia, so my impression of Moscow was of a rather grey and dreary place. Even so, Gavin did a great job of describing what he could see. I was struck by the image of the onion-shaped domes on St Basil's Cathedral in Red Square, even if the church bells sounded somehow tinnier than the more sonorous and sweet-sounding bells of churches in the UK.

In our hotel we were often asked whether we'd like to trade our jeans, bags or shoes, or anything else that seemed strange or exotic, to our Russian hosts. One team member thought he had done some great business when he sold his kit bag for 40 Russian roubles. The only problem was he didn't get an opportunity to spend the money in Russia, and when we got home no bank was willing to take roubles for sterling.

We ran in the Lenin Stadium in Moscow, the same stadium that hosted the 1980 Olympics. Over 100,000 spectators had packed into the stadium then to see Seb Coe and Steve Ovett battle it out in the 800 m and 1500 m Olympic finals. In contrast we ran in front of a couple of hundred soldiers who I think were paid to be there as supporters rather than for any security reasons. With the stadium so empty it was impossible for me to picture how vast it actually was, but despite the eerie feeling it was still great to run on the same track as Coe and Ovett. I won the 1500 m and 5000 m, and then had my first race against a Russian in the 800 m who gave me a scare. He tracked us until the last 300 m when I managed to open a gap to win in 2:03.

One bright Saturday morning in May 1987, my nan collected the mail and found a letter for me stamped with a postmark from the Houses of Parliament. 'Oh, it's from the Prime Minister,' she joked. When she opened the letter she was stunned to read that it actually *was* a letter from the Prime Minister's office. The letter informed me that I was to be honoured with an MBE, or Member of the Order of the British Empire (although I do sometimes jokingly refer to it as recognition of a 'Mad Blind Englishman'). The letter insisted that I keep the news strictly private, and even though I wanted to shout it to the world, I managed to keep it a secret, more or less.

The great day arrived and I set off for Buckingham Palace with Mum and Dad. I was all dressed up in my top hat and tails, feeling and, if I'm honest, enjoying the stares as Henley and I led the way through Charing Cross station. The thought ran through my mind that a century earlier, the interested looks from passers-by would have been for a dog wearing a harness, seeming to guide this gentleman. However, Henley couldn't come all the way with me to the palace — perhaps it was feared he would chew one of Her Majesty's corgis — and instead he stayed with one of Dad's work colleagues.

The three of us grew more excited as our taxi passed through the gates of Buckingham Palace into the quadrangle. Hearing the change of surface from metalled road to the crunching of gravel made the moment more real for Dad and me, while Mum for the first time in her life was able to see the palace from 'the other side' of the railings. I then felt the taxi turning right and, as it braked to a halt, I knew we were there — we had arrived at Queen Elizabeth's front door.

Mum and Dad were ushered into the ballroom to watch the investitures while I was met by a page who, during the next hour or so, gave me some tips on etiquette. He told me how I should nod, as I didn't know how to bow properly, before taking the last three steps up to the Queen. He instructed me to stay silent while Her Majesty pinned the MBE on my lapel. I asked the page how tall she was because I like to look people in the face when they are talking to me. 'Her Majesty is five feet, two inches,' the page informed me. As I'm six-foot-two (1.88 m), I reminded myself to look down when she was presenting the MBE. However, the page hadn't told me that the Queen would be standing on a podium. Too late! Next thing I knew the Queen was pinning the MBE to my lapel, but when she spoke her voice came from my eye level, and I realised with a jolt that she was standing on something and I'd been ogling the royal bosom.

It was incredible to think that the most famous person in the world, our monarch and someone I greatly admired, was the person presenting me with the MBE. I was 26 years old, and the first Paralympian to be awarded with the MBE. What an unforgettable and proud moment.

Chapter 8 – Driving blind

Just as everything seemed to be going smoothly, Vic Smith, who had been my main guide runner from 1984 to 1986, injured his knee, effectively ending his career and our running partnership. Thanks mainly to Vic, I had set six world records during this period. His dedication and commitment meant that I was able to train hard four times a week. His knee injury was a cruel blow, and although he did make a comeback in 1989 when he shared guiding duties with Matt Lawton when I set my last two world records, it was a sad way to end what had been a hugely successful running partnership.

With Vic out of action, I quickly realised how dependent I was upon having regular access to good-quality guide runners. Without Vic I struggled to find anyone to run with locally until I moved to Hereford a few years later. It taught me never to take anything for granted and that nothing lasts for ever. I still went for slower, steady runs with Vic and the occasional track session, but I desperately needed more guides to push me if I was to successfully defend my three Paralympic titles in the Seoul Paralympic Games in 1988. Enter Barry Roydon, who became one of my fastest guides; by January 1988 we were regular training partners. Barry was an exceptional runner; he could handle a hard cross-country race on his own on a Saturday and still guide me around a 10 mile (16 km) road race on a Sunday.

Away from running, my job with the personnel department in Lloyds Bank in the city was ticking along nicely. Henley and I enjoyed our daily commute, especially when it was shortened by ten minutes when the department moved to Black Horse House directly above Cannon Street station. However, in early 1988, rumours began to circulate about cost-cutting measures and, sure enough, within a few weeks, it was confirmed that personnel would be moving to Bristol. This wasn't an option for me — the upheaval would be too great — but luckily I was offered a job with Black Horse Life Assurance, a subsidiary of Lloyds Bank Plc, at their office in Chatham, where I would be working with 12 girls. I thought I had died and gone to heaven.

I got on so well with the girls in the office that Jane, the office manager, occasionally had to remind me, gently but firmly, to do my work and to keep quiet and let the girls do theirs. All the girls were great fun, but I thought one girl in particular was special. Her name was Tracey, and we would chat and flirt throughout the day. It certainly made going to work more fun.

Black Horse Life did something no previous employer had done — they bought me a computer. Not only did it have a screen reader (reading exactly what was on the screen) but it also had VersaBraille, an electronic 80-character Braille display which, at a press of a button, moved up or down a line. This computer revolutionised my work because for the first time I could edit and spellcheck my own work. I was more productive, quicker and more accurate at what I did, and for the first time I was honestly able to say I was good at my job.

On my third day with Black Horse Life I was excused to go to Brands Hatch to meet a potential sponsor. This was the first time any company had shown an interest in sponsoring me. Two years before I had written to all the major sportswear and footwear companies to request sponsorship. I always got the standard rejection letter in reply: 'We receive many similar requests, etc etc . . . so thanks, but no thanks.' I hadn't realised there were so many world-record holders and gold medallists in the UK looking for sponsorship.

So when the Canterbury Mortgage Centre asked to meet me to discuss a 'mutually beneficial partnership', I went for it. The deal was I would make media appearances organised by their public relations officer and, in return, they promised to pay me for my services. I was chuffed that they saw some potential in me. As it turned out, my first and last promotional role for the Canterbury Mortgage Centre was at Brands Hatch because, before the contract had been drawn up, the company went into liquidation. Still, at least I had a memorable day out at Brands Hatch on the company.

TVS (the regional television station) and Radio Kent were there to capture the 'blind man driving'. Rob Walker, who was obviously a very trusting mate, had given me some driving lessons in his car at West Malling aerodrome. Another mate, Martin Komorowski, also let me drive his car, which he often borrowed from his dad, in the local car parks. My lessons with Martin ended abruptly one evening when I hit a curb and damaged the chassis. Sorry, Martin's dad!

Whilst I had prepared as well as possible for my maiden drive around Brands Hatch, I was still very nervous. I was introduced to Rick, the chief driving instructor, who told me about the car I would be driving. It was a Honda Civic CRX with 16-valve fuel injection, which I took to mean that it was very quick. After the pep talk and photos, I was helped into my crash helmet and firmly strapped into the passenger seat. The first thing that occurred to me was how basic and spartan the car was inside. There wasn't a lot of padding on the seat, no arm rests, and even no door panels. Everything that could have been stripped out had been stripped out. All this was forgotten when Rick started the car and we set off around the Brands Hatch racing circuit.

Driving at a moderate speed over the first two laps, Rick described the circuit, the turns, the chicanes and the speeds the car would reach in a race. He told me: 'When we come to the third lap, I'll show you what the car can do.' I am a speed freak, so this was music to my ears. As we approached the start of the third lap, I braced myself in anticipation, and then felt the thrill as Rick floored the accelerator and the seat punched me in the back. I could now appreciate the need for a harness as I was pinned to my seat by the G-force as Rick threw the car around the track. This has to be one of the most amazing experiences of my life.

All too soon Rick braked to a halt, and we swapped places. I waited with nervous anticipation behind the wheel of the car with the engine running, while the cameraman, who was either brave or stupid, squeezed into the back. The car wasn't tuned just to sit idle, and I was about to stall it when I remembered just in time from my driving lessons with Rob that he had told me to dip the clutch and touch the gas. It could have been an embarrassing start to my driving career.

At last we were ready to go. Rick used the clock face to describe which direction I should steer: when he shouted one or 11 o'clock, it meant a slight turn right or left. Ten or two o'clock indicated a tighter turn, and so on. It was a wonderful experience, and with more practice I would have done better than 50 mph (80 kph), but nevertheless, it was a remarkable day.

Another memorable day was the time a mate took me for a spin on the back of his 1000 cc motorbike. I jumped at the chance, but held on tight as he accelerated from 60 to 100 mph to overtake some cars. I definitely felt more vulnerable than I did strapped into a race car, but it was so exhilarating.

Although I enjoy travelling at speed and it gives me a huge buzz, my favourite way to travel and experience new places is on a tandem bike. Sampling new smells, sounds, and, just as important, having new scenery described as I pedal past is so exhilarating. My first opportunity to tour on a tandem came when Matt Lawton, one of my mates and guide runners, asked if I'd like to join Kay, Matt's sister, himself and two friends on a week's cycle around Brittany in Northern France. We borrowed a tandem from the Metro Sports Club for the Visually Impaired in London. Matt is a good cyclist and, after a couple of trial rides, we were confident it wouldn't be a problem for me.

This was the first time I'd sampled the French countryside, and I loved the atmosphere of the place. It was heaven to pedal through the countryside, pick up a baguette and some cheese, and eat lunch in a village square or on a river bank. I was less impressed, however, with my first experience of oysters, and I swallowed mine as quickly as possible. I didn't quite understand what all the fuss was about; they just felt slimy to me, with little taste.

After we pitched our tents at the end of a long, hard day on the bike, Matt and I would go for a run. Apart from the tiredness, making the transition from cycling to running was tough, and it gave me a much greater respect for what triathletes do. However, when we ran some of the tiredness out of our legs, we put in some good sessions. We needed to — the Seoul Paralympics were five months away, and Matt had high hopes for his own track season.

Perhaps the tandem tour was a risky strategy only a few months out from the Paralympics, but I appreciated the benefits of cross-training and believed the hard cycling helped my strength and stamina for the Games. The free physiotherapy I received from Sue Blunt at the Alexandra Hospital in Chatham was also a big part of my preparations for Seoul; Sue's healing hands certainly helped prevent my minor niggles becoming major injuries. As well as being a top-class physio, Sue also offered to look after Henley while I was in Seoul.

Shortly before leaving for the Paralympics in South Korea, Steve James, who would be my running guide and room-mate throughout the Games, myself and a few other members of the Paralympic team had the pleasure of meeting Princess Diana at a small send-off party. The heavyweight boxer Frank Bruno was also there. What a contrast! One moment I was shaking Princess Diana's slender hand, the next I was craning my neck to look up at big Frank Bruno who enveloped my hand in his great big paw.

This was the fourth and last time I would meet Princess Diana. The first time we met was in the Buckingham Palace quadrangle along with Prince Charles, and on the previous occasion, in April 1988, the princess had presented me with the Evian Health Award.

'How is your swimming going?' I'd asked her, because I knew she was a regular in the royal pool.

She replied that she had just been swimming that morning. 'In fact, I wouldn't be surprised if you could still smell the chlorine,' she laughed.

Our flight to Seoul seemed to take for ever. We had a brief stopover in Jeddah, Saudi Arabia, where those who could walk were allowed off to stretch their legs before our next stop in Bahrain. The unfortunate wheelies had to stay put in their seats. Finally we reached Seoul, a full 18 hours later.

After travelling halfway across the world safely, we nearly didn't make it from the airport to the Paralympic Village, as our coach driver had to take sudden evasive action to avoid a suicidal maniac who cut into our lane on the motorway. We just assumed that that was how they drove in Asia.

I was intrigued to see what the food would be like in South Korea. I love my food — I don't eat to run, I run to eat. Of course, having been an elite athlete for many years allowed me to eat more than most without piling on the kilos. Doing a hard run at lunchtime worked best for me because it meant I could have a normal breakfast three hours before I ran. However, for a hard run in the evening I couldn't eat anything heavier than a couple of sandwiches at lunchtime. I avoided cucumber and onions which are slower to digest and have a nasty habit of repeating.

Fridays used to be a real treat for me, because after my lunchtime run with Jim in London, I had the evening free from training. It meant I could sit down with Mum and Dad when I got home at 7 p.m. and eat one of my favourite dinners, Mum's steak and kidney pie with mashed potato, cabbage and gravy. The rest of the week I had to settle for a microwave dinner on my own when I got home from evening training, usually well after 9 p.m. After my long run most Sundays, I looked forward to a pub lunch washed down by a couple of pints. I really felt as though I'd earned it, which made the meal taste so much better.

When travelling to a new country, one of the things I look forward to is sampling the food. I was disappointed with Bulgaria and Russia, but everywhere else I've travelled the food has been great. I would never have thought to put maple syrup over scrambled eggs and bacon, which I enjoyed on Darling Harbour in Sydney. In the US I enjoyed my first taste of pumpkin pie and bagels, and the ice-cream was to die for.

I didn't really know what to expect in Seoul, but I was intrigued, even if I had to be cautious about what I ate ahead of competition. The first thing I tried was some unusually sweet rice cakes which were quite nice. I avoided most of the more dubious-looking food until after the racing. The Koreans did their best to provide plenty of western-style food, although they never really got the hang of scrambled eggs, which were usually served runny and raw.

Steve, my guide runner, lived 150 miles (240 km) away in Birmingham, and because of this we had done relatively little training together, apart from the occasional track session. Still, I was fit and confident and knew that I had the best man for the job running beside me. We had eight days to work together before the competition started, and by the end of our pre-competition training we were running so smoothly together that I was no longer aware of the rope linking us.

The athletes' village was the best and safest place for our slow, steady runs and our recovery runs. The only drawback was not being able to avoid listening to 'Hand in Hand', the theme song for the Paralympics and Olympics, which was played over the public address system again and again. We came to know that song pretty well. The only running track available for the athletes to train on was the warm-up track next to the main Chamsil Stadium (now referred to as the Jamsil Stadium). During our allocated session it was crowded with wheelies, amps and blindies, all trying to find some space — it was like running the gauntlet. Steve needed eyes in the back of his head to avoid colliding with anybody, but still we came close to being run over by a few wheelies.

We weren't able to train in the main stadium as most of the track was covered with the paraphernalia of the opening ceremony, but we were allowed to walk along the home straight. I remember standing in lane five, the same lane that Ben Johnson had raced in earlier that summer to smash the 100 m world record, only to be later disqualified. It was also special to remember that on this same track just a few weeks earlier, the flamboyant (and now sadly departed) 'Flo-Jo', Florence Griffiths Joyner, had had the world talking about her impressive, if contentious, performances in the women's 100 m and 200 m, not to mention her fabulous fingernails.

My good build-up to the Games got even better after I got back to the athletes' village following a training run. Bill Berry, now one of the assistant managers for the Great Britain team, told me I had been selected to carry the Union Jack into the stadium at the opening ceremony. This was incredible! I would be leading the Great Britain team into the stadium at the Seoul Paralympic Games. The news came totally out of the blue for me — it was such a privilege and a thrill.

Steve and I needed to attend a 'dry run' along with all the principal players in the opening ceremony. Thankfully, as it was hot, it wasn't a full dress rehearsal and we didn't need to wear our suits. I was given tips on how to carry the flag and how to rest its weight when stationary by placing its foot on my hip to give my arms a rest. Protocol dictates that you shouldn't ground the flag pole at any stage during the ceremony, as this is considered disrespectful. Although only a glassfibre pole, it still felt rather weighty to this puny middle-distance runner.

On the morning of our first final, Steve and I helped ourselves to a soda from one of the numerous drink dispensers scattered around the village. As I went to take a drink I received a really sharp pain in my lip, which turned out to be a wasp sting. Instinctively I jerked the cup away from my mouth and showered some poor unfortunate with the contents. Still, I was worried it would affect my running, so I went straight to the first-aid room to have some antihistamine cream applied before it swelled up and became a problem. Fortunately, I suffered no reaction and I was ready to race.

The night before, I'd dreamt that I would win only silver in the 5000 m. I'd heard a Brazilian runner had been reclassified to race in my T11 category (no sight, up to some light perception), and that he was fast. However, instead of feeling nervous before the start of the race, I felt inexplicably calm and confident, and I won in 16:19, outsprinting my old mate Toffiri from Norway over the last 300 m, with the Brazilian nowhere to be seen. I progressed to the finals of the 800 m and 1500 m without incident, and won the 800 m final from the front in 2:02.

I now had two more gold medals to add to my collection, but incredibly I hadn't even raced in the main stadium yet. In order to squeeze the athletics into seven days, the Korean organisers had seen fit to put the 'lesser' races on the warm-up track. I was determined to enjoy my one and only appearance in the main Chamsil Stadium so we hit the front early, which had the added advantage of avoiding the melee as athletes and guides fought for position. However, my pace had been a little over-eager, and I was beginning to struggle with more than a lap to run. Then Steve shouted for me to 'pick it up'. Lovas, a new threat from Norway, had come from nowhere and was trying to overtake. I suddenly became aware of the noise from 20,000 spectators — it was like someone had switched the volume on — and then the sound of the bell signalling the last lap rejuvenated me.

Somehow, from somewhere deep down, I managed to find another gear. I wanted this more than Lovas did. The pain would be over very soon, and there was no way another blindie was going to beat me, no matter what it took. I held on to win by a second in 4:09; Toffiri won the bronze in 4:14. I lapped up the applause and excited chanting, but what was that crazy rattling sound? Steve explained it was the Koreans banging sticks together to show their appreciation.

Later, Steve and I were invited to the Lloyds Bank head office in the centre of Seoul. We were amazed when they showed us the front page of *The Times* newspaper from England — the main picture was of me winning my third gold medal. They also presented both of us with a recording of the theme song 'Hand in Hand'. Steve and I tried not to laugh — the last thing we needed was to hear that song again. It had been thrashed morning, noon and night at the athletes' village, and I could sing every word in my sleep.

Chapter 9 – Forget golf, stick to running

Our journey home from Seoul was a lot quicker and easier, with just the one stop in Anchorage, Alaska. It was quite a novelty to get out and stretch our legs and taste the snow outside on a viewing deck. When we got back to London, my physio's partner, Chris, drove us straight from Heathrow to the Alexandra Hospital to pick up Henley from Sue. Chris suggested it would be a nice touch to wear the medals around my neck, and although I felt self-conscious, I thought Sue might be keen to see them.

What I didn't know was that it was all a set-up. When I walked through the hospital doors I was greeted by a huge round of applause, and Steve told me there was a television camera in my face. TVS, the local regional television station, was there to film my homecoming, along with the hospital staff, the girls from my office, a few of my guide runners, my physios, Mum and Dad, and three Gillingham Football Club players, who also received physio treatment at the Alexandra. It was a totally unexpected and humbling experience, and I was just glad I'd decided to shave at Paris airport that morning.

It was the first of a number of receptions, including an invitation to Downing Street for the British Paralympic team where I got to meet the Prime Minister, Margaret Thatcher. She was as dominant a character in person as she came across on the radio and television. I thought she and I were having a conversation — just as I was starting to talk on a subject, I found myself listening to her as she'd totally taken over. How did that happen?

I was having a great time. Rochester City Council held a civic reception in recognition of my achievements in Seoul. The Lord Mayor presented me with a really nice briefcase, complete with an engraved plaque inside. On my first day back at work, the girls threw a surprise party for me. It was good to be back in the office. I was great mates with everyone, but my friendship with Tracey moved to another level. There was definitely chemistry between us — it was the first time I'd felt like this about anyone. I remember telling her she was 'endearing', which was quite a bold step for me at the time.

Nothing happened between us until the dust had settled following my return from Seoul, but a month later we started seeing each other. I was elated, barely able to believe this cute, pocket-sized girl with curly dark hair and a lovely laugh had fallen for me. Maybe my wave of success and popularity swept her off her feet, but for the time being I was on cloud nine. She was my first long-term girlfriend and I thought all my Christmases had come at once. First my success at the Paralympics and now my first real girlfriend — I was a different man, one with new-found confidence. I was on a high, I was working with some really good-quality and willing guides, so my running was going as well as ever. Things were looking good for the 1989 season.

Six months later, Tracey phoned me to say she wanted to end our relationship. I wasn't prepared for it, and I certainly hadn't seen the writing on the wall. Yes, we'd experienced some tensions, but I still thought we were getting on really well. I was stunned and, for once, I was speechless. Being dumped isn't a nice feeling for anyone. Like all things in life, though, we don't become the people we are without taking the knocks along the way.

At least I had my running to help me get over it, and I channelled all my hurt and frustration into my running, pushing myself even harder than before. Just two weeks after Tracey and I broke up, I ran 15:43.4 for the 5000 m at the Crystal Palace, knocking 18 seconds off my world record. A couple of weeks later I was back there, this time in the 1500 m. I improved my previous world record by two seconds, crossing the line in 4:05.11. Vic and Matt shared the guide running duties on both these occasions.

At the time I felt I could have run the 1500 m a lot faster, but subsequently I've realised what a good performance that was. I am proud to say this 1500 m world record still stands today. I would have been 37 seconds behind Steve Cram when he set the world mark.

That summer, Matt and I travelled to Switzerland for the European blind championships at the Letzigrund Stadium in Zurich, which is famous for hosting the Weltklasse (World Class) Athletics Grand Prix. I don't remember much about the opening ceremony, but Matt has fond memories of that night. Some of the girls in the ceremony changed their costumes right in front of us, stripping naked in front of what they assumed was a group of blind athletes, not realising that at least one of us had nothing wrong with his eyesight! It was almost too much for my 19-year-old guide to describe, but he did his best.

Somehow we managed, with the aid of a cold shower or two, to shift our focus back on to the running and our tactics for our first race. I was in the form of my life and felt very confident. However, I wasn't the only one. My Norwegian rivals, Toffiri and Lovas, were also going well, and both had come close to my 1500 m world record time. The concern, particularly in the 1500 m, was that they might try to race as a team. Our first final was the 1500 m and, after much debate, Matt and I decided to run from the front. Our concern was that the Norwegians might attempt to block me off and make me run very wide, which is much easier to do in a blind race because of course it involves four athletes, not just two.

Later Matt admitted he was terrified before the race, as I had never been beaten in a major championship, and he did not want to be responsible for my first defeat. The pace was pretty quick from the start. Matt and I sprinted to the first bend to secure pole position before we settled into a more sensible rhythm.

After 300 m I asked Matt, 'Where are they?'

'Right behind you, mate,' he replied.

The next two laps passed in a blur. The field bunched up and the

Norwegians seemed poised for an attack. I could sense they were there, and responded to the sound of the bell by picking up the pace a fraction. With 300 m left, as we'd arranged, all Matt had to say was 'straight' and we surged. Matt said later, 'You pulled half a yard ahead of me with that sudden, awesome, injection of power.' It felt fantastic.

'Five metres clear,' Matt said with 200 m left. I managed to accelerate again.

'Ten metres clear.'

As we hit the home straight we were flying and I felt great. After we crossed the finishing line, John Anderson ran over to tell us we'd run the last lap in 58 seconds and the last 300 m in 42 seconds.

After that, Matt and I won the 800 m and the 5000 m with relative ease, but I wasn't finished yet. For the first and last time, I was also running in the 400 m. The last 300 m of the 1500 m had got the other athletes worried about my speed. In training, Matt and I had run 40 seconds on each of 4 x 300 m repetitions, so 53 seconds should have been achievable. I got through the heat, but we were knocked out in the semi-final. Afterwards John Anderson said: 'Had you not waited until the others had covered the first 50 m before starting to run, you'd have made the final.'

I wasn't too disappointed, though. At last we could pig out on the fabulous ice-creams Matt had been describing all week, and I could listen to his story one more time about the pretty girls who had taken their clothes off in front of him.

In March 1988, my sister, Sue, had travelled to the West Indian island of St Maarten, in the Netherlands Antilles, to work in a bar part-owned by our cousins, Deidre and Michael. She'd initially planned to stay for three months, but three months became six months. She loved the lifestyle, and was in no hurry to come home to an English winter, so she stayed. She has lived there

Wearing black-out glasses
with the Union Jack on them,
Sydney 2000, post-marathon.

'00 10 28

Silver medal in the men's marathon, Sydney Paralympic Games, 2000.

Kath and I cycling around Ireland with the Birmingham Irish Cycle Appeal.

Abseiling in Wales.

Honorary Master of Arts degree, University of Warwick, 2001.

Inducted into the BBC Hall of Fame, 2004.

With my sisters, Ange and Sue, at our pre-wedding ceremony in St Maarten.

Wedding reception, Mantells, Auckland, 2007.

With Bruce and Sharron Kerr, my new in-laws.

Seeing my beautiful bride, Sarah, before the wedding ceremony, 2007.

With my three-day-old son, Thomas, October 2007.

Holidaying in Fiji with Thomas aged 10 months, 2008.

My beautiful family in our Auckland home.

At the 2008 British national championships at Watford with guide Paul Harwood.

Swimming with Spencer Vickers, 4.6 km from Rangitoto Island to St Heliers beach.

The guide rope.

Rob Matthews MBE.

I was your typical gormless, gawky teenager.

Early days out running.

Playing goalball in
the Netherlands.

My first guide dog, Henley.

Quando, the legendary guide dog.

Jemma, my third guide dog.

Joy, my current guide dog.

Awarded the Disabled Sports Personality of the Year in 1984, with Mum.

With my father,
Aubrey Matthews,
and his infamous
pipe.

At Buckingham Palace, having been awarded the MBE, 1987.

MBE medal.

Meeting Princess Anne
when presented with
the Disabled Sports
Personality of the Year
award in 1984.

Meeting Princess
Diana at a charity
lunch, 1987.

Meeting Margaret Thatcher at Downing Street, 1989.

Flag bearer at the Seoul Paralympic Games, 1988.

With legendary Olympic decathlete
Daley Thompson, 1989.

Playing golf at Leeds Castle in Kent, 1991.

World championships in Assen, the Netherlands, 1990.

European championships
in Caen, France, 1991.

Marrying Kath, 1994.

UK guide runners — Derek Jones, Martin Komorowski, Steve James, me, Vic Smith, a friend, and Gary Heath.

A hard training run with Paul Harwood through the Warwickshire countryside.

Finishing the London Marathon with Mike Peters, 2000.

Lap of honour after winning gold in the 10,000 m with Paul Harwood, Sydney Paralympic Games, 2000.

ever since, and I've been lucky enough to visit her several times.

As an international athlete it was difficult to juggle training with holidays, and even when the track season ended, I was reluctant to spend too long away from running without a guide runner. Thankfully some of my guide runners, including Neil Peerson, Rob Walker and, years later, Gary Heath, were more than willing to come to the West Indies with me to relax and run in the sunshine.

With the European championships over, it was time for some well-earned rest and relaxation. It was great to be able to have a holiday and to run almost every day, although we still let our hair down from time to time. No sooner had we cleared the arrival area at the airport than Sue pressed an ice-cold bottle of Heineken, the St Maarten equivalent of water, into our hands. This was obviously going to be a tough break.

It was brilliant to stand in the back of Sue's boyfriend's pick-up truck, enjoying the smells, sounds and the excitement of the wind in our faces. The only thing Rob had to keep an eye out for was low-flying branches. Getting in the mood (or should that be the spirit?) one evening we sat on Sue's terrace, enjoying 'apple pies', a cocktail of vodka and apple juice with cinnamon. Thankfully I felt fine the next day.

I was getting right into the holiday atmosphere in the West Indies when I tried my hand at waterskiing and scuba diving for the first time. Bernard, a powerful West Indian, showed me on the beach how I should stand up on my skis when I felt the boat moving. He demonstrated this by pulling me into a standing position, as though he were lifting a baby, as I kept my knees slightly bent and anchored my feet in the sand. On the water I remembered what I'd learned, and next thing I knew I was rising out of the water like Neptune and skiing across the water like a pro. I even learned to cross the boat's wake, but I did this once too often, lost my balance, and hit the water which felt like concrete at the speed I was travelling. The impact also ripped my shorts down the seam, something I didn't realise until I was halfway down the high street.

The next adventure was scuba diving. My instructor was a very nice-sounding Canadian girl who gave me a quick lesson on the beach and then held my hand as we swam along the seabed through the beautiful warm water. It was wonderful to be able to breathe underwater — I felt like Jacques Cousteau. It was marvellous to feel the different texture and ripples in the sand as we glided over it, and my guide managed to find a starfish which she placed in my hand to show me. It took me a while to get used to not being able to hear underwater, as this is one of the senses on which I'm totally reliant.

In the late summer of 1989 I received an invitation to compete in the Australian Blind Sports Federation's (ABSF) national championships in Melbourne. It was an opportunity of a lifetime, but I was worried that finding a guide runner and the money to pay for the air fares would be a big obstacle. A couple of phone calls sorted things out. Gavin Burren, my young guide from the 1987 European championships, said yes straight away, a decision that led to him emigrating less than a year later.

The air fares were taken care of by Melanie Boyd, a contact I had in London who found us an anonymous sponsor. The whole trip was booked and paid for, including six nights' accommodation on our way home, and to this day I don't know who paid for the trip. Whoever it was, I can't thank them enough for their incredible generosity and kindness (and thanks, of course, to Melanie for putting it all together). All we had to do now was try to adjust from our winter of endurance training in England to the speed work that would be needed to race in the sunshine of an Australian summer. I took the trip to Australia very seriously, not least because a private businessman had paid my way. I wanted to do the right thing by him, as well as for myself. I watched what I ate and what I drank in the lead-up to Christmas, which was quite hard after a long, tough season.

If I thought the flight to the US was a long time to be sitting still, the journey to Australia seemed to go on for ever. About ten hours into the flight, we were hit by the numbing thought that there were still two hours to go to Bangkok, and we weren't even halfway to Australia. It seemed impossible that we would ever get there. Eventually we arrived in Melbourne, 27 hours after leaving London.

Only mad dogs and Englishmen go out in the midday sun, right? Gavin and I chose to go for our first run around midday, not realising how hot it was. After just a couple of miles we had to stop and recover before we ran home. We got up much earlier to train after that, but it didn't make much difference. The temperature was often up around 40 degrees, and when the northerly breeze, which was hot and dry, blew from the hinterland, it felt even hotter. The weird thing was that only a couple of hours later, the temperature dropped to the low 20s and we were shivering.

In the Australian blind championships, I competed against partially sighted athletes as well as the few totally blind ones. Unfortunately, I found there are relatively few quality totally blind athletes anywhere in the world, and I won the 5000 m with a sprint finish, beating a partially sighted Aussie. Ten years later he competed as a T11 (totally blind) in the Sydney Paralympics. We also won the 800 m, but I never relaxed; I felt tired for the whole race. A couple of days later I won the 1500 m in 4:12 which I was disappointed with at the time. In hindsight, it was a decent performance as I wouldn't run any faster for another six years.

Michelle Harrington was a guide and helper at the ABSF and she offered to put Gavin and me up at her family home for the remainder of our time in Melbourne. The serious business of racing was over, so Gavin and I had quite a bit of spare time, which the four Harrington sisters helped us to fill. I say four, but it was really three — Gavin took a shine to Jo, the youngest sister, and I didn't see quite as much of her (or Gavin) for the remainder of the trip. Eleven months later he migrated to Australia and married Jo; they still live in Melbourne where they have three children.

We spent two nights in Sydney on our way home. We were there for such a short time, but I did manage to gain an impression of the Opera House and Circular Quay, and I was impressed with the efficiency of the monorail. We also visited a number of bars in a memorable pub crawl. In one bar, our beers had just arrived when Gavin whispered urgently, 'Drink up, fast as you can. I'll explain outside.'

On the pavement he told me that the bar was full of Freddie Mercury look-a-likes. Now as much as I like the music of Queen, neither of us fancied the idea of getting drunk in a gay bar. Later that evening, we found a genuine English pub and a couple of pints in there just about finished me off. I can remember being slightly surprised to find myself in some shrubbery, and Gavin struggling to help me up as we were both laughing so hard. It was one of the first times I was genuinely blind drunk.

On our stopover on the way home, Bangkok was hot, noisy and smelly, and the humidity was unbelievable. We travelled around in a tuk-tuk, which I found quite exhilarating as it swerved in and out of the traffic. However, Gavin had the disadvantage of being able to see just how close we were to being maimed for life. We stayed in a pleasant hotel with a swimming pool, but we couldn't run as the city's pavements had huge gaps between the slabs, making it a nightmare for Gavin to guide me. There was also a non-stop traffic jam from 7 a.m. until 9 p.m. and the stink of the open drains didn't help either.

We thought it safe to book a trip to the Temple of the Emerald Buddha as it was only 10 km away. The journey took over two hours through the traffic, and although impressed by the buddha, we opted to give the bridge over the Kwai River (supposedly the railway bridge from the famed movie of the same name) a miss, as that was 100 km away. I had a suit and two shirts made to measure for the first, and probably the last, time for a 'very good price' and we were both impressed with the finished article, although maybe the monogram on the breast pocket was a little over the top.

After four days in Bangkok, it was quite a relief to be heading home, not least because Dad had told me over the phone that Henley had required surgery to remove a fatty lump from near his armpit where the harness would have rubbed. When we picked Henley up from Wokingham on our way home, I was delighted to see that he was as right as rain again.

I'd missed Henley while I was in the West Indies and Australia, and I particularly missed the independence that he gave me. Little did I know that I was about to become even more independent. In my absence Mum and Dad had decided to put the old family home up for sale. Dad had retired over a year earlier, and they had decided it was time to move somewhere nicer and less built-up. They'd seen and eventually bought a place in Tickhill, South Yorkshire.

It was also time for me to let go of their apron strings. Before leaving for Australia I had half-heartedly applied to the local council for a flat, and when I came home I found it had been processed and I had been successful. So in February 1990, aged 28, I finally left home. I moved into my own flat in Chatham, 3 miles (5 km) from home and a 10-minute stroll from work. I had lots of good intentions, and it was initially very exciting. Dad and I walked into town to shop for some useful items for the flat. I was so keen that I even bought an ironing board. However, nearly four years would pass before it was used.

This was the first time in my life I actually had my own place with my own furniture and my own stuff. It was a spacious bachelor pad with plenty of room for me and my running machine. Until their move up north in May, it was also close enough to Mum and Dad, which meant I was still in the fortunate position of being able to go home for company, a chat and some decent food whenever I liked.

I'd quite enjoyed doing my own thing at home when Mum and Dad were away on holiday, but living on my own, even with Henley for company, proved more difficult than I'd expected. It took me a while to realise that I didn't particularly enjoy my own company. Even before Mum and Dad moved, I often felt very lonely, and the day they moved to their new home some 220 miles (352 km) away, it was with a heavy heart that I returned to my flat alone. I could have cried.

But I learned to cope, and slowly became more organised, especially with my washing. I worked out a system of pinning the shirt together with the matching tie and a plastic label I'd created in Braille, telling me the main colour; I did the same with my socks. Henley and I soon became friends with Eny, a sweet, elderly lady who lived in the flat above mine. She insisted on ironing my shirts and trousers as she felt it wasn't something a man should have to do for himself.

I had a couple of cooking lessons from the Kent Association for the Blind, even managing to make an excellent lasagne. One evening after work I set out to make the lasagne at home. Four hours later, I was tired and no longer hungry, and realised that either I needed to speed up significantly, or find less complex dishes to make for dinner.

After my evening training run and my dinner, Henley and I would often pop upstairs to see Eny for a cup of tea and biscuits. I was grateful for the company. Eny was very fond of Henley and, when I gave her permission, she liked to give Henley saucers of tea. I did put my foot down, though, when she asked whether she could give him food.

With me it's very black and white — either a dog has tit-bits or he doesn't. There is no grey area. I don't believe it's fair to give tit-bits only occasionally. In the past I have been accused of being cruel as I don't give my dogs anything to eat away from their meals. On one occasion at the beginning of an organised walk through the countryside (referred to as a ramble), two elderly ladies stopped to admire Henley, and chastised me when I told them I never gave him treats, telling me how their dogs looked forward to their tit-bits. When I asked where their dogs were, they laughed, saying, 'Oh, they couldn't do this, they're too fat.'

To try to avoid spending too much time alone in the flat, I looked for other interests to broaden my horizons. I was introduced to golf that summer by Mike, a nearly blind chap from Maidstone. Mike arranged for me to meet Chris, a golf professional, at Leeds Castle in Kent, who gave me some lessons and sold me a half-set of clubs. After a few lessons he asked me to give a demonstration in front of Princess Alexandra of Kent, the Queen's cousin, who was visiting that day. Using a six iron I managed to chip a few balls 60 metres, and surprisingly got them pretty close to one another. Her Royal Highness seemed quite impressed, anyway.

However, I soon found golf wasn't my game. I was too impatient and restless to appreciate it, although I must say it was lovely walking around the course at Leeds Castle, one of Henry VIII's old haunts, in the early evening, with Dave Sancto and Colin Nethercote, two mates from work. I enjoyed listening to the birds' evening song, hearing the breeze in the trees, and picturing in my mind the lake and the ripples caused by yet another of my attempted chips falling short.

The beginning of the end of my golfing career came at a Black Horse Life tournament. Dave was my guide and we were scheduled to play two rounds of 18 holes. The morning round went fairly well, but being dedicated to my sport I had to get out for a run before lunch. By mid-afternoon, I was physically and mentally drained, and I was playing awfully, even by my terrible standards. I was so bad we called it a day after only ten holes. Playing another tournament with Matt Lawton, I only managed 12 holes before

Matt suggested we give it up. I was playing so poorly that Matt said it was like 'flogging a dead horse', and recommended I stuck with athletics.

I took his advice, but it was getting harder. I was going through a lean patch in terms of guide runners, and was forced to run more and more frequently on the treadmill. The treadmill was only intended to be a means to an end, something to use a couple of times a week when I was stuck for training partners, but by 1990 I was training on it so much that it became something I resented. I was doing up to five sessions per week on it, but it was mind-numbingly repetitive and I was finding it increasingly hard to motivate myself. In my desperation I was forced to travel to Yorkshire and Birmingham to find training partners.

It was incredibly depressing to find my running career in freefall, and there seemed to be nothing I could do to reverse the situation. Shortly after returning home from Australia, my options for guide runners became even more limited when Gavin picked up a serious injury, effectively ending his running ambitions. Vic had never fully recovered from his knee injury, and Mick Banfield and Rod Smith had stopped running. Given how poor my training had become, I had no chance of regaining my form or coming close to the times I'd run the previous year.

Luckily enough I found a solution to my problem in the village where Mum and Dad were now living. Tickhill, just south of Doncaster, was a great improvement on Strood, and their house had a layout remarkably similar to the house we'd grown up in at Poplar Road. I had few problems finding my way around, other than the juxtaposition of the small bedroom and bathroom, which confused me a couple of times. After Strood, Tickhill was amazingly quiet, with no road or railway line at the end of the garden. It was on the edge of some lovely countryside, and it was fantastic to be able to run the dogs with no fear of roads.

Whenever I hear church bells I'm reminded of where Mum and Dad lived in Yorkshire. St Mary's Church in Tickhill rings three verses of a different hymn each day, every four hours. Living less than 200 m from the church, Dad had grown familiar with the pattern. 'Hark at the bells,' he'd say. 'It's Wednesday, so it'll be "the Minstrel boy".' I love hearing cathedral and church bells ringing on festive and even solemn occasions, even just chiming the hour — somehow it seems so 'English'.

The other reason I liked Tickhill so much was it meant I was able to run fairly regularly with Martin Roscoe who lived in Leeds, 40 minutes by train from Doncaster, the nearest station to Tickhill. We'd met in Zurich the year before and Martin had offered to run with me if I was ever in Yorkshire. At that time neither of us thought it very likely, but with my parents' move up north and my dire shortage of quality guide runners, Martin helped me out of a hole. Although it meant I had to travel to Leeds, the commute was made easier when I stayed with Mum and Dad for long weekends. Once again, Black Horse Life was incredibly supportive, giving me extra leave to train and race which allowed me to take long weekends in Yorkshire.

Not only did I take Martin up on his offer to train, I asked him to guide me in the world championships in Assen, the Netherlands, in July 1990. For me, the championships couldn't have started better when I won the 1500 m final. An Australian runner shot off from the start and built up a lead, but I managed to catch and pass him, and held on for the gold medal. I won the 5000 m by sitting behind Toffiri and kicking over the last 300 m, but the 800 m didn't go to plan. I felt flat warming up. I had no energy and I didn't feel the usual rush of adrenalin before the race.

Nearing the bell, my sluggishness forgotten, we moved out to take command of the race when an Italian suddenly drifted out in front of me. Had I been sighted, I could have used my arm to nudge him out of my way, but I didn't know he was there, and there wasn't even time for Martin to warn me. We made contact, and the next thing I knew I was flat on my face, wondering what the bloody hell had happened. After Martin had retrieved the guide rope, we started running again, but finished 19 seconds behind the winner. This was my first-ever international defeat and it hurt.

Initially I was stunned and couldn't understand what had happened. Later on I felt frustrated as it would have been a good race if I had stayed on my feet. My frustration increased when the Italians protested and claimed I should have been disqualified. Thankfully their appeal was rejected. Someone said to me I should have counter-protested as he'd clearly tripped me, but by that time it seemed pretty unimportant. 'Such is life,' I thought. I knew I was going to be beaten at some stage in my international career, and at least I had a good excuse and some nasty-looking spike marks on my shins to show off to my sympathetic team-mates.

Chapter 10 – Blind love

By this time I was 30 years old and was ready for a change. I'd been feeling out on a limb and rather lonely in the flat, and I'd been working at Black Horse Life for three-and-a-half years and was feeling restless. There just wasn't the same atmosphere in the office any more, as quite a few of my closest friends had moved on. Then there was the lack of willing, good-quality guide runners in the Medway area, which meant I was resorting to the treadmill more and more often. Things were, to say the least, frustrating.

I'd heard of a remedial massage course at the Royal National College for the Blind at Hereford, the same school I'd attended in my late teens, and the idea of training for a new career really appealed. Once confirmation came through that my local authority would fund the course, all I had to do was pass the assessment which was scheduled for April 1991 at the RNC. On the day, Henley and I arrived at Hereford railway station with plenty of time to spare, so I decided to walk. I was confident of remembering the way to the RNC, although it had been ten years since my last visit when I was still using a long cane, which was much slower than walking with a guide dog.

Five minutes into our walk, nothing seemed familiar. Perhaps I should have given up and found a taxi rank, but that would have been too easy. I wanted to be independent and prove to myself I could manage. I had to ask a couple of times for directions, but at last we reached a landmark I remembered, a triangular island in the middle of Pengrove Road. Then I knew the college gate was just around the corner. The first person I met as I entered the entrance hall was my old principal, Mr Marshall, who was in his final term before retiring.

The prospective students were shown to a room to await the first part of the assessment. The first person I chatted to was Cara

Stevens, a quietly-spoken, partially-sighted Irish woman. While we were chatting, Cara proudly told me about her family, especially her son, but I was more interested in her daughter, who sounded intriguing and happened to be unattached. I remember hoping at the time, even though it seemed ridiculous, that Cara and I would both pass the assessment and maybe I'd get a chance to meet her daughter. Little did I know what destiny had in store.

The first question in my assessment from the lecturer, Jane Hyder, was a little disconcerting. 'Show me how you fold a towel,' she said. I had helped Mum fold the washing when I was growing up, and I'd been living on my own for a while now, and felt I was a tidy and competent housekeeper. Besides, how hard could it be to fold a towel? So the lecturer's comment surprised me.

'Well, I suppose with plenty of practice we might be able to teach you how to fold a towel properly,' she said. She emphasised then, and during the course, how important it is that a massage therapist and their couch are neat and tidy at all times. I obviously had a lot to learn. Despite this, I must have impressed her enough as I was accepted onto the course.

The emphasis of the course was more hands-on than theory-oriented, and I felt it provided me with the ideal opportunity to utilise the experience of years of running and the hours I had spent on the physios' benches. Physiotherapy had always intrigued me, and I had picked up a lot through my inquisitiveness, peppering the physios with lots of questions along the way. I had explored the possibility of studying physiotherapy when I was younger, but didn't have the qualifications at the time. This course would give me the chance to work at something I loved and an opportunity to help people, and I felt I had something of a head start because I already appreciated just how important massage can be when done properly.

The move to Hereford also worked out well for my running. I

was incredibly fortunate that Bill Berry, one of the Great Britain coaches, was now living in Hereford. I asked him if he could find me anyone to run with, and he introduced me to some brilliant guide runners, two of whom — Gary Heath and Derek Jones — became close friends.

On the last weekend in August 1991, my guide runner from Leeds, Martin Roscoe, drove to Kent to do some last-minute training with me and guide me in what sadly turned out to be my last race in a Medway AC vest. We had ten days before the European championships in France. The next day we drove the 250 miles (400 km) to Hereford, somehow managing to squeeze the two of us, Henley, and most of my worldly goods into Martin's saloon car. We went straight to the RNC to register for the course where I was pleased to meet Cara again. Leaving Henley guarding the luggage in my room, Martin and I went to the running track.

The all-weather running track in Hereford lies in the centre of the horse-racing circuit and, as such, has sparse protection from the wind, which could add an unpleasant dimension to track sessions. Still, when I think about running and my life in Hereford, I remember the evocative smell of apples cooking around November time, which is when Bulmers turned the fruits of their orchards around the county into cider. Similarly, the smell of coal smoke in the breeze on a freezing-cold evening from those houses with open fires reminds me of my time spent on work experience at Credenhill, the nearby Royal Air Force base. These smells in a way are my photograph album, bringing back nostalgic memories of a couple of important years of my life — years in which I met Kath, I was running free of injuries and setting new world records, as well as forging lifelong friendships with Gary, Derek and their families.

Once I'd got my bearings, Hereford became much more familiar. The roads and their crossing points, along with the shops and pubs, all slotted into place in my mind-map. Hereford hadn't changed as much as I had thought. The college had changed, however. Gardiner Hostel, where the girls had stayed and from which I had been banned 12 years earlier for being sick in the corridor, was now the accommodation for mature men and women. Initially, Henley and I stayed in Armitage Hall, where I had once shared a lounge area with Mark Rochford, and later moved into Gardiner Hostel which felt weird at first. I couldn't adjust to sharing bathrooms with women, and found myself unable to relax when a woman came in. I'd be in a cubicle, minding my business, but then a woman would come into an adjacent cubicle, and I'd be out of there like a shot. Stage fright, I think you'd call it.

On the first morning of the course I met the rest of the class, which included Cara and four other women, plus three guys — Andy, Richie and myself. Over the next nine months we learned massage techniques and studied anatomy, physiology, aromatherapy, reflexology and shiatsu. As a small group we managed to learn quite a lot about each other over the course of the diploma. Our tutor, Jane Hyder, encouraged us to talk about ourselves and why we were doing the course. I learned that Cara's husband, Bill, had died suddenly and unexpectedly two years ago at the age of 50, and she hoped this course would help her become more independent and get her out of the house.

Cara and I got on really well, and she told me her daughter, Kath, whom I was yet to meet, had asked her to pass on the message that she would like to buy me a drink for each gold medal I won in France that year at the European championships.

The championships in Caen, in Normandy, nearly didn't go ahead; the National Organisation of the Spanish Blind (ONCE), which used to be a major sponsor of the Tour de France, had to bail out the French at the last minute. Spain had the largest team at the championships, so I guess their national body felt it their duty to step in, but it was obvious the Spanish team were given preferential treatment in the dining room. They always seemed to have finished their meal before we saw any food, and we were restricted to two croissants each whereas the Spaniards' plates were loaded — not that this rankled at all!

In the final of the 1500 m I came under real pressure. Entering the final straight I could hear a gaggle of athletes queuing up to have a go at me. If confirmation of my predicament were necessary, my guide runner, Martin, told me to 'kick like f***' and I did. We just hung on to win from a new threat, Paulo Coelho from Portugal. Where once I felt invincible, I now realised that the chasing pack were coming up fast. I managed to win the 5000 m as well, but victory came at a price. Just 50 m into the race, someone ran into the back of Martin and ripped his shoe off. The all-weather track was rough and abrasive, and I really don't know how he managed to complete the distance on one bare foot, which was a bloody mess at the end of the race.

He didn't look like he would be able to run for quite some time, but with laser treatment from the team physio and obviously some good healing genes, Martin was back up and running in four days. Unfortunately, this wasn't soon enough as the 800 m final was in two days' time. Andy Curtis's guide, Jason, agreed to step into the breach, and we ran really well together and led until the last bend when we were passed by two athletes. Jason is proud to tell anyone who will listen that he was the first person to guide me to a non-gold medal.

His foot now fit to run on, Martin and I joined the 4 x 400 m relay team in our last race together, and again we won gold. A few team members overcooked the post-competition celebrations big time, including my guide. Fortunately for Martin, a physio placed him in the recovery position. I was so grateful I hadn't been tempted to hit the spirits the night before, as the boat crossing back to England the next day didn't particularly help the symptoms of those who had.

When I rejoined the course the massage teacher wasted no time in bringing me back down to earth, saying, 'Whilst you have been away gallivanting, the class have moved on, and you have some catching up to do.' With the support and help of my friends and classmates, I caught up pretty quickly. Things were good, a new chapter in my life had started, and despite my indifferent form leading up to the championships, I had still won three gold medals — and there was the intriguing prospect of three drinks with Cara's daughter, Kath, to look forward to.

Finally, my chance to meet Kath came on Monday, 23 September 1991, when Cara told me Kath would be driving over to join the yoga class that evening at the college. Striding across the familiar room, I could hear a few of the girls were already waiting for the yoga teacher to arrive. With my sonar switched on, I zeroed in on Cara's voice, assuming Kath would be near her. When I came to a halt, I realised I'd stepped on a foot. 'Oh sorry,' I said.

'That's all right, I've got another one,' Kath replied. 'Hello, you must be Bob.'

'And you must be Kath. I'm pleased to meet you,' I replied gallantly, taking my foot off her foot. Shaking hands, I was struck by how petite her hand seemed in mine. 'She sounds nice,' I thought. I'd have to wait a while before I could ask someone reliable and impartial as to what she looked like.

Although I can't see, I still like to know what people look like. I can tell quite a lot about a person by shaking their hand: a firm, dry, not too brief grip I find is usually a good sign. When Ray Charles, the famous blind singer, met a girl, apparently he slid his left hand up her arm to get an idea of what she looked like. Were I to do this, I reckon I'd be considered a dirty old man, so I content myself with a handshake, the voice, what height it's coming from, and whether the person is looking directly at me or not. And my first impressions of Kath were all good. She had an attractive-sounding voice, well spoken with a slight Essex accent, and I could hear the smile in her voice; she also laughed easily.

With that, we went into the gym and I was pleasantly surprised to find she'd put her mat next to mine. I hoped this boded well.

Over the years I had misinterpreted friendly signals from girls as something else entirely, so I had learned to ignore them. Still, I asked Richie, whose sight was reasonable, as subtly as I could what Kath looked like. Unfortunately he wasn't very helpful as he hadn't been able to see her properly. Later on that evening, I was trying to explain to Kath how I visualised people when Richie joked that she had a big nose. Strongly denying this, she invited me to look for myself, but I was too shy to accept her offer.

As a class we went out for dinner quite regularly, with Kath often joining us. After a few nights in her company I started to realise that I was very attracted to her. I used to hang around in the bar, insisting the others were seated first for dinner, hoping she would be the one guiding me to a seat, which would leave her no alternative other than to sit beside me. It's very difficult, trying to get a girl's attention when you can't see her and don't want to make your interest in her too obvious. More often than not, though, Kath did sit beside me.

The best technique for guiding is for the blind person to take the guide's elbow. The guide then stays half a step in front, so you get some prior feel, along with verbal instructions, of how high a step up or down is. This is the second physical clue, after shaking their hand, of what the person looks like. You get a fairly accurate idea of how tall they are, for instance, and whether they keep themselves reasonably fit. Kath was 5 feet 4 inches (1.63 m) tall and did seem in good shape. After Derek met her, he told me she had long, thick, dark-brown hair, blue eyes, and a 'peaches and cream' complexion. 'She's lovely, Bob,' he said.

Another evening the class all went to a concert at Hereford Cathedral, which is home to the Mappa Mundi, a map of the world which dates back to the late 13th century. I've always enjoyed listening to a cathedral's organ, especially when it is loud, and the feel of the notes reverberating all around the venue. I'm able to get an idea of the size of the church or cathedral and the height of the ceiling as the sound fades.

After the concert, Cara invited us all back to her house in

Wistanstow, a gorgeous little village between Hereford and Shrewsbury. It was a beautiful 17th century cottage, which used to be the village shop; it even had its own stable and bakehouse, and plenty of rooms for us all to sleep over. Next day, Kath gave me a guided tour of the house, of which she was obviously very proud. She pointed out the low, solid wood beams, warning me to look out for my head. Later Jo, Andy's wife, surprised me by saying, 'Kath likes you a lot.' Jo, with her woman's intuition, had noticed the preferential treatment that Kath gave me. She said I was the only one she'd given the tour to. This pleased me immensely, but I was still determined not to let my hopes run away with me.

It took me a couple of weeks before making, what was for me, a pretty bold overture to Kath in the not very romantic surroundings of the college dining room. The opportunity came during one of the few pauses for breath in conversation between the women. I tested my luck and cheekily asked Kath, 'So when are you going to buy me those drinks then?'

I nearly fell off my chair when she replied, 'Any time you like.'

I was all but tongue-tied, but I managed to blurt out, 'Maybe next weekend? I'll give you a call during the week.'

A few days later, having borrowed 50 p from her mum for the phone call, I nervously dialled Kath's number, and it was a done deal. I took her to the Orange Tree pub for our first date. Sitting on the back seat of the taxi on the way to the pub, I felt something nudging my hand, and I thought she was getting a bit friendly by edging her hand towards mine. Emboldened, I edged my hand closer, only to find it was her handbag! Towards the end of a very nice evening, Kath leapt to her feet and ran off, leaving me bemused and wondering what I'd said. Luckily she returned shortly after, explaining that a lady had mistakenly picked up her coat and was disappearing with it.

For our next date, Jan, Gary's wife, recommended the Restaurante Ferenze as a good place to take a girl on a first dinner date. Taking Kath out, it was important to me to look as good as possible, so I was only too keen to accept Cara's offer to help with my ironing. It became one of our favourite haunts during our time in Hereford, partly due to the great Italian food and friendly staff, but also the nostalgic memories it held for each of us, and we had a lovely first evening there.

Back at the college after dinner, Kath asked me to give her feet a rub. She explained that she knew we'd been learning the technique on the course, and joked that the practice would be helpful. Afterwards, as she was leaving, Kath said, 'I'm going to be very forward now and kiss you goodnight,' and before I could object, she had kissed me on the cheek, which sent me into a bit of a spin. I hadn't dared hope for this — I'd been about to shake hands with her. Having closed my door, a little disoriented, instead of sitting on the bed I sat on the bedside table, breaking my alarm clock.

For our first Valentine's Day together, I took Kath for a romantic weekend (she drove, with me directing) to the Cottage of Content, a delightful family-run hotel in the Herefordshire countryside. It was heaven to lie in bed, listening to the birds and sheep and no traffic. On a walk around the country lanes before breakfast, Kath described the green pastures, the trees and the traditional wattle and daub (black and white) houses. With the fresh air in my nostrils and Kath's little hand in mine, I could hardly have been happier, and I was finding out for the first time what falling in love was like.

Kath told me that she'd moved back home to be with her mum after obtaining a transfer from London to the Shrewsbury army barracks where she was an administrative officer for three majors and a colonel. Since her dad's early death and with her brother, Shaun, away at university, Kath had been Cara's companion and rock, so with Kath spending more and more time with me, Cara was having to adjust once again.

While my relationship with Kath was going from strength to strength, my running situation had also improved. Soon after I moved to Hereford, Bill Berry introduced me to Gary Heath who became one of my closest friends and most important guide runners.

The most difficult aspect of guiding is the knack of both guide and blindie moving their arms together. It should be pretty easy, but thinking about it too much can create problems. In common with most of my best guide runners, Gary got the knack of guiding confidently straight away. Knowing I would be able to give him a reasonable workout, Gary was keen to run with me regularly and help me towards my goal of making the Barcelona Paralympics in 1992. Very quickly, Kath and I became close friends with Gary and his wife, Jan, along with Derek and Liz Jones. Derek, the last piece in the jigsaw, and I had started running together in October 1991.

Gary, Derek and I ran together at least once a week on the Hereford running track. During the cold winters there was often a bitter wind blowing across the track, but most of the time the sessions were really enjoyable. Most importantly, during my first winter in Hereford I was able to run consistently, week in and week out, with the same guide runners. With Bill as my coach sometimes encouraging, occasionally needing to cajole, there was much more emphasis on strength and endurance, making me a much tougher runner mentally.

Without Bill's advice, support and friendship, everything I achieved at that time would have been impossible. Although I intended doing so at the time, I deeply regret not giving Bill the thanks or credit he deserved for his time, patience and friendship.

It's funny — because our hands are so close together, my guide runners and I often get funny looks and sometimes comments, as well as abuse, mainly from passers-by, who assume we are holding hands; they don't seem to notice the guide rope. On one memorable occasion, Vic and I were running in the Bath half-marathon to raise awareness of 'sport for the blind' and were wearing vests saying as much. From the 9 mile marker, a runner repeatedly pushed past us, cutting in front of us, and making us go around him. Vic was about to have a word, when he abruptly turned to us and said, 'What is it with you two — are you queer or something?'

'No,' Vic replied, 'he's blind!'

'Oh, sorry mate,' he said, rather sheepishly. 'Well done — keep going. Hey, clear the way!' he shouted, 'blind runner coming through.'

One of my best running performances came with Gary in the Bulmers Woodpecker Cider New Year's Day 10 km road race. The course was a really good one for me, no uneven ground or sharp corners to navigate, and the last 2 km were slightly downhill, which suited my track speed. Derek and I had run the course just before Christmas, which helped me visualise where I was during the race and to know what to expect in the way of hills. I was the only blind athlete in the race, but still finished fifth and shattered my personal best by nearly two minutes, running 32:47 which was a world record.

While I was working hard on my running, I also qualified with a credit in remedial massage at the RNC, and set up my own business at a gym in town called the Factory Health and Fitness Centre. I rented a room off the physio and started off by charging the ridiculously low price of £6 (NZ$18) for a one-hour massage. The plan was to get my name out there and build up a customer base. The low price worked well. I had people queuing out the door for a massage. Unfortunately, combined with all the training I was doing I was knackered by the end of the day. Something had to give, so I raised my price to £8 (NZ$24) and, whilst I lost a lot of clients, at least now I wasn't so busy.

I settled down in Hereford. I had Kath in my life; my loyal and close friends, who were also my training partners, were here; and I'd set up my own business. Henley and I lived with Derek and Liz and their daughters, Laura and Helen, who quickly became like family to me, and still are. Having said that, I was convinced one day that Henley, a notorious scavenger (he was a labrador after all), had pushed the boundaries of our friendship to the limit. Liz was a fabulous cake-maker and was often asked to make birthday and wedding cakes. She even made a cake to celebrate my achievements in Barcelona, adorned with models of Bill, Steve and myself. This one particular day she had spent hours working on a wedding cake before heading off to do some errands.

Left alone in the house, I heard the unmistakable sound of a Henley conquest. I found him devouring what was left of a cake in the kitchen. 'Oh my god,' I panicked. 'How do I explain to Liz that Henley has just eaten her nearly completed wedding cake?' Not having the guts to face her, I wandered the streets with Henley for a couple of hours before finally calling in to Derek's office to tell him first. While I was there, Liz rang to ask Derek whether he'd seen me.

'Yes, he's cowering here in my office and is afraid to go home and face the music,' Derek laughed.

It was such a relief when Liz said that Henley had only got his paws on a sponge cake she'd made that morning.

Chapter II – Barcelona

In the early 1990s, Anneka Rice, a famous television presenter, had a series on BBC1 called *Challenge Anneka*. She took on all sorts of projects, ranging from providing water to a village in Africa to accepting a challenge issued by the British Paralympic Association, which was to make a 60-second commercial to publicise and help raise funds for the British team competing in the 1992 Paralympic Games in Barcelona. The real challenge was that she had to fulfil these tasks in only 24 hours.

Eighteen months before the Games, Anneka hired Crystal Palace to do the filming and assembled a selection of British Paralympic athletes, including my guide runner, Martin Komorowski, and me. She arranged for the actor Tom Conti to do the voiceover. She'd also hired Westminster Cathedral and its choir, who would sing the backing track for the commercial — a recomposed version of Handel's 'Zadok the Priest' (which she'd also managed to arrange).

As the music built towards the climax, the commercial featured close-up shots of 'normal-looking' athletes held in their starting blocks, running and jumping across the screen, until at around 50 seconds into the commercial the choir came to a rousing crescendo, with which the camera pulled back to show these athlete were actually Paralympians. The runner in his blocks had a prosthesis; and the two athletes running alongside one another were connected by a rope — yes, that was Martin and me.

Anneka managed to coordinate everything, including editing the commercial and rushing it across to Thames Television to be screened in time for that evening's *News at Ten* ad break at 10.15. Everyone involved was at the post-*Challenge Anneka* party where a big television showed the commercial live. Even though I couldn't see it, I had goose bumps — it was really evocative and moving.

The Barcelona Paralympic Games in 1992 were a landmark event — for the first time the Paralympians had parity with the Olympians. Not only did we share the same stadia, but also the same accommodation. The athletes' village was much more impressive than anything any of us had ever experienced. Our third-floor apartment was spacious, with two bathrooms, a kitchen, lounge and two bedrooms. Steve James, who'd acted as my guide runner in Seoul, had agreed to return for Barcelona, and he and I shared one room, with three wheelies in the larger room.

Our apartment also had a video intercom which, to me back in 1992, seemed way ahead of its time. The 'touch screen' information screens were also impressive. I certainly hadn't seen or even heard of anything like it. Steve was able to get all sorts of information from these about any sport, including profiles on all the athletes. Remarkably — and for the first and only time to date — we were able to get results in Braille. This would have been due to the involvement of ONCE, the National Organisation of the Spanish Blind.

The main building, and the focal centre of the village, was only a short walk from our apartment, and in the basement of this building was the food hall which was open 24 hours a day. The village also had a music and video library where you could select a CD and listen to it on headphones. You could even watch a video of your event just 24 hours afterwards.

Sometimes the time spent waiting around for the racing to begin can seem like a prison sentence, but the Barcelona village was like a holiday camp. You can't do much sightseeing as this drains the energy, and it's important to stay out of the sun for the same reason. So you sit around, waiting for the next meal or training session; it's so important to be disciplined and not eat or train too much. Steve tried to distract me when he knew I was thinking too much about the racing to come.

With the heat of Barcelona, we were very aware of just how important it was to keep ourselves well hydrated, and there were always plenty of empty water bottles lying around our apartment. No matter how long I might be out of our room, Steve got a kick from assembling the bottles like so many skittles and waiting for me, the bowling ball, to return to see if I got a 'strike'. Another game and diversion he played with me was the authentic version of 'blind man's bluff'. He was incredibly good at creeping silently around the room, making it really hard for me to hear, let alone catch, him.

Kath was in Barcelona to watch me, along with Derek and Liz, Gary and Jan, and we enjoyed some memorable times together, eating in one of the many restaurants along Las Ramblas, Barcelona's most famous street, being entertained by the buskers. It was a difficult time for Steve as Lauren, his first child and my god-daughter, was three months old, and he wanted to see her progressing day by day; three weeks away from her meant he missed a lot, including seeing her roll over for the first time.

Barcelona was a fantastic games for me, but I have one recurring regret — that I didn't listen to Bill when he suggested I run hard from the front in the 1500 m. I was certainly fit and strong enough to do it, but instead I'd decided to wait until the last 300 m before making my move. Just before we were introduced to the crowd, Steve told me that the camera was following us and we were on the giant screens at the end of both straights, as I was the reigning Paralympic champion and world record holder.

Instead of feeling warmed up and raring to go, though, I felt cold and numb. Ridiculously, I felt far less confident in my ability and fitness than I should have been, just for a change, and this was probably responsible for my first-ever defeat in the Paralympic Games. A Russian led out the first lap at little more than a jog and then, with the pace constantly changing, disaster nearly struck on the second, and again the third, lap as I tripped on the heels of an athlete ahead of me, nearly falling, after which my legs felt like jelly.

Running along the back straight for the last time, we hit the front as planned, but the acceleration took a huge physical effort. Entering the home straight I had absolutely nothing left. My legs were shot, and when first Paulo from Portugal and then Lovas from Norway came past, there was absolutely nothing I could have done about it; I was treading water. Steve virtually had to stop just before the finishing line, as crossing it before me would have resulted in a disqualification. The Americans obviously weren't convinced, and asked to view video footage to decide whether I should have been disqualified. They lodged a protest — if successful, their man, Tim Willis, would have been promoted into the bronze medal position — but it was cleared, and I held on to the bronze medal. (If only I'd remembered this lesson four years later in Atlanta.)

I didn't consider I had won a bronze medal; in my view I'd lost the gold. I was pleased for Paulo, as well as Lovas who, although he had only won silver, celebrated as if he'd won the gold. I later realised how his elation demonstrated just how much it meant to my rivals to beat me. For the moment, however, I was just devastated with my mental weakness beforehand, my risky race plan, and then my performance during the race. There were a great many 'if only's going around in my head, but I didn't have the luxury to dwell on these, and feel sorry for myself for long. The 5000 m final was just around the corner, and I had to get my focus back.

Losing the 1500 m put some more pressure on me, but at the same time, it gave me an even greater incentive to do well in the 5000 m. I told Steve half an hour before we stepped on the track that I was afraid of not being up to the challenge. Obviously this could have been a significant moment in my running career, as who knows what might have happened had I run badly again? Steve, putting his hand on my shoulder, said, 'I know you can do it. I believe in you, and so do Kath, Derek and Gary.'

I started concentrating and believing again, and was determined to do whatever it took to win. I was prepared to control the race from the front, but it wasn't necessary. I stayed in second place, with Steve telling me what was going on, following every move from my rivals, with Paulo Coelho following behind me. With 500 m to go, I hit the front, winding up the pace. At the bell, I don't know whether it was real or imagined, I visualised a bright light, and Steve said, 'Let's go!'

I thought, 'Oh God, this is it,' and I kicked.

With 300 m to go, I could hear Paulo behind, and just kept kicking, feeling strong. Up the home straight, I felt powerful — I wasn't going to let anyone pass me. Nor did I. I ran that last lap in 62 seconds to win the gold medal, and in doing so set a new Paralympic record of 16:03. Boy, did I enjoy that lap of honour! Carrying the Union Jack, I ran over to the spectators' stand to see my team-mates, but especially Kath and my friends who had shared my despair over the 1500 m. But that was now forgotten. I'd won the gold — my third Paralympic 5000 m title in successive Games, and my seventh paralympic gold medal, the one of which I was most proud. I had proved to myself that anything was possible, if only I would believe it.

I shall never forget my last race on the penultimate day of competition, the 800 m final on Saturday afternoon. We were made to wait at the mouth of the tunnel on the edge of the track while the women's T11 800 m final was run. It was nerve-wracking and very exciting. There were over 80,000 people in the stadium, and I was able to follow the athletes' progress around the track by following the cheers as they rang out around the stadium. It was like following a Mexican wave.

During our race the crowd were so noisy that Steve had to shout to give me instructions. Whilst we ran a good race, a Cuban runner passed me in the home straight to win the gold medal. Amazingly, he ran without a guide rope linking him to his guide runner, and yet still managed to run a perfect line; he was able to move into lane one, leaving his guide in lane three, and yet somehow manage to run perfectly straight. For a totally blind athlete to run a perfect line in that kind of noise, at the end of that punishing distance, when your legs and your rhythm start to go, was a miraculous feat.

There was no proof the Cuban was cheating, but it was the last time in the Paralympics that athletes running in the track events, up to the 1500 m, were permitted to run without wearing blacked-out glasses, something that guarantees a level playing field. Incidentally, four years later at the Paralympics in Atlanta in 1996, the same Cuban ran in the T12 (partially sighted) events, yet he'd beaten me in Barcelona in the T11 (totally blind) race.

I left the stadium for the last time with Kath, Gary, Derek, Liz and Jan, and as we made our way out of that magical arena at the top of the hill looking down over the city, the fountains started dancing and the theme song of the games, 'Barcelona' by Freddie Mercury, started playing. It was a very moving and emotional end to my 1992 Paralympic Games.

Everything about that evening was perfect. We went to a small restaurant, and it may have been the emotion of the night, but we all agreed it was the best spaghetti and some of the finest beer we had ever tasted. To cap it all off, for the first time Kath told me she loved me.

On the flight home the pilot congratulated the Great Britain Paralympic team on their achievements and 'in particular Bob Matthews who got the clean sweep — gold, silver and bronze medals'. I took some good-natured abuse from my team-mates about the special treatment given to me by the pilot, but it was a nice touch.

Kath had a surprise waiting for me soon after we got home. One evening she asked me to come to Wistanstow for the weekend to show off my medals to a school friend of hers — of course it was really me she wanted to show off. We arranged to meet on the Saturday afternoon at the Plough Inn. Derek and Liz dropped me off early at Hereford station wearing my Great Britain tracksuit, because Kath wanted her friend to see me in all my finery.

After picking me up, Kath explained that her friend would meet us in the pub. As soon as I got in the door and before I was able to order a pint, I was accosted by a young lad who said, 'Aren't you Bob Matthews? Can I have your autograph?' I readily agreed, then turned to Kath, feeling pretty good about being recognised, and remarked, 'How about that?' But then a young girl came up to me, asking whether I was Bob Matthews, and could she have my autograph too. My pleasure turned to bemusement. Of course I was pleased, but this was an amazing coincidence — it's not every day that I'm recognised, let alone asked for my scribble.

We took our drinks to a table, but no sooner had we sat down than I heard Mum's distinctive voice, and there she was with Dad and, as I soon discovered, 20 or so of my friends who had travelled there for a surprise post-Barcelona party. The daft thing was that Derek and Liz were also there — they could have given me a lift instead of dropping me at the station. I don't quite understand how Kath managed to fool me so easily, but it wouldn't be the last time.

On 19 April 1993, 18 months after we'd first met, I finally plucked up the courage to ask Kath to marry me, and thankfully she said 'yes'. I couldn't believe it! Growing up, I never imagined myself married, and now shortly before my 33rd birthday, I was engaged. I was proud of myself and happier than any man deserves to be.

Kath was amazing how readily she shared herself with everyone in her life. Be it me, travelling the world to support and cheer me on in competitions, or dropping everything with no hesitation to be with her mum whenever Cara needed her — this incredible, giving and considerate woman was going to be my wife.

Since we were now engaged, Kath felt it was time I met some of her Irish mafia, her mum's family. I had been due to run in Dublin at the European blind championships, but I couldn't because I was injured. Nevertheless, as we'd already planned to go, we decided it was a great opportunity to visit Ireland to meet Kath's aunts, uncles and cousins.

We caught the ferry across from Wales and drove into the Irish countryside. Kath's family were wonderful and we had great 'craic' with them, even if there was sometimes a 'satellite delay' while I processed what had just been said; sometimes I had to ask them to repeat it. There were a few good nights out in McGuire's, the village pub, sampling the Guinness, but I think Kath's relations probably considered me something of a lightweight on our first night out, as by 2 a.m. I couldn't drink another drop of the 'black stuff' and needed my bed.

We toured around a little of Ireland's beautiful countryside, taking in the 'Ring of Kerry', which starts at Killarney and heads around the Iveagh Peninsula. The Cliffs of Moher, rising 214 m above the Atlantic Ocean, in County Clare were another highlight. From a viewing platform Kath told me she could see the Aran Islands in Galway Bay and the valleys and hills of Connemara.

Kath said she felt frustrated that she couldn't give me a true picture of what she could see, although from her description I felt my view was pretty good, especially as it was enhanced by the feel of wide open space and the breeze on my face, or the sound and smell of the sea, as well as the brightness of the sun which I can still see. Arriving in the town of Blarney I was keen to kiss the Blarney Stone, which is a block of bluestone built into the battlements of Blarney Castle, near Cork. According to legend, kissing the stone endows the kisser with the gift of the gab, or great skill at flattery. I had the collywobbles as I trusted some stranger to hold my legs as I dangled upside-down to kiss a piece of stone with over 30 m of empty space between myself and the ground.

Things were to change for me once again shortly after our trip to Ireland. Henley, my trusted guide dog, had been my companion and eyes for 11 years, but he was now considered to be of retirement age, so I wasn't surprised when I got the call from the Guide Dogs for the Blind Association (GDBA), telling me they had a replacement guide dog. I was introduced to Quando, a beautiful, 18-month-old, long-haired, three-quarters golden retriever, one-quarter collie at the Leamington Spa training centre.

I later learned how lucky I had been to be offered Quando. He had been on a shortlist of three dogs being considered for an English citizen who lived in New York and worked for the United Nations in war-torn Bosnia. He may well have been the best of the three dogs, but fortunately for me, a golden retriever was chosen instead as it was more visible. Quando was nearly all black, which is considered to be an unlucky colour by Muslims, so instead of ending up in Bosnia, Quando ended up with me.

Over the past year, I had let Henley dictate the pace, as he had obviously slowed in his later years. Imagine then the difference when I gave Quando the 'forward' command — it seemed to have the same effect as a starting pistol on a sprinter, and he took off. I felt as though I'd climbed out of Mum's old Austin 1100 into that racing car at Brands Hatch. It was like travelling at warp speed — it was the fastest walk I've ever had, but once I was confident and relaxed, it was exhilarating.

The realisation that Henley would no longer be my guide after we had worked so well together for so long was sad, but at least I would see him regularly, as Gary and Jan were delighted to have him as their pet. Henley had drastically improved my independence and my confidence; he had made it easy for me to strike up friendships, and had even helped me meet a couple of girlfriends. Being together practically 24 hours a day, seven days a week, we had become incredibly close. I will never forget Mum's horror when she discovered Henley had polished off the last few slices of my 21st birthday cake; amazingly, he had even eaten the key.

The awful news I had been dreading came one year after his retirement in January 1994 when Henley was 13. The vet felt it was time for Henley to be put to sleep. It was extremely important to me to be there, to be with him at the end, so Kath and I jumped in the car and headed for Hereford. In the waiting room, it seemed as if Henley was saying goodbye, as he went over to Jan and Gary, then came to Kath and me. After one last cuddle, I lifted him onto the vet's table. It was a peaceful and dignified goodbye. I stroked and held him as he drifted off to sleep.

Henley had been a fantastic guide dog, and Quando was shaping up to be unbelievable, but guide dogs aren't infallible, especially when finding the right location. Estimating the location of a particular shop can also be awkward. I often have to open quite a few shop doors, have a sniff inside and a listen, and maybe even a feel, and if it doesn't smell, sound or feel right, out we go to try next door. A chemist is easy, with its distinctive odour, but going into a travel agent to see whether they have any cheap deals is a little embarrassing when you discover you are standing in a ladies' underwear shop.

Shortly after moving to Yorkshire, Dad and his second guide dog, Josh, were still learning their way around the village when he thought he'd drop in to the local pub for a pint. Opening the door it seemed very quiet and smokeless. Still, he went up to the counter and asked for a pint of bitter, only to be told by the girl that the Red Lion was next door — Dad was in the bank!

I was engaged and had a new guide dog; my life was really changing. It was around that time that I spotted an advertisement for a Braille secretary/receptionist at the Leamington Spa guide dog training centre. This job would be more sedentary, and so better for my running, but more challenging for me than just audio typing. Having talked it over with Kath, I applied for the job, and in September, Kath and I drove to the interview. We had just walked in the door back at home in Hereford when I received a call, offering me the job.

Eight months after training with Quando at Leamington Spa, we were back, this time on reception as the first faces the public saw and spoke to on the phone. Kath got a transfer to a Ministry of Defence facility about 10 miles (16 km) away and started work there in January 1994. We decided it was time to look for a house, and as this was our first time of doing this together, it was initially very exciting, but by the time we'd looked at the 20th house, we were over it. Eventually we found the place we wanted where we would live together — a three-bedroom, semi-detached, 1930s-built house in a cul-de-sac 3 miles (5 km) from work. We moved into our new home in May, and turned our focus to organising the wedding we'd scheduled for 20 August.

My injury was allowing me to run, but frustratingly it had been impossible to find anyone good enough and willing to run with me in Leamington Spa. Fortunately, Gary and I managed to get together to run four times a week, but it meant a 140 mile (224 km) round trip to be able to train with one another. It was a necessary evil though, with the world championships in Berlin looming.

These were the first world championships to be organised by the International Paralympic Committee (IPC) and were the largest event for Paralympic athletes outside of the Paralympic Games. It had been warm in England leading up to the event, but nothing like Berlin, where the temperature climbed to 35 degrees during the day, and didn't fall much below that at night. Again I shared a room with my guide runner, Gary. The first room we were allocated was relatively shady and quiet, but then the management decided to move us so the athletes could receive a good broiling on the south-facing side of the hotel overlooking the square with its outdoor bar and busy road. This would have been fine if we had air-conditioning, but we didn't, so while the athletes tossed and turned and struggled to sleep, the team management had no problems getting some shut-eye in their cooler north-facing rooms, which they retired to after their hard evenings of carousing.

I won silver in the 1500 m and bronze in my debut over 10,000 m, but I also picked up a new injury, which was diagnosed as a stress fracture of the fibula, the non-weight-bearing bone between the knee and the ankle, and forced me to withdraw from the 5000 m. I couldn't believe it — for the past year I'd had hamstring and buttock pain, and now this. To take our minds off the disappointment, and for a change of scenery, Gary and I wandered around the city centre and enjoyed the sights, including 'Checkpoint Charlie', the well-known crossing point through the Berlin Wall between East and West Germany. We eventually finished up at a restaurant where we enjoyed bratwurst with sauerkraut, washed down with some very good German beer.

I had my stag night at the end of July 1994. Kath took Quando down to Sussex where she enjoyed a fairly sensible hen night. She was an understated person, not wanting a big bash. However, I spent the evening in Leamington Spa with mates I hadn't seen since leaving Kent, with Vic, Glenn, Jim and Matt, as well as Steve, Derek and, of course, Dad. Starting at the bar of the GDBA, we did the obligatory pub crawl; I even had a stripper who arrived in police costume. She was very understanding, realising that 'what the eye couldn't see, the hand should feel for', and there is a photo to prove it, which a mate left strategically placed for Kath to find. It also shows Dad's hand reaching for a look as well. We had great fun playing drinking games, but unfortunately Dad became either tongue-tied or was enjoying himself so much that he often earned the penalty drink, which Steve James, my best man, reduced to half-measures.

As our wedding day drew closer, I had several sleepless nights, worrying over seating arrangements, and who would get on best with whom. Derek, Shaun, Steve, Quando and I stayed overnight at the Leamington Spa training centre prior to our wedding day. We had a nice evening, but I drank a little too much Irish whiskey and woke up on the big day with a hangover. Steve surprised me with a bottle of champagne and we added orange juice to make Bucks Fizz which went down very well. Kath, who had stayed at home, was also spoiled by Liz and the bridesmaids, Laura and Helen, who brought her breakfast in bed. Later a beautician applied Kath's make-up and then the girls helped her into her wedding dress. Shaun was giving Kath away, and was probably as nervous as anyone, given that he trod on Kath's hem a couple of times, earning himself a few well-chosen words of advice from his sister.

Liz found the material for the tailor to make the cravats for Steve, Shaun, Dad and I, who were wearing morning suits, and a bow for Quando who was the 'page boy'. Steve, Quando and I arrived at St Peter's Church in Leamington Spa with plenty of time to spare for photos of the best man, the groom and his dog. Walking into the church I got a shot of adrenalin a few minutes before 2 o'clock, as the organist started to play 'Trumpet Voluntary'. My legs started quivering and my heart-rate hit race pace. But then I heard the rustling of Kath's dress as she arrived at my side, and she whispered, 'Hello, Bobby.' It was a magical moment.

Thanks mainly to Kath's organisational skills and desire to keep things simple and understated, the day went off without a hitch and everyone got on well where they'd been seated — why I'd been so worried, I don't know. It was a beautiful day.

I was determined to drink within my limits, bearing in mind that too much beer can hinder the wedding night! Kath was never a big drinker, only having a little champagne and wine during the afternoon. However, Sue and Ange cornered her at the bar later in the evening, and they started drinking tequila shots. By the time we got to the bridal suite, Kath was far too poorly to think about conjugal rights, and she was still pretty poorly the next morning. Thanks, girls!

She had just about recovered sufficiently to drive to Poole Harbour that afternoon en route to France, where we enjoyed two weeks of driving around Brittany and Normandy for our honeymoon.

Chapter 12 – Abominable Atlanta

It is easy to forget just how much pain you put yourself through during training. It's not until you are preparing for the next track session that you remember just how much it's going to hurt. That is the time when your motivation is really tested. How much do you want it? I find the hardest part of going for any kind of run is actually putting on my running shoes. On a cold, wet and windy night, it is best to put them on without thinking about what's waiting for you outside the door. As I've said before, 80 per cent of running is your state of mind, and in the build-up to the 1996 Atlanta Paralympic Games, my mind wasn't in the best place.

I knew there would be a lot of gruelling training ahead of me before I was anywhere near fit enough to do myself justice, and I was struggling with the recurrence of my leg injury. I had no excuses in terms of guide runners — I trained regularly with Paul Harwood and Steve James. Neither of them was available to run at the Atlanta Paralympics, but I was certainly no worse off when Paul Rowe stepped into the breach to guide me in the Games.

It was actually a hot summer in England that year, and the week spent acclimatising in Florida with the British Paralympic Team before the Games could well have been done at home. After one particularly painful track session in Birmingham, Kath, Paul and I watched the highlight of Great Britain's Atlanta Olympics, the gold medal performance by the men's coxless four. It was the only gold medal Britain won at the 1996 Olympics in what was a very disappointing Games for the team.

The Atlanta Paralympic Games were hyped as being better than any that had gone before, but in fact they were an anticlimax after Barcelona, and just about everything was backwards. Even while the Games were still on, people were already looking forward to Sydney in four years' time. The bedrooms were rather cosy-sized twin rooms, which were too small for the wheelies to manoeuvre their chairs. The facilities and local organisation were equally shambolic. As the late Helen Rollason, the BBC presenter, put it in her autobiography, we Paralympic athletes 'had to put up with organisation and accommodation way below that offered to the athletes at the main Olympics'.

The flags around the perimeter of the roof of the stadium had been taken down and sold to the Sydney Olympic Committee. The computers had been literally ripped out. The flagpoles just outside the athletes' village had been chopped off just above pavement level, a perfect height for tripping unsuspecting blindies. The athletes' leisure swimming pool had been filled in. Centenary Park, the site of the Olympics, was a building site and all the sponsors had packed up and gone home. NBC had paid US$456 million to secure the television rights to broadcast the Olympics, whereas the Atlanta Paralympic Organising Committee (APOC) had to pay NBC US$1 million to show some of the Paralympic Games. At least we did have parity with our Olympic peers in that the transportation was crap for us as well.

Anyway, there was no point in dwelling upon the many and varied shortcomings of the Atlanta Paralympic Games. We were there to run around the track which, fortunately, had been left for us. Ironically, that too was later ripped up to be replaced by a baseball diamond.

By far the best aspect of the Games in Atlanta was the media coverage in Britain. Finally, the Paralympics had started to be taken more seriously, and we were in demand for television and newspaper interviews. Best of all, the BBC broadcast a series of 30-minute highlight programmes during the Games. Not surprisingly then, there was a great deal more interest shown by the general public in Britain which is a trend that has continued in successive Games.

My first race was to have been the 1500 m semi-final. Paul and I made sure that we were on the warm-up track in plenty of time as we were so wary of the shabbily-run transport system in Atlanta. We registered, as usual, one hour beforehand, and were escorted the short distance to the final check-in, but then the administrators discovered the Honduran athlete hadn't registered. After some consultation and a long wait, the officials finally told us the heat was cancelled, and all six athletes and their guides were straight through to the final two days later.

Athletes betray their nerves in a number of different ways before a major final. Some become hyperactive, jumping around and chattering, no matter how hard they try to stay calm. During my career, I tended to be lethargic, uncommunicative and heavy-legged, and had a nasty habit of chewing my fingernails. Waking up before a big race, my first thought was always, 'Oh shit,' before the adrenalin started to course through my body and I began to get excited about what lay ahead. But very soon after the excitement kicked in, the doubts would come banging down the door again. On my way to breakfast I would obsess about how my legs were feeling, and worry about how heavy and taut my calves and thighs felt.

I often had to remind myself to lighten up: 'This isn't death row, for crying out loud, this is what you've trained for,' I used to say to myself, but still I found it an effort to eat anything on the morning of a race.

An hour before a race you have to register officially. Failing to do so means you're out of the race, and in some cases out of the Games. For runners and guides alike, when you walk into the first call room to register, that is when the big race pressure usually hits hardest. It is like the point of no return — a lot like walking into the lobby of the Hotel California: 'You can check in any time you like, but you can never leave.' Officials in this area check the length and number of spikes screwed into your track shoes. The maximum allowed in each shoe is six and they can be no longer than 6 mm. They also check you have the correct competition numbers on your vest.

Once this is done, you can complete your warm-up in a designated area beneath the stands where you are acutely aware of the roar of the crowd. Then, about 20 minutes before the race, competitors are directed to the second and final call room. This is the most difficult time as six athletes and their guides are crammed into a confined space. This is where the deep-breathing exercises come in handy. You are only permitted to leave the room under strict supervision to answer the call of nature, and not surprisingly the supervisors are kept pretty busy. Then you are given your lane number which has to be stuck on your hip for the photo-finish equipment (number one being on the inside of the track).

Then comes the moment of truth, as the athletes are instructed to line up in ascending lane order and form a procession into the Olympic Stadium. Walking to the start line can leave you feeling weak and floppy. At this point you need to have a word with yourself and focus on why you are there. You've got a few minutes to jog around and loosen up, and then you are summoned to the start line. In the last moments, poised for the gun with your toes on the line, there's a feeling of unreality. Then the gun fires and the waiting is over, worries and tired legs are forgotten, especially if you find yourself in the lead, as I did in the 1500 m in Atlanta.

We went through the first 800 m in 2:16 which is when I started pushing hard, trying to shake off Paulo Coelho who was following every move I made. As we passed 1000 m, Paulo moved out, making me dig deeper — there was no way I was going to let him dictate. At the bell, I had opened a gap. Had I found a little more effort at that point, perhaps Paulo would have found it harder to rip past me on the back straight, but that's exactly what he did with 300 m to go, and there was nothing I could do. He finished four seconds ahead of me, setting a new Paralympic record of 4:08.52.

I was disappointed not to get the gold, but a silver medal was still a good result, given my recurring-injury-hit preparations and being less fit than in Barcelona. Besides, the silver medal seemed a good way for Kath and I to celebrate our second wedding anniversary. Kath had been staying in a youth hostel and, thinking we'd be allowed to have until the next morning to celebrate, had booked a hotel room for us that night. Unfortunately, I had to return to the athletes' village that evening, anniversary or not, as no one was allowed to stay overnight outside the village whilst still competing.

Still, we made the most of it, with a southern-style meal and an excellent pint of Red Brick ale, which came from a local micro-brewery. I always presumed that it was only the British who appreciated real ale, but this tasty drop made me realise that some Americans had taste after all.

My mate, Noel Thatcher, a partially-sighted athlete, made all the headlines in Atlanta after winning the gold, despite having been diagnosed during the Games with a stress fracture of the fibula. The media loved it as they could write about the blind athlete winning with a broken leg. The story was even more sensational when 'Thatch' also won the 5000 m a few days later.

On the same day as Thatch's race, my 5000 m final was scheduled for 9 a.m. so we set the alarm for 5 a.m., giving us plenty of time to get up, eat breakfast and get to the stadium an hour before the race. Once again, I found myself in front until the lap marker showed five laps to go, when I lost the lead for the first time to Willis (USA), Paulo (Portugal) and Ledesma (Mexico). I increased my pace and thought I was keeping in contact, but in fact a gap of 30 m had developed by the time we started the last lap. I wound up for my famous last-lap finish, expecting to hear athletes ahead at any moment, but it wasn't until we were approaching the home straight that I at last caught 'sound' of the breakaway bunch. Sprinting flat out, we managed to move up into the silver medal position, but it was too little, too late, to catch Paulo.

After hugging each other, Paul and I congratulated our fellow competitors and then turned our thoughts to the warm-down. One of the problems Paul and I had solved by training every day in America was how to keep our synchronisation in the final 100 m when sprinting flat out for the line, so during our warm-down we talked about being satisfied with staying together, especially as we'd sprinted from 200 m out, making up a great deal of ground.

Paul headed off to find out the official results and when the medal ceremony would be held, but a short while later he returned. He sounded bewildered when he told me he'd seen the results, but beside my name were the letters DQ. I'd been disqualified, and Willis, USA, who'd finished fourth, was the fortunate recipient of a bronze medal.

Blind athletes running with a guide runner can be disqualified for one of four reasons: firstly, if the athlete changes guide runners more than once during a race (I was unaware of this rule at the time, never having had to change guides before, but I became familiar with it seven years later); secondly, if the guide runner is seen to be pulling the athlete during the race, and the athlete is deemed to have gained an advantage; thirdly, if the athlete and guide runner are more than one metre apart at any stage in the race; and finally, if the guide runner crosses the finish line ahead of the athlete. We were accused of breaking the fourth rule.

Despite being aware of the rules, disqualification wasn't something I'd thought much about because my guides and I run stride for stride and always cross the finish line shoulder to shoulder. This time we had got it wrong, and Paul crossed the line fractionally before me. I have certainly never blamed Paul; we had done relatively little training, in which time he had become a great friend and guide. This disqualification was a valuable lesson, and from that day on my guides have practised for races by easing off just before the finish line in training to ensure I cross the line first.

Bill Berry, who was now the Great Britain team manager, pleaded mitigating circumstances, but his appeal fell on deaf ears. The judges have always been very strict on the rules and, in many cases, have even used the photo-finish equipment to adjudicate. In our case it wasn't necessary.

In the swimming events, blind swimmers are tapped on the head by their coaches as they draw close to the wall at the end of a length. It is referred to as 'bonking'. If they time it right, they can do a tumble-turn and push off the wall without losing any momentum. In Atlanta, one coach slightly mistimed her signal to her swimmer and apologised to her out loud. The swimmer clearly wouldn't have heard in any case, and she went on to win gold, but she was disqualified because coaching is strictly prohibited during a race, and the coach's spoken apology was considered a form of coaching.

We were devastated, Paul more so as he felt responsible. I was just grateful to have found such a good guide runner at short notice, someone I had got on well with and who had quickly become a great mate. We had no further time to indulge ourselves in self-pity, though; we were due to run in the 800 m final that same evening.

The 800 m athletes usually run the first bend in lanes and only on the back straight are they allowed to break and jostle for position on the inside lane of the track. For some reason, the officials in Atlanta decided to use the much less safe 'waterfall' start. This meant five blind athletes and their guide runners started in a curved line, standing shoulder to shoulder, and instead of staying in lanes, it was a 'free for all' for the inside lane from the off.

When the starter's gun fired, there was a stampede of bodies.

Paul and I were drawn in the inside lane, which meant that every other athlete outside us was gunning for our lane. Inside the first 30 m we were cut up by the faster starters, and to avoid a collision we had to break our stride, virtually coming to a standstill. In an 800 m race, we had no chance of making up the deficit and, try as we might, I had to accept my first non-podium finish (barring a fall) in a major championship.

While it wasn't the best Games from my point of view, the Great Britain Paralympic team enjoyed outstanding success, finishing fourth in the medal table behind the USA, Australia and Germany, with 42 gold medals. When competition was finally over, it was great to be able to get back to normality and to spend time sightseeing with Kath. We went to Williamsburg, an 18th century period town with the old shops, signs and menus, but very modern prices. In Washington it was interesting to see and walk around the White House and Capitol Buildings and sample the eclectic cuisine. One evening, emerging from the subway, Kath and I stopped to listen for a while to an impromptu solo performance from a jazz trumpeter, then moved on to enjoy an outdoor meal of New Orleans-style food.

Our flight home was delayed by 24 hours by the close passage of a hurricane. Shortly after lifting off, there was a moment when we both felt our time had come to an end when the plane plummeted for a couple of seconds in the turbulent aftermath of the winds. It took a few flights to forget that scary experience.

Once again, Kath took me completely by surprise by organising a party for me soon after we got home from Atlanta. On the day of the party, before I went for a run with Paul, I heard banging from the street, which Kath said was our next-door neighbour doing some work in his front garden. I thought no more of this as our neighbour, Jeff, liked to keep himself busy. However, when Paul Harwood dropped me home after our run, I got out of the car to cheers and applause. 'Bewildered' doesn't come close to describing how I felt. Jeff had been putting up some street decorations, and Kath had organised a street party to celebrate my silver medal in Atlanta. As well as most of our neighbours, Mum and Dad were there, along with Ange and Sue and a number of guide runners, including Paul Rowe and Vic Smith, not to mention the Mayoress of Leamington Spa who said a few words and made me feel acutely embarrassed. It was brilliant, though. I tried to respond, but for once, words didn't come easily.

I was in for another pleasant surprise shortly afterwards when I learned I was to be honoured by the Royal Mail as the Paralympian who best embodied the Paralympic spirit. Considering Steve Redgrave, the rower, was nominated as the Olympian who best embodied the Olympic spirit, I was in exalted company indeed.

After Atlanta, I had my second opportunity to visit Downing Street, this time to meet John Major. He seemed like a nice bloke; he was slightly taller than me, at 6 feet 3 inches (1.9 m), and had hands like shovels. He looked straight in my eyes when he spoke to me, and gave me the impression he was interested in what I had to say. Of course, being a Chelsea fan helped me warm to him.

Before leaving for Atlanta, Kath had been seriously considering a change of direction in her career. She wasn't the type of person to rush into decisions, thinking long and hard before making them. She certainly didn't hurry into making the decision to marry me, nor the decision not to have children as she felt the risk of them inheriting RP was too great.

Not surprisingly, then, she took her time to consider moving on from the Ministry of Defence. Having spent nearly eight years sitting behind a desk, working as an administrative officer, she was tired of pushing pieces of paper around, dealing with the never-ending bureaucracy, as well as the difficult army officers who she felt 'needed to get into the real world'. The one positive outcome of Kath working in the army was that she introduced me to Paul Harwood, who became one of my best friends and is still one of my main guide runners to this day.

Kath was more determined than ever to find a job she enjoyed, rather than endured. As Kath had lived with her mum and helped her cope with her deteriorating vision, and was now living with me, a confident, totally blind person, she approached the rehabilitation department of the GDBA, confident that her first-hand knowledge and empathy would make her an ideal employee. On the two-day assessment to become a rehab worker, Kath and the other hopefuls were assessed in different situations, such as guiding a competent blind person, as well as one less skilled, around a building, dealing with opening doors, and tackling steps.

Kath was accepted onto the rehab course in October 1996, but it meant that for the 18 months of the course, she wouldn't be earning any money. We'd always lived within our means, and we knew if it came to it we'd just have to tighten our belts. As it turned out, the outgoing general manager of the GDBA came up trumps, and offered Kath an £8000 bursary, which paid for her educational costs during the course. He also offered her a job on her successful completion of the course, so there was lots of good news.

The bad news was that the course was in Surrey, which was 110 miles (176 km) from our home in Leamington Spa, and meant that Kath would have to spend four days a week away from home. For the next year and a half, we would just have the weekends together.

Of course I missed having my wife and best friend around, but I wouldn't have dreamed of not supporting Kath. She had certainly made her fair share of sacrifices in support of my running career. The phone calls to Kath in the evenings helped me get through the separation. To be honest, I guess I had become a bit lazy with Kath there to take care of most of the household tasks. I am not bad at cooking, but when both of us were working full-time, she did the majority of the cooking as she was so much faster. With Kath gone during the week, I dusted off my old Braille cookbooks, donned the apron and got cooking.

When Kath began her rehab course, I wasn't doing any running — my old injury had flared up again — so I had far too much free time on my hands. I started to find ways to fill it by going to the gym a few times a week, and meeting up with mates for dinner or a drink in the pub. But it wasn't until I started running again that I became more settled. I realised running had become so much a part of my life and identity.

Weekends, though, were great. Kath and I were able to enjoy the benefits of 'a weekend marriage' (her words, not mine). It was fascinating to listen to Kath talk about her course. She was given some experience of what it's like to be blind when, wearing a blindfold, she was guided along a busy street. She said how frightening she found it. Once, when we were on holiday, we passed some workmen cutting stone slabs in the street. I felt confused and disorientated by the noise, and desperately needed to get away from it as fast as possible. Kath hadn't understood my anxiety at the time, but having experienced something of what I had felt, she apologised for thinking that I had over-reacted at the time.

The class was also given an idea of what partially sighted people could see of the various fields of vision by wearing simulator spectacles, or SIM specs. Of course, a fully-sighted person plunged into a world with less or no vision finds it incredibly difficult to adjust and is often scared to move, whereas the person living with blindness or poor vision has no choice but to learn to adjust to it.

One of the first skills Kath and her peers learned was the sighted-guide technique, or how to guide a blindie properly. They did this by taking turns to be guided by one another, wearing a blindfold or SIM specs. She also learned how to use and teach the long cane, Braille, and living skills, which involves teaching a newly visually-impaired person relatively simple tasks like how to boil an egg safely and make a cup of tea.

Kath gained a great deal of job satisfaction and pleasure from using the skills she'd learned. One of her many successes was working with a deaf and partially-sighted lady who had her application for a guide dog turned down as she was unable to get out independently and safely, and she was low on confidence. Kath went to see her, gained the lady's trust and got her using and practising with the cane. As she became more confident, she was able to walk further and faster with the cane. A few months later, the lady was reassessed by the same person who had originally turned down her application for a guide dog. He found it difficult to believe that he was reassessing the same person, as the transformation Kath had helped bring about was incredible, and he had no hesitation recommending her for a guide dog.

One benefit of Kath being able to read and write Braille was that we could now leave each other Brailled messages. On the flip side, it meant I would no longer have any secrets.

To spend some quality time together, Kath and I invested in a tandem bike, thinking how great it would be to tour together. We discovered that a tandem is traditionally built for the tall person to ride on the front and the shorter person at the back. With Kath standing five-feet-four (1.63 m) in bare feet and me at six-feet-two (1.88 m), there was no way Kath would allow me to steer the thing, so we had to get a tandem custom-built. We found a local bicycle builder who built a tandem that would fit. It was great fun making decisions about the size and type of wheels, brakes, gears, colour, pannier carriers and so on, and it certainly looked the part in Ferrari red. We christened her Molly — now all we had to do was learn to ride her.

Nearly 30 years earlier, Mum and Dad had bought me my first bicycle as a Christmas present (never would I have guessed that my next pair of wheels would be a tandem). It had been a touring style, five-speed bike, also painted red, and was my pride and joy.

I was so proud when I took my Cycling Proficiency Test in the school playground. It was only a case of steering in and around bollards and between lines, but I thought I'd done reasonably well, only bumping a couple of bollards. I was annoyed with myself as I'd seen the bollards and thought myself clumsy, which was only partly true as my sight obviously wasn't as good as I imagined. I didn't pass — the teachers felt I wasn't proficient enough, but said I could try again another time after a little more practice.

Initially, Kath and I struggled to get moving on our tandem, with plenty of false starts, but after five minutes as we worked out how to start in unison, we got moving, albeit slowly and a little unsteadily. We were beginning to wonder whether this had been a fool's errand and if we had wasted £1200 getting a tandem custom-built, but we weren't going to let it beat us. A couple of rides later we regarded 15 miles (24 km) as merely a long warm-up. With new-found confidence under our belts we started planning a tandem-biking and camping tour around Ulster in Northern Ireland.

We started off at our friends James and Mel Brown's place in Portaferry, near Belfast. James had been a bicycle mechanic, so was able to teach me simple tasks such as repairing a puncture. It is embarrassing to admit I hadn't really thought through how Kath and I would cope if we had a mechanical problem, but James was always at the end of a phone if we couldn't find a bike shop. Throwing caution to the wind, we set off.

Our adventure went really well, apart from one minor accident when we were coasting down a hill to catch a ferry, and the front wheel slid from beneath us on a metal rail. Thankfully, only our egos were bruised, and only a herd of cows witnessed our downfall. Heading back south along the east coast was particularly lovely, with the sound of the North Sea on our left, and the lush green countryside on the right where I could hear the long grass stirring in the breeze.

Ten days and 500 miles (800 km) later we rolled back into Portaferry two very happy campers. We'd met some wonderful people, enjoyed the Guinness and eaten a lot of great food. We'd also seen much of Ulster's beautiful countryside and famous landmarks, such as the Giant's Causeway just outside the village of Bushmills in County Antrim. Our cycling trip of Ulster was finished off by us polishing off a litre bottle of Black Bush whiskey (well, mostly James and I). Amazingly, neither of us had a hangover the next morning — obviously this was a much better drink than the stuff which had put me in the sickbay back in college all those years ago.

Chapter 13 – One last drink

Christmas 1996 was the last Christmas I spent with my dad; the festive season has never been the same since. That Christmas Eve, Kath and I met my parents at Leamington Spa station as they were spending a few days of the holiday with us. Arriving home from the station, we were greeted at the front door by the fantastic and delicious aroma of Kath's freshly made mushroom soup. The sun streaming through the windows created a warm, comfortable, almost intoxicating atmosphere. It was perfect.

At 4 p.m. we listened to the Christmas carols from King's College, Cambridge, on Radio 4, which had been a family tradition for as long as I could remember. We passed around a plate of cheese and crackers, and a glass of port which Dad was always fond of saying was 'just something to wash the cheese down, you know'.

After we picked Ange up from the station we all went to midnight mass at St Peter's Church, where Kath and I had been married. Next day we all had a great Christmas lunch at Eathorpe Park, where we'd had our wedding breakfast. Dad and I got the lunch off to a good start in the bar with a couple of pints of We Three Kings, a really good, locally brewed ale. The only thing that marred the day for Ange was my refusal to put *Eastenders* on the television. Well, it was Christmas Day! I couldn't understand why anyone would need to glue themselves to a programme in which everyone always seems to be shouting, fighting or hopping into bed with best friends and other people's wives/husbands. I couldn't think of anything more depressing, so I put on something more Christmassy instead.

After seeing Ange onto her bus back to London on Boxing Day, we all went for a walk and conveniently ended up at a newly opened pub bearing the unusual name of the Benjamin Satchwell (named after one of the founding fathers of Leamington Spa). Surprisingly for a new place, it had some atmosphere, and Dad and I particularly enjoyed the guest ales. It was a special, magical Christmas.

After Mum and Dad had gone home a few days later, I was doing the washing up when, inexplicably, I felt a deep sense of loss and became very emotional. It was almost as though I'd had a premonition that we had just spent our last Christmas together. Rationally, there was no reason to feel that way. Kath consoled me by saying it was because we'd just had a really nice time. Whether it was a premonition or not, sadly it proved to be right.

In April I received a call giving me the scary news that Dad had been taken to hospital, having passed out. Talking with him on the phone later, he described how he'd dropped in for a pint at his local pub, the Travellers' Rest, after doing a little shopping. He said he'd felt 'a bit queer' and the next thing he knew he heard someone say they'd called an ambulance. His faint turned out to have been caused by cancer which was in its early stages. The doctors had found a shadow on his lung and feared it was malignant.

I was stunned, not able to comprehend the far-reaching effects of this news. Surely this couldn't be happening? My dad, a man I'd always been able to talk with about literally anything, had cancer? He'd always seemed so strong. The closest he'd come to being sick, as far as I could remember, was when I was seven, and he had to spend a week prostrate, having hurt his back. Of course he'd always had a distinctive, musical cough since contracting yellow fever in his teens, but it had never affected him.

As a boy, at bedtime he would usually come into my room for a chat. He'd sit on the floor or lean against the door and the two of us would just yap away about anything that cropped up — from a girl I'd just met and liked the sound of, to the incomprehensible size of the universe. Sometimes we'd get onto the subject of the finality of death and what came after. We couldn't imagine there being just 'nothingness'. I remember him saying, 'I can't believe everyone who dies goes to the same place. Imagine meeting Henry VIII — it seems fantastic.'

Devastatingly, Dad's cancer turned out to be one of the fastest-growing forms of the illness, and even with treatment, he had been given just months to live.

On Kath's 32nd birthday, a week after Dad had collapsed, Mum, Dad, Ange, Sue, Kath and myself met up for a lovely weekend at Ange's house in London, just before the start of Dad's first course of chemotherapy. Sue and Guy-Pierre, a Frenchman whom she'd met on St Maarten, had planned to get married in the West Indies later that year, and of course we were all looking forward to making the trip for the wedding, but they decided to bring the date forward because we didn't know how much longer Dad would be capable of such a long flight.

Obviously I had no intention of missing my baby sister's wedding, but it would severely affect my preparation for that summer's European championships unless I could take a guide runner with me, which Sue and Guy-Pierre agreed would be no problem, so the arrangements were made and off we all went. Kath had some exams to take and so had to miss the first four days of the fortnight's holiday; it felt longer, and it was so nice to see her when she did arrive.

Dad and Kath were very close, and were delighted to see each other. She was pleased to see how well he was looking. Dad was determined to enjoy himself as much as possible, which meant sampling anything he could get his hands on. We weren't particularly surprised therefore to find him smoking a joint at the beach bar. He was a little disappointed, though, as it didn't do very much for him. Even more than ever, he had a devil-may-care attitude, so when Ange and Sue kept daring him to strip on the beach, he did. Guy-Pierre was really angry with them, though; unbeknown to Dad, he'd bared his bum in front of the beach bar where Guy-Pierre worked.

Mum wasn't enjoying herself, though. She was trying to cope

with Dad's cancer, and on top of that, just before she'd travelled for Sue's wedding, she'd had to have her pet dog, Toby, put down. The stress really got to her in the first week of the holiday, but fortunately a local doctor put her on Valium, so she was much more relaxed and happier in the second week of the holiday. Dad was much more down to earth and was able to talk about his cancer, saying 'I hate the thought of this bloody thing growing inside me', and how determined he was to fight it.

On the morning of Sue's wedding, I got a knock on my door from my guide runner who told me he was going home to England because the high level of stress wasn't exactly the relaxed Caribbean holiday he'd had in mind. Without a guide runner, I would be unable to run for a week, and it was only two months out from the European championships. Kath agreed that, if we could change our tickets, we should fly home after the wedding as I had to be able to run. With that mini-drama settled, we resolved to enjoy Sue's special day.

It was such a wonderful day, which was made even more special because of how different it was to a standard British wedding. We all met at the harbour on the morning of the wedding, where a large motor launch waited to take the wedding party to the British-owned island of Anguilla, which is smaller and less commercialised than St Maarten. We drank champagne on the way over, trying hard not to spill it on each other as the boat bounced up and down on the waves. The church was also unusual, with a cool, prevailing breeze blowing through it. It was fantastic that Dad was able to give Sue away, and very emotional for her when they danced together later at the wedding reception.

Kath and I flew back two days later, leaving the family festivities, not to mention the sun, sand and sea, to arrive back in a very cold and very wet England. As it turned out, I had to pull out of the European championships with a recurrence of the leg injury.

With the benefit of hindsight, I made a selfish and entirely wrong decision to return home to train. Kath had only been there for four days, and Dad only had months to live. I was so focused on running in the European championships that I didn't really comprehend the severely limited quality time I had left to spend with Dad.

I'm not very religious, but during those months I had a few discussions with a greater power. I would stand in our back garden just before turning in for bed, asking for some sign, anything, to indicate how much longer Dad had, and even whether the cancer could be held at bay. I remember one night a church bell in the distance chimed 11 o'clock. Was that a sign of how many months Dad had to live? I was clinging on to the hope that we could still fight this thing. Dad had always been my rock, and I couldn't imagine life without him.

The thought of losing Dad was more numbing than anything else. I just couldn't understand why this could be happening to my dad. He was more like a mate to me than a father, especially in my later years. Kath was there with me every step of the way and was my shoulder to cry on. I don't know how I would have coped without her.

Towards the end of August, Kath, Quando and I drove to Tickhill to spend a few days with Dad. He'd always had a thick head of hair all his life, whereas I had been losing mine steadily since I was 20, but after the chemotherapy treatment, Dad and I now had something else in common — we shared the same hairstyle.

By now Dad was considerably lighter and weaker, but his sense of fun and purpose in life didn't desert him; he really did have an amazing 'never say die' attitude and determination not to let anything get him down. However, he was a little frustrated that the chemo had numbed his sense of touch, making it difficult for him to read Braille. He was doing as much as possible to keep himself active, walking every day with his guide dog, and doing some woodwork. He was quite proud of the wooden rack he'd made for his pipes over a few visits to the woodwork room at the hospice centre as a day-patient. At home he enjoyed going out to his shed where he worked on the seven pine shelves he was making for Kath and me, which fitted in the alcove of our living room.

Later, Dad and I had a 'man to man' drink, which tragically proved to be our last one together, just the two of us. We went to his local where he had always enjoyed a pint or two of Bass. The landlord's name was Ted. On seeing Dad come through the door, he always called, 'Hello Aubrey, what'll you have?'

Dad always replied, unable to hide his grin: 'A pint of bas'ted.'

Three pints later, Kath and Mum picked us up on the way to the restaurant where we'd booked to have a meal. I'd failed to realise that with Dad's reduced body mass, those three pints had affected him as much as six would once have done. When we got home, he bent down to take his shoes off, lost his balance and landed in the broom cupboard. Thankfully he wasn't hurt.

A few weeks later, when Kath and I went up to see Mum and Dad again on Saturday 18 October, Dad had very little strength left. We walked into their bedroom and found Sue sitting on the bed next to Dad, giving him a manicure. He was still in good form, recounting childhood memories and talking about family holidays. We laughed about our experiences as a family of five crammed into the family car, and the time we'd camped for a change, having caravanned the past four years, and the performance it took to erect the tent.

We reminisced for hours about Dad and I playing football and cricket. We talked about him reading us bedtime stories from Braille books, one of our favourites being the golliwog stories, which are seen as being politically incorrect nowadays. We used to collect the golliwog labels off Robertson's jam jars, and send them away for a badge. Dad told us how, aged 15, he'd played the banjo on stage in Chiswick, West London, and wondered what had happened to his banjo. We had a good giggle, remembering

Dad sleep-walking into my bedroom in the middle of the night when I'd had a girlfriend home. He'd walked over to the radiator under the window, had a real good look at it, then turned around and walked out, closing the door behind him. He'd been gob-smacked when I'd told him the next morning.

On Sunday, Dad made one last visit to the Travellers' Rest for a drink, with Sue and Ange taking it in turns to push him in a borrowed wheelchair. He probably hadn't expected such an exciting ride. I asked Dad if he'd heard any strange noises or had dreamt of 'the other side'. I guess I wanted to get an understanding of how long it would be before he passed away. Dad claimed there was nothing unusual to report. Throughout Dad's illness he had never complained about any discomfort, nor felt sorry for himself; he'd borne the illness stoically and extremely bravely. After 42 years of marriage, his main worry was about having to leave Mum alone.

Kath and I headed back home on Sunday to get back to work on Monday, but on Tuesday morning I received a phone call from Sue, telling me to 'come back up here, it doesn't look as if Dad has very much longer'. Sue and Ange met me off the train at Doncaster, and on the way to Tickhill we stopped for a drink at the Travellers' Rest, taking a pint back for Dad — one last drink — which went down well. I asked him, 'Would you like us to pour a pint of Stones (a local beer) on your grave?'

Laughing, he said, 'Oh yes, I should like that!'

Turning in for bed later that night, we said goodnight to Dad, as it turned out, for the last time. He was unconscious the next morning. Ange, Sue and I went for a walk, and arrived back in his bedroom when he drew his last breath. It was 12.20 p.m. on Wednesday, 22 October 1997. Dad was 73.

I wanted to be one of the pallbearers at Dad's funeral, so Shaun, Kath's brother, offered to stand beside me to help me bear the load.

Mum chose Elgar's 'Nimrod' for the organist to play as we carried the coffin into the church, and we also sang 'Jerusalem' which I found uplifting. Ange chose 'All Things Bright and Beautiful' and Sue gave an oration. At Dad's wake in the Travellers' Rest I recited one of his ditties I could remember, and I had one of Dad's favourite maxims engraved on a brass plaque to go on the wall: 'What the eye doesn't see, the hand should feel for.' Then Sue, Ange, Kath and I carried a pint to his grave, took a sip each, and took turns pouring it over the grave. It was our final drink with Dad.

I feel lucky we had some warning that Dad wasn't going to be around for very much longer, because you try to make the most of whatever time there is left, but as a friend of mine warned me, 'there will always be something you wished you had said' and he was right. There is still plenty I'd love to be able to say to Dad. I have so many fond memories of him and his idiosyncrasies. For instance, I can still see him lighting his pipe with his flame thrower-like lighter, inhaling deeply, exhaling a pall of smoke and disappearing into it like a genie. This ritual was peculiar to Dad; I've never seen or heard of anyone smoke in quite such a way.

Maurice Tucker, one of his friends from college days, described in Dad's obituary how, lighting a friend's cigarette, Dad was chuckling, thinking the friend's hair was burning, only to discover that it was his own. Dad was always a fun and positive person to be around. The vicar told his own story during the service of how, shortly after his arrival in the parish, he had bumped into Dad strolling through the village with his guide dog. Dad had heard how the church was having problems with its plumbing. With an impish grin, Dad said to the vicar, 'I hear you've got problems with your waterworks.'

He was a tall, handsome man who was loved by everyone who met him. I don't blame Dad in any way for passing on RP to me, but I do thank him for making me see that being blind is far from the worst thing that can happen to anyone. Dad showed me I could have a normal life. He was a fantastic husband and father.

He worked hard to support the family, and he always enjoyed a good joke and an ale. I think of Dad a lot, especially since I too have become a father. I wish my son, Thomas, could have known his grandfather, but I can't help but feel that he isn't far away, reciting a ditty or two to Thomas while he sleeps.

Rest in peace, Aubrey Thomas Ellis Matthews.

Chapter 14 – Tour de France

This was getting beyond a joke. It was 1998 and looking like it would become another frustrating year for injury, but at least it enabled Kath and I to have a normal summer holiday for a change. With our appetites whetted by our tour of Northern Ireland three years earlier, Kath and I opted to take Molly, our tandem, on another adventure, this time cycling off the ferry at Cherbourg in the north of France and planning to make it all the way down to Marseilles in the French Riviera. Did I really say a normal summer holiday?

We had set ourselves quite a task with 680 miles (1088 km) ahead of us, but had planned our trip on the secondary roads, which are much quieter and more scenic. The plan was to get to Marseilles to meet Sue and the newest introduction to the Matthews family — her daughter, Ella.

I'm still convinced we could have made it, were it not for the mechanical issues we experienced early on. I was now competent at changing an inner tube if we had a puncture, but there was nothing I could do when the gear block disintegrated early on our third day. Bloody hell, there were ball bearings all over the road — not good — plus the bike shop wouldn't be open until the next morning as it was a Sunday. By the time Molly was fixed, we'd lost three days. I couldn't help but feel responsible. It was up to me to make sure Molly was roadworthy — I'd actually had the local bike shop replace the old, worn gear block before we left home. Still, despite the setback we made it as far as Figeac, a distance of 545 miles (872 km) in 10 days, before we realised we were never going to get to Marseilles in time to meet Sue, who was due to fly back to the West Indies.

Despite the problems, we still had a great, if tiring, time. Carrying everything on the bike, we travelled as light as possible. The tent and bed mats went on the back; everything else, including our sleeping bags and changes of clothes, fitted in the four panniers. Having flogged this weighty machine up the last hill of the day to reach the campsite, we would arrive tired but exhilarated, with a huge sense of achievement. It was my job to set up the tent while Kath unpacked what we needed. Staying in the tent really made those nights we opted for a soft bed at a bed-and-breakfast even more special.

Looking back now, it is amazing we avoided being kicked out of at least one campsite when I decided to let loose with my new-found French. On our first night, instead of asking the campsite manager, 'Do you have a shower?' I said, 'Voulez-vous une douche?' which translates into 'Would you like a shower?' We still got to camp there and we had a shower without him. Afterwards, we had to jump back on the bike to find a restaurant and some more great French cuisine.

Our route through the French countryside in many places was really quite hilly; it was hard at times to stay enthusiastic as we slogged up yet another climb. However, the hard parts were more than made up for by the beautiful fresh croissants for breakfast which got us off to a good start, and cycling along the quiet idyllic lanes and through the quaint villages. The fields were full of sunflowers and wheat, and there's nothing like baguettes and cheese for lunch whilst sitting on a river bank on the edge of an ancient village with fortified walls and a 12th century castle as a backdrop.

On the sixth day of cycling, our path crossed that of the Tour de France. What an experience, but what an anticlimax. Choosing a good vantage point we were able to look back at a bridge where the cyclists had a gentle climb up to us. We'd been waiting a couple of hours when, at last, the peloton appeared. The bunch flew past in a blur of colour with a huge mass of cyclists riding wheel to wheel; we barely had time to shout, 'Go on, Chris Boardman!' It didn't matter — we later learned that Boardman, the British rider, had crashed out on the first day.

The farther south we went, the hotter it became. We were up by 6 a.m. every day so we could get as much cycling in as possible before the heat kicked in. In one of the villages I had escargots for the first time since my 18th birthday. I enjoyed the taste of the meat with garlic butter, as long as I avoided thinking about the concept of eating a slimy snail.

We had come so far, but realising we were never going to reach Sue in time, we determined that we would have to catch the train south. We soon discovered that French trains don't like bikes, especially tandems. We tried to hire a car instead, but again were thwarted as there were no hire cars available in the area for three weeks. Finally we accepted the fact that we weren't going to make it to Marseilles to see Sue and baby Ella, so we turned around and headed back towards England. Our attempt to make it to Sue was a little ambitious, but we certainly had fun trying.

Back home again, it was now Quando's turn to be in the limelight. I had been asked to show him at the Crufts Dog Show, held at Birmingham's National Exhibition Centre, to demonstrate how a guide dog and his owner work together by weaving in and out of artificial obstacles. Later, to illustrate that guide dogs don't live in their harnesses but have a lot of fun, I ran around the arena with a guide runner whilst Quando entertained the crowds with some free running, all the time showing off how much faster than us he could run. There is no doubt Quando would have been the fittest guide dog in the UK, possibly the world. He was always out in front of us on any runs up to 10 miles (16 km), exploring and investigating, often running back towards us to make sure we were keeping up, and encouraging us to greater effort. If we ever got in front whilst he was relieving himself, he'd come surging past to reclaim his position at the head of the bunch.

Life was about to change significantly. Early in 1999, I became one of the elite disabled athletes to be granted funding from the

Lottery through its world-class performance plan. This financial support afforded athletes the choice of working either part-time or giving up work completely to concentrate on their training. I had been competing and winning gold medals for Great Britain for 16 years, not only fitting my training in and around my working hours, but also with my guide runners' schedules. After a long day at work, plus all the travel, 'running my eyeballs out' wasn't always the easiest prospect at 7 o'clock in the evening. I had to keep reminding myself that the hardest part of training really is putting my running shoes on; no matter how knackered I felt, it had to be done.

Feeling as though I was stagnating behind the reception desk at the GDBA, I looked for an opportunity to do something more challenging and satisfying. I discovered a great bicycle mechanics course at the Queen Alexandra College for the Blind in Birmingham, 25 miles (40 km) away, and knew this would provide plenty of challenges and satisfaction. After our experience of cycling through France last year, learning something of the mechanics of the bicycle seemed an excellent idea, especially if Kath and I were to achieve our ambition of touring the world on the tandem.

Being recognised as an elite athlete gave me both the opportunity to enrol on the 18-month course and the chance to find good-quality guide runners in Birmingham. I wasted no time in handing in my notice at the GDBA. I could now concentrate on training for the European championships in September before the build-up to the 2000 Sydney Paralympic Games. Whilst I wasn't any worse off financially, I did miss the routine of working regular hours and the friends I'd made.

Paul Harwood was my most regular guide runner by then, but he could only fit in a couple of runs per week with me. I was fortunate in that Paul Rowe, my guide runner from Atlanta, was still fit, keen and living quite close to the Queen Alexandra College, and he agreed to train with me for a few months.

That April I started the course, boarding nearby as otherwise it would have involved four hours' travel a day. I ran with Paul Rowe during the week and did the really hard training sessions with Paul Harwood at the weekends — it was almost a perfect scenario. The only downside to my change in direction was spending so much time away from Kath. Ironically, she had just finished her studies in Surrey and now it was my turn to study away from home during the week. Once again we had a weekend marriage.

Life at the Queen Alexandra College wasn't too bad. Kath was able to visit during the week, and Paul Rowe introduced me to a couple of idyllic old country pubs. It's amazing that within only a couple of miles of the second-largest city in England, you can be in the countryside.

Towards the end of 1999 I started running with Mike Peters who soon became a very good guide. It was such a coincidence that he had married Zara Hyde-Peters whom I had known years earlier. Mike became a great friend and made a tremendous difference to my racing and training whilst I was in Birmingham over the next six months or so.

The stepping stone to the Paralympics was the European championships in Lisbon. Tim Redman agreed to be my guide runner, although he couldn't travel until the day of our race. I was very nervous, wondering whether he'd make it on time for the race or not, and he arrived just three hours before the 1500 m. To compound these jitters, most of the Great Britain team went down with upset stomachs and diarrhoea to varying degrees not long after arriving in Lisbon, and it took a while for the realisation to dawn that the time I spent in the bathroom wasn't just caused by pre-competition nerves.

The 1500 m didn't quite go according to plan. I felt fatigued from the start, and my pace was relatively much slower than the times I had been doing in training. I still managed to do a 64-second last lap which thankfully was good enough, because it was all I had left. With the memory of my disqualification in Atlanta, I warned Tim about not crossing the line ahead of me as we came into the home straight for the final time. I was in a bit of a daze afterwards, thinking how lucky I had been as I hadn't expected a time like 4:17 to have been good enough for the gold, but it was.

Apparently the race looked a lot more impressive than it felt. Afterwards, Noel Thatcher congratulated us on a superb tactical race with an impressive last lap. Winning the 5000 m two days later made these championships my most successful in eight years.

Chapter 15 – Blind ambition

The year 2000 was to be a momentous and memorable one for me. I was 39 and it was the year of the Sydney Paralympic Games. Almost every waking hour was spent training, or thinking about training. The Sydney Paralympics were to have been my sixth and final games, so as well as the 5000 m and 10,000 m, I was determined to run in the historic marathon, which dates back to 490 BC.

It was also the year that the television drama, *Blind Ambition*, was made, starring Robson Green. *Blind Ambition* tells the story of an 800 m runner whose hopes of qualifying for the Sydney Olympic Games are dashed when he is blinded in a car crash. After a period of convalescence, he stuns everybody by deciding to try to run in the Sydney Paralympic Games as a blind 800 m runner. The author of the story told me he was inspired to write it after he watched me win the 800 m in the Seoul Paralympics in 1988.

I was flattered to be the inspiration for a movie, and I was also chuffed to be asked to show Robson Green and his guide runner, Mark Womack, the ropes. They both came to Leamington Spa to watch me train and then tried to copy the way my guide and I ran together. Both actors ran a few laps with me to get a feel for what it was like, and both adapted to it quite quickly, proving that running with a blind athlete isn't all that difficult. I also got to appear in the television drama as an extra. I'd expected glamour and excitement and some acting, but I was disappointed. We hardly saw the actors as we sat around and waited for the cameras and the lights to be set up, drinking endless cups of tea in the catering bus to pass the time.

Although Robson played the part of a blind man really well, the script writers had some weird ideas about how blind people lived. Of course, it's easy to pick holes in something of which you have an intimate knowledge, but where did they get the absurd idea that blind people have no doors on their kitchen cupboards in case they walk into them? Another glaring error was the scene which showed a rehabilitation worker teaching Robson how to use a white cane. He'd have got more bruises than I ever did the way he was taught to use it.

As well as being quite boring, the days on the film set were also quite tiring. In the first scene, Mike and I had to let Robson and Mark pass us just before the finish line in an 800 m race. The next scene was harder to shoot, as I had to play the part of a sprinter running pell-mell towards my caller, Mike. We needed quite a few takes, 12 in all, before the director was satisfied. My legs felt pretty stiff by the end of the day's filming — not the best preparation for my first marathon in five days' time.

The London Marathon was a very important race for me. I really wanted to run this historic distance at the Paralympics, but to qualify I needed to run below 2 hours 55 minutes. I was chuffed to hear from a respected coach of marathon runners that he felt I was ultimately capable of running a 2:32 marathon, although for my first attempt at the distance he reckoned 2:42 would be a more realistic goal.

Starting in Blackheath in the southeast of the city, the London Marathon covers a distance of 26.2 miles (42.1 km) and takes in many of the famous and historic sites on the way to the finishing line at Westminster Bridge. Despite the serious nature of needing to run the qualifying time for the Sydney Paralympics, Mike Peters, my guide runner, and I had a great time for the first half of the race. Until we reached Canary Wharf at 16 miles (26 km) there were street bands and spectators all making themselves heard. *The Times* newspaper had run a story on me, telling how this would be my first marathon, but even so, I was amazed that so many people recognised me. At the pace we were expecting to run we knew there'd be many runners around us, and had wondered about the logistics of Mike being able to pass bottles to me at the water stations. As it turned out, we had no problems, even if drinking on the run wasn't at all easy.

Passing the 20 mile (32 km) marker, I entered uncharted territory. I'd never run further in my life. Only a mile later, I hit the proverbial runner's wall — the wheels, doors and everything else seemed to fall off. Everything below the waist just seized up, and my speed dropped from averaging 6 minutes 13 seconds per mile (3:53 per km) to over 8 minutes. Mike was a seasoned marathon runner, and his experience helped keep me going while I struggled to put one foot in front of the other. The crowds were fantastic and played their part, calling my name; they were terrific, so much so that Mike was glad of his sunglasses to hide his emotion. Still, the last few miles seemed to take an eternity as I struggled along the Embankment, Pall Mall and Bird Cage Walk until at last Mike told me we only had 400 m to go. I could have kissed him.

We crossed the line in 2:53:18 which should have been good enough to earn selection for Sydney, but my immediate concern was, 'How can I possibly get back to the hotel on these legs?' Having wound my legs up to a shuffle, Kath, who had taken over guiding duties, was very patient, although I had to ask her to slow down a couple of times. We eventually made it to the steps leading down to the Tube, which I could only negotiate using the hand rail. Getting off the train was another dilemma as neither leg seemed capable of handling the large step down to the platform. In all my years of running my legs had never been this stiff, and on the train journey home my bum ached so much that I wasn't able to sit still or get comfortable.

The soreness was gone from my legs in a matter of days, but I reckoned I'd earned some time away from running and I took two weeks off. It turned out to be a terrible decision. I compounded this mistake by pushing myself too hard, too soon, when I did get back into it. On three consecutive days I went for a 40-minute run and on my third day back I felt a twinge in my right foot. I hoped it would heal itself, but it was another three weeks before I eventually went to see a physio. By the time I was up and running again, I'd lost six weeks' hard training, and there were only 16 weeks left to peak for the Sydney Games.

Despite the fact that my time in the London Marathon was well inside the qualifying time for the Sydney Paralympics, I was in for a shock. I was told my time was six seconds too slow, and it was only (!) the fourth quickest time in the world that year. I was gutted. I'd fallen in love with the idea of being able to run in at least one Paralympic marathon.

The national governing body, UK Athletics (UKA), is responsible for the development and management of Olympic and Paralympic athletics, and it turned out that the director of disabled athletics at UKA, Ken Kelly, wanted the team to improve on the tally of medals brought home from Atlanta, targeting 45 gold medals. With the intention of concentrating their efforts, it was decided that athletes would no longer be able to compete in more than two events. When it was realised that this would result in Great Britain losing out on a significant number of gold medals, this decision was reversed. Shortly afterwards I received notification that I could indeed run in the marathon as well as the 5000 m and 10,000 m. This was fantastic news, especially as I would never get a better opportunity, or a better vantage point, to enjoy a cheap sightseeing tour of Sydney.

Back from injury, I was able to begin the build-up to Sydney with Paul Harwood. I postponed my bicycle mechanic studies in Birmingham because for the next 16 weeks I would eat, drink, breathe and sleep running. I spent over £100 per week on taxis to train with Paul. The training was gruelling: 9 mile (14 km) runs in 53 minutes on the road or through the countryside around Paul's house; sprinting up a hill for 60 seconds, jogging back and then doing it another 11 times; not to mention the 300 miles (480 km) or more we put in on the track.

In the interests of my sanity, most of our track sessions have been erased from my memory, although I do remember running 10 repetitions of 1000 m with 90 seconds' recovery between each. Another favourite session was six one-mile reps. I particularly enjoyed our recovery runs which were anywhere between 9 and 17 miles (14 and 27 km). We were able to step out of Paul's front door and run for miles along lanes through the beautiful Warwickshire countryside with very little traffic to bother us. I can still see the brightness of the sun rising, hear the dawn chorus and remember the beautiful freshness of the early morning.

Paul made a huge commitment to help me get to Sydney, and of course travelling to Australia with me was a massive sacrifice to make. I didn't have children of my own at that time, so I wasn't able to fully appreciate then just how much of a wrench it was for Paul to leave behind his daughters, Lucy, aged six months, and Sally, aged three. His family were really supportive, and I certainly appreciate now the sacrifices they made for Paul to spend a considerable amount of time training with me over the years.

As the Games drew closer, I wasn't confident I had done enough speed endurance work to win the 10,000 m. The favourite for the event was Carlos Ferreira from Portugal, who was also the world record holder for the marathon. I felt my best chance of a gold medal was in the 5000 m, as no one was likely to run away from me before the bell, and I felt I still had enough speed over the closing lap to run away from the field. How wrong I was.

I have always worked on the premise that the next competition will be tougher than the last. Before every big race meet there are always rumours about unknown athletes — runners you've never heard of seemingly appearing out of the woodwork. Before Sydney, the rumour mill was running hot about a Kenyan runner —

rumours that would prove to be correct. Still, I knew that if I ran sensibly and well, I could win three medals. If I were to run out of my skin, then I could possibly emulate the great Emil Zatopek who won three gold medals in the 1952 Helsinki Olympics in the same events I was running in Sydney — the 5000 m, 10,000 m and the marathon.

The Great Britain team spent a week on the Gold Coast, near Brisbane, to acclimatise and adjust to the time difference before heading south to Sydney. We arrived at the Radisson Resort in time for breakfast, and chose to have steak as we'd heard that that was what Aussies eat for breakfast — we wanted to assimilate, after all. Then we went to bed for two hours to help speed up our adjustment to local time. I found it difficult to wake up, and during that first 40-minute run I felt as though I was on sedatives.

The Sydney organisers were extremely efficient. No sooner had we landed than we were bussed to the Paralympic village, processed, and given our accreditation which provided us with access to the village and to the stadium in which we'd be competing. Paul and I shared a small tin bungalow with Danny Crates, an arm amputee competing in the 400 m, and Steve Payton, a runner with cerebral palsy who was competing in the 200 m and 400 m. We were issued with Olympic duvets, which we obviously wouldn't need — Australia was always hot, wasn't it? Wrong. The first two nights it was freezing, and we were glad of the radiator and the extra duvets that Paul had managed to purloin. The dining room was massive with six serving areas and lots of choice — perhaps too much. Not being able to see what's being served up or to read a menu, I am sometimes indecisive about what I want to eat. During the Games, Paul and Mike simplified things for me by offering me a choice of three options or bringing me what they thought I'd like.

Before the Games were officially opened, the Great Britain team were asked to wear our posh Paralympic gear to a reception in Sydney, where dignitaries eulogised and our Minister for Sport, Kate Hoey, spoke a few words. We had a team photograph with the Sydney Harbour as the backdrop. This is where we had expected to catch up with Mike who should have just arrived from England. Mike was my second guide runner. Because I was running the 5000 m, 10,000 m and the marathon, I was given the luxury of two guides because the chances of one guide getting injured trying to cope with such a heavy workload were much higher. I guess that if I injured myself, it was just my bad luck.

Being a school teacher, Mike was unable to join us until half-term had started. We didn't find him until the next day, though, when he told us that after his flight to Sydney he had spent the day in hospital undergoing tests, having experienced a recurrence of heart palpitations. He was perfectly OK and had been given the all-clear to train by the doctors. Our management team were much more anxious about the situation than Mike was, and as far as I was concerned, if he was happy and confident, then so was I. They spoke about flying another of my guides out, which would have been silly — even if Mike was unable to do much, I had done most of my training with Paul, and he was the faster guide and would be doing most of the work.

It was great to see Mike again, not just to have someone different to talk to on training runs, but we were also close friends, and I enjoyed his banter. Next day the three of us ran to Stadium Australia's warm-up track in Olympic Park, which was like a stadium in its own right, and did some acceleration runs, practising changing guides as this is what we would be doing around the mid-point of the 10,000 m and at the 30 km mark in the marathon. It went very smoothly each time, with me barely noticing that Mike had turned into Paul, and then back to Mike.

The opening ceremony of the Paralympic Games was on the evening of 18 October, and once again we all got dressed up, this time with a lot more enthusiasm. The teams had to wait while the organisers sorted them into alphabetical order. We waited in the main basketball arena, and if that was anything to go by, then the rest of the stadium would be incredible — the arena was massive, seating up to 18,000 people.

The anticipation of stepping on the track was exhilarating, and I got the familiar nervous buzz as the team drew closer to the growing cacophony from the stadium, until at last Great Britain was announced. The noise was unbelievable — with 100,000 people clapping and cheering, and the music blaring out, I had to ask Paul whether we had actually stepped onto the track yet, and when he replied that we had, I got the biggest thrill.

After the main ceremony, Mike and I walked back to the athletes' village as we didn't want to stay up too late — the 10,000 m was only 36 hours away. Unfortunately we missed Kylie Minogue who entertained the crowd afterwards, but I guess some sacrifices are necessary. Paul, who was 10 years younger and a bit of a party animal, rolled up a little later.

Mike and Paul are both ex-army. Their kit was always organised and tidy, everything in its place, and they were always ready at least ten minutes early — as Gary, another guide runner who was also in the forces, used to say, 'If war's going to break out at 8 a.m., you've got to be ready at 7.50 a.m.' I could have done with some of that kind of discipline. If there was a war, I'd aim to be ready for 8 a.m. so I wouldn't have to wait around. I've missed a few trains, buses and even the start of a race in Hereford once because of my attitude, and even after my years of international experience, Mike and Paul still had to take it in turns to hurry me along.

I walked out for the start of the 10,000 m with Mike who was guiding me over the first 13 laps. Paul and the other relief guide runners were led to the designated change-over area on the home straight. As we were introduced to the crowd, rather embarrassingly the BBC camera pan from my shoes up to my face showed me nervously chewing my thumbnail.

At last the starter fired his pistol, and the first track and field final of the 2000 Paralympic Games was underway. We'd talked tactics ad infinitum beforehand, and I felt that the longer the race went without too much pace being injected, the stronger my chances of winning. If I could hang on until the last half-mile, I knew I would be able to finish faster than anyone else. There were approximately 30,000 people in the stadium, and during the race there seemed to be a strange and exhilarating atmosphere. Although I could hear the athletes immediately around me, I visualised them as spectres in a mist.

The first 5000 m took just over 18 minutes, which suited me just fine. I was running easy and I remember asking Mike whether he felt we should take the lead. Luckily he said to wait. The positions towards the front of the race were constantly changing, and Mike did a great job of keeping me out of trouble as it's so easy to trip in that situation.

Coming into the home straight for the 13th time, Mike told me to accelerate slightly as we moved out wide. The next thing I knew was Paul saying, 'Eh up, Bobby. Time to start racing.' He'd moved between us seamlessly and caught Mike's end of the guide rope as we moved to the front for the first time. My acceleration had the effect of stretching the field. I stayed in front, even though I didn't feel particularly comfortable. Then, with five laps still remaining, the two Mexicans and the favourite, Carlos Ferreira, made their move and eased past me to relegate me to fourth place. I felt like I was running in quicksand, and the gap was growing all the time.

A lap later, I managed to find some inner strength and halted the slide to keep them within 20 m, but it was so incredibly hard. Paul did a fantastic job as my eyes, and kept telling me how far behind we were, and that the other athletes were looking pretty rough too, in particular Ferreira. He kept asking me, 'How much do you want this?' During our training sessions, we'd practised increasing the pace over the last two laps of every race, no matter how knackered I was. With just over two laps left to run, the gap started closing and my confidence grew. The tiredness started to fall away as we increased the pace. My scalp tingled slightly with adrenalin as with 600 m to go I moved into third place and Carlos Ferreira hit the front. I felt another shot of adrenalin as I heard the bell, and moved into second place as I overtook the leading Mexican. I was now just five metres behind Ferreira.

Gathering myself for the acceleration, Paul told me, 'Relax . . . wait.' Later he explained that there was no need to push Carlos too early by trying to pass him. So I waited . . . and waited. All along the back straight and around the last bend, Paul kept saying, 'Wait . . .' Coming into the home straight, I felt Paul drifting us wide and then he shouted, 'Straight . . . go, go, go!' I went. I knew we had changed pace well, and had passed Ferreira, but I wasn't certain about the victory until I felt Paul easing back behind my shoulder, just like we'd practised over the hundreds of track efforts, ensuring there would be no repeat of the disqualification in Atlanta. We won by three seconds in a new Paralympic record of 35:18.

It would have been so easy to have said to myself when those athletes passed me, 'I can do no more, let's save it for the next race,' but I didn't. I concentrated and believed in myself, and ultimately proved that I was still the best after 17 years as an international.

Paul and I found Kath, Cara and Debbie (Kath's friend who was on her world tour) in the crowd, and after hugs and kisses they gave us a Union Jack to take on our lap of honour. It was an incredible moment, one that I had dreamed about but also one that I secretly feared I would never experience again. As we celebrated we realised that Mike was nowhere to be seen. He should have been with us on the lap of honour. It turned out that as Mike watched the end of the race, he'd tried to jump over the barrier to join us, but an official advised him that if he did, then his athlete would be disqualified.

After those initial celebrations, an amazing and seemingly never-ending series of interviews began. First up was Jon Ridgeon, who was working with Paul Dickenson on BBC television, then came a string of miscellaneous interviews. After what seemed like five minutes, but was probably an hour, we were summoned for the ultimate accolade, the medal ceremony.

As medallists and guide runners were being sorted out to stand in the correct place to walk to the medal podium, the news filtered through that there were disqualifications. We were positive that we weren't affected. Unfortunately, the Mexicans who had finished third and fourth had been preceded across the line by their guides and, just like in Atlanta four years earlier, Tim Willis from the USA benefited. This would take some time to sort out, so Paul and I made our way back to Kath and the others.

At last we found Mike and we all retired to the Homebush Bay Brewery, our 'local' within the Olympic Park, for a couple of beers and something to eat. Before the race I'd anticipated having quite a few beers, whatever the result, but after two I couldn't manage another drop. It was partly tiredness, but I also felt a little sick as a hard race can be tough on the stomach.

Late that afternoon the disqualifications and appeals were sorted out, and the first three were called to the medal room. As expected, our result wasn't affected, and Paul, Mike and I enjoyed a bit of banter with the girls who accompanied us to the podium where they explained the procedure for receiving our medals (guide runners don't receive a medal themselves whether their athlete is successful or not). They led us through a long tunnel which finally arrived at a lift which delivered us onto a platform 20 m above the crowd. The sense of looking out over the stadium, with all that empty space, the dramatic music which introduced the medal ceremony, the stadium announcer booming out the results, first in English, then in French, and the audible hum of the crowd were truly magical.

The ceremony was very moving. To receive a Paralympic gold medal for the first time in eight years and hear the national anthem whilst visualising the Union Jack flying in my honour, was very emotional, and my eyes were wet. I was so incredibly proud, and the crowning glory was this was the first gold medal won on the track at the Sydney Paralympics by Great Britain.

It took us at least 20 minutes to get back from the podium as people wanted to congratulate us, see my medal and get my autograph. An orderly queue formed every time I showed someone the gold medal, and Mike developed a system whereby he wrote '10,000 m Gold, Great Britain', only leaving me to sign my name. It had been a long time since I'd had to do so much writing, and I never expected to get writer's cramp. In the end Mike suggested that I hide the medal or we would never get to the other side of the stadium where most of the British team and our friends and family were waiting.

At 7.30 a.m. British time, straight after the news, I did a live interview with Victoria Derbyshire on the sports news on 'Radio 5 Live'. Immediately afterwards I talked to Steve May on the Radio 4 sports news. I felt like I had made it! I would have loved to have got hold of a copy of one of those interviews with the sound of Stadium Australia in the background.

I was still proudly wearing the gold medal an hour or so later when Kath and I headed off to the train station on our way to a celebratory meal in town. It took us an hour as we were constantly stopped by passers-by asking to see the gold medal. OK, I admit it, I milked the occasion a bit, but everyone seemed to want my autograph and to have their photo taken with me. The pleasing thing was that many of them had actually seen the race and were very complimentary. Climbing on the train I received a spontaneous round of applause from the passengers. I was having a marvellous time!

Towards the end of our meal, my neck started to ache from the weight of the medal, and I reluctantly took it off and placed it on the table beside my plate. I still wasn't ready to put it away. It was hardly surprising I should have been struggling to wear it for so long — it weighed in at nearly 8 ounces (249 g).

Kath was sharing a room with Cara, her mum, so that night the two of us decided to go wild and book a room at a nearby hotel for the night, despite the very real threat of being sent home for spending a night outside the Paralympic village. Damn it, there was no way I was going to spend that night in the 'little love shack' I shared with Paul! We're great mates, but we both needed a break for a night — and besides, he wasn't my wife.

Early the next morning we learned I'd been on all the major television news bulletins in England. I really enjoyed my five minutes' worth of fame, and to me it reflected just how far the Paralympic movement had come in terms of media coverage since the 1984 games in New York and the Seoul games in 1988. The extent of the media coverage then was a few column inches on the sports pages, and a patronising 45-minute highlight programme shown months after the games. Now 12 years on, the UK media were giving the Paralympic Games much more extensive coverage and, more importantly, the same respect which had always been afforded the Olympic Games.

We enjoyed our success for a day or so and then turned our thoughts towards the next challenge, and focused on the 5000 m, which was five days after the 10,000 m. With the success of the Africans in middle- and long-distance running, I'd often wondered when they would break through onto the international stage with their blind athletes. We had heard there was a Kenyan running in the T11 1500 m and 5000 m, and that he looked very good in training.

And so it proved to be. Despite running 16:09 in the 5000 m which was my season's best, the Kenyan, Henry Wanyoike, beat me resoundingly into second place. I was disappointed not to win a second gold, especially as Paulo Coelho, the excellent Portuguese athlete, hadn't been able to maintain his fitness into his third Games. I'd beaten Paulo in Barcelona and he'd just beaten me four years later in Atlanta. I knew the Kenyan would be tough, but had reckoned I had a good chance of getting the better of him. Pretty soon after the starter's gun, though, I had to accept the fact that the rumours about this new athlete hadn't been exaggerated, and come to terms with second best on this occasion.

However, his victory didn't pass without controversy. Reviewing the video footage, you could clearly see that, as Wanyoike and his guide crossed the finish line, his guide collapsed in a heap, at which point Henry did a victory lap around the poor guy. He then ran over towards the stands by himself, jumped over a speaker and grabbed a Kenyan flag off someone in the stands. Mike pointed out that, with his guide flagging over the last three laps, Wanyoike was able to run a perfect line all the way around the track, towing his poor guide along.

There was a great deal of talk amongst many guide runners and spectators about how miraculous a feat this was in the T11 category, which was for athletes who were totally blind with no helpful vision. The Portuguese and Canadian guides were incredulous. Mike, who was close to the finish line, couldn't believe the Kenyan's antics. 'How come you can't do that?' he asked me. Kath couldn't understand it either. As part of her role as a rehabilitation worker for the blind, she had learned how to assess the amount of sight a person had, or didn't have, so she could best understand their needs. There was no doubt whatsoever in her mind that the Kenyan had some useful vision, and had therefore gained an unfair advantage over the other athletes. By no means was she suggesting Wanyoike had much sight, but he had enough to give him some assistance. To a sighted person (which he had been until four years before), he would be considered to be blind, but if a totally blind person was given that amount of vision, they would think it was Christmas!

Before being retested, Wanyoike ran in a 1500 m heat. The rules state that competitors have to wear blacked-out glasses or blindfolds for the 1500 m and the shorter distances. I have never understood why they don't apply this same rule to the longer distances of the marathon, 10,000 m and 5000 m races, thus ensuring a level playing field. In his 1500 m heat, it seemed clear, even to those with no experience of guiding blind athletes, that Wanyoike was running in an unfamiliar situation — his guide runner seemed unable to guide him properly. Throughout the race, Wanyoike banged into his guide and hit the raised curb on the inside of the track. He was still good enough to make the final, but only just.

The medal ceremony for the T11 5000 m took place a day-and-a-half after the race, but this bizarre set of circumstances had one more twist. Henry Wanyoike turned up to collect his gold looking zombie-like in a wheelchair, and the people with him explained he'd had a recurrence of malaria, which apparently was the reason for him not racing in the 1500 m final.

Even though I had lost the chance of emulating Emil Zatopek's feat in the Helsinki Olympics, I was still pleased with the silver — it was a Paralympic medal after all. Now we shifted our focus to the next event, the marathon.

The start line of the marathon lay a kilometre north of the Sydney Harbour Bridge. The morning of the marathon was cool — ideal conditions — although the day had warmed up by the last hour of the race. Mike was taking over the baton at 30 km, so he and the other replacement guides were whisked off to their respective places just over half an hour before the race start. Paul and I made our final preparations: we made sure our shoes were tied correctly and that our numbers were on properly. We had a few last sips of water, and tried to empty our bladders. Shortly before we left the warm-up area to go to the start, Farny, who was running in the T13 (partially sighted) category, came over to say he felt I had an excellent chance of winning: 'Ferreira has just been coughing and clearing his lungs like an old man. There's no way he sounds as though he could run a decent marathon.'

However, this proved to be just wishful thinking.

Each category had a cyclist for the whole distance equipped with a walkie-talkie to relay the race situations. The T11 cyclist was none other than Mike's wife, Zara, who was the endurance director at UKA. Unfortunately I didn't see her as much during the race as I would have liked, as the cyclists were supposed to stick with the leader. Paul kept me in the picture about landmarks as we moved along the marathon course. I enjoyed running over the Sydney Harbour Bridge and then passing the Opera House and Darling Harbour. I could visualise them, as they were all areas in which I'd trained and walked around. It was good to have some distraction from the race in the early stages as it is such a long way, but by the time we got to Hyde Park, about 10 km into the race, I was in fifth place and concentrating pretty well.

By this time Ferreira had put his foot down and disappeared into the blue yonder. Paul wouldn't let me go with him, instead keeping us at an even pace of four minutes per kilometre, encouraging me and telling me what was happening ahead and behind, and using the experience he'd gained running with me for five years and from running 30 marathons by himself. He coaxed me through my first sticky patch, assuring me that I'd come out of it. Running freely again, I moved into second place at 25 km, which is where I stayed. Mike did a great job of getting me through the most difficult period of the race, between 36 and 40 km, when the Italian closed to within two minutes of me, but then I found some more strength and finished strongly in a new British record of 2:47:38 to win my second silver medal of the games.

I was delighted with my performance in Sydney — one gold and two silver medals. It was a great comeback after such a disappointing time in Atlanta.

The following year, 2001, got off to a good start when Paul, Kath and I travelled to London to meet the Queen at Buckingham

Palace. The whole British Paralympic team had been invited, but only the gold medallists were specifically presented to Her Majesty and the Duke of Edinburgh. Later we would have the opportunity to meet with other members of the royal family, including Princess Anne, Prince Charles, Prince Andrew and Prince Edward.

We were assembled into a horseshoe shape whilst the Queen worked her way around the room, being introduced to each athlete by Helen Potter, the chef de mission from Sydney. As the Queen got nearer, both Paul and I became increasingly nervous. I had learned from our previous meeting, when Her Majesty presented me with the MBE, that the Queen was a foot shorter than me, so I now knew where to look. When it came to our turn, the Queen made us feel really at ease, and she congratulated me on my gold and two silvers. She seemed genuinely interested in our partnership, asking Paul about his role as a guide runner, and commented how difficult it must be. I managed not to say anything too silly, fortunately, as etiquette dictates one shouldn't ask Her Majesty a question, only respond. The lad next to me asked her about how it felt to wear her heavy crown at the opening of Parliament, and the Queen answered that she wore a different one, weighing about six ounces (170 g), and moved on. Shortly after, the lad fainted — divine retribution for daring to ask our monarch an unbidden question, perhaps?

Six months later, I was able to add the initials 'MA (Hons)' after my name, as the University of Warwick awarded me an honorary Master of Arts degree in recognition of my achievements in the Sydney 2000 Paralympic Games. I was given my own mortarboard and gown, which I wore with pride at the presentation in front of a large audience.

My achievements were further recognised when the National Policing Improvement Agency (NPIA) named the sports and fitness facility at their new training centre at Ryton, just outside Leamington Spa, after me: The Bob Matthews MBE Health and Fitness Suite. I was humbled to have such a well-equipped fitness centre named in my honour where future generations of police officers and recruits would do much of their health and fitness training. It was kind of crazy being able to train in my own gym!

I restarted my studies as a bicycle mechanic to finish the final six months of the course. I had lost time due to preparing for and competing in the Sydney Paralympic Games, which meant I had to retake all the tests I had already sat successfully, but I passed them all again without too many problems and could now call myself a bicycle mechanic.

In 2001, again I was injured and unable to run, so I started tandem cycling with Russell Burrows who also ran with me occasionally. To get a measure of how fast we could go on the tandem, we competed in time trials recording 10 miles (16 km) in 24 minutes, and 25 miles (40 km) in under an hour. It got me thinking: if I couldn't conquer this recurring injury, I should give tandem cycling a go at a future Paralympic Games.

With this downtime in running, Kath and I took the opportunity to go on another tandem adventure in July as part of the Birmingham Irish Cycle Appeal (BICA), an annual cycle ride which was aiming to raise £25,000 for a children's charity. We cycled from Birmingham to Donegal on the west coast of Ireland, a distance of 400 miles (640 km). We cycled through the beautiful countryside of England and Wales, where the highlight was the ride through Snowdonia, before catching the ferry across to Ireland. The cycling around Lake Vyrnwy was wonderful, where the paths were flat and made for pleasant, easy riding. The sound of streams cascading into the lake and the fresh smell of the water spray are things I will never forget. It was even more pleasant in the shade where we were cooled by the closeness of the water. That first night we stayed in the Royal Goat Hotel, which was built in 1798. It was a hotel with a lot of character, and apparently it was haunted by its first landlord who died suddenly before he was able to tell his wife where he'd stashed the savings. We were too tired to search for the hidden treasure, or to be bothered by any ghosts.

There were 35 cyclists, mostly Irish, some of whom possessed a wicked sense of humour. We were followed by a van which carried provisions, spare bicycles and parts. After cycling up to 80 miles (128 km) every day, it was bliss to stay in a comfortable hotel and luxuriate in a bath, soaking away some of the stiffness from tackling the undulating roads and challenging hills. Sampling the Guinness with dinner in the evening once over in Ireland was another highlight. I enjoyed my first one when we got off the ferry, and I later discovered that it tastes so much better in Ireland than anywhere else in the world. It was worth all the miles we put in. However, I drank in moderation because I knew I would pay for it the next day if I didn't — it was difficult, though!

One day in Ireland we had a break from cycling, and enjoyed the sights of Dublin. Kath and I went to Croke Park, the national stadium, where I saw my first game of hurling between Wexford and Limerick. Beforehand, I upset the locals by describing the game as little more than 'a glorified egg-and-spoon race'. In fact, it was a very exciting and incredibly skilful game, which ended in a flurry of excitement with a last-minute winner for Wexford.

I really loved the smell of peat fires as we cycled through the Irish countryside, and of course the scenery was impressive. Kath described the large grey boulders which contrasted against the lush green paddocks and hills. I often heard the sounds of babbling streams and what seemed like millions of sheep. The roads, however, weren't always the best maintained, and sometimes it felt like a giant had dragged his fingernails across them. I shared my opinion on the roads with the mayor in one of the towns where we stopped one night, and he wasn't best impressed with me, saying, 'I'm rather proud of them.'

After six days' cycling, we finally made it to Donegal. What an achievement — we'd covered 400 miles (640 km) and put money in the bank for the charity. The journey was so enjoyable and incredibly well organised. It was such a treat to have someone to provide the fuel every day and book the accommodation each night. It really made a difference having a support crew and not having to worry about breaking down, even though I now knew how to fix our bike myself. But the highlight of the tour was the new friends Kath and I made, like-minded people with the same sense of adventure. We looked forward to the next cycling trip with them. However, neither of us could have known then that our trip to Ireland would be one of our last together.

Chapter 16 – Things change

By 2002, I was 41 and had been running for 20 years. Running was my life and it gave me a true sense of purpose — you could say running defined who I was — but it didn't come without its frustrations. I knew that if I had been able to see, I could have done so much more. I could have run further and faster. I could have trained where I wanted, when I wanted. I wouldn't have had to keep looking for guide runners who were fit enough and fast enough to keep up with me and, more importantly, who were willing to train with me. And I wouldn't have had to run over 10,000 miles (16,000 km) on the treadmill that I loved and hated in equal measure for 14-odd years.

Still, I also knew that if I had been able to see, I might not have had the focus and determination to create the equivalent opportunities and enjoy as much success that I had as a blind runner.

Paul Harwood had been my main guide runner for seven years at this stage of my career, and was certainly one of the toughest and most uncompromising guides I'd run with. Paul is a very focused athlete in his own right, and has represented Great Britain in ultra-distance races. As well as being an outstanding runner, he was a superb guide runner. The only problem was that, at times, he was too fast for me — or should I say I was too slow for him.

I realised I wasn't quite the same athlete I had been. The years were starting to take their toll, and I needed to train on my own to keep up with Paul. That meant pounding the treadmill which I found monotonous and soul-destroying. About that time, a company called PowerSport gave me an alternative treadmill, called a Powerjog, to prepare for the Athens Paralympic Games. It was a high-tech piece of machinery, and helped enormously with my training. It was able to talk to me via my computer, letting me know the gradient and speed I was running and the distance I had covered. In theory, this marvellous machine meant I could rely less on my guides, but in reality it was still treadmill-type training.

Just because I am blind doesn't make running on a treadmill any easier. One of the reasons I run is to feel the wind, the sun and the rain on my face. I may not be able to see where I am running, but the scenery and environment matter as much to me as to any other runner. I know when I am running somewhere beautiful. I can feel it. I can hear the birds singing in the countryside, and I can hear the hum of the traffic in the city. I can smell the trees and the flowers when I am running along a forest trail, and the twists and turns, the hills and dips, all play a part in making a run interesting and enjoyable.

In early 2002 I wasn't enjoying my running like I used to. I wasn't able to keep up with Paul on long runs or speed work. I had spent so much time on the treadmill that when I ran on the track, my legs felt like Bambi's — they were heavy, weak and floppy. An injury was inevitable really, and running along a bridle path in April I twisted my ankle quite badly. I would have advised any client of mine to rest, ice and elevate their ankle for a few days, but like many so-called experts I ignored my own advice.

I was under immense pressure to get fit enough to run the qualifying standard for the world championships in July. Having missed the 2001 season through injury, failure to qualify for the world championships would have placed my Lottery funding in jeopardy. This funding made up 50 per cent of our household income, with Kath's salary making up the rest. Extensive physiotherapy on my ankle along with pure determination and hard work helped me to achieve the qualifying standard by the end of May, and proved to the British team selectors that I was in good enough shape to compete in the world champs.

Before the worlds, I went to Illinois in the US for some warm-weather training. While I was there I competed in the Steamboat Classic, a four-mile (6.4 km) road race. It was great to be able to run in the sunshine again. With the temperature around 30 degrees and 90 per cent humidity, ironically, all of that treadmill training paid off, as training indoors with little or no cooling breeze is perfect for acclimatising to hot, humid conditions.

Now, at last, I was in decent shape, but unfortunately my lower left leg was feeling progressively worse from all the intensive running. It didn't help that I hadn't listened to my body and taken the time to rest after my ankle sprain like I should have done. An MRI and bone scan confirmed that I had a stress fracture in my fibula, plus both my ankles were less than 100 per cent. Just a month out from the 2002 world championships, I was restricted to running just three times per week. The rest of the time was spent on my exercise bike and in the gym. It wasn't enough — despite taking it easy just a week before the world championships, my lower leg was still painful, and as if in sympathy, my left hamstring had started to act up. I had little choice but to pull out of another international meet. 'Not again,' I thought.

To make up for the disappointment, Kath and I spent a week in the south of France with our great friends, Gary and Jan. We were in our element, eating the local fare and drinking the French wine. I loved the early morning trip to the village markets for a coffee and a day's supply of croissants, baguettes and cheese. My French isn't the best, but you don't need to understand the language to enjoy the tastes, smells and the atmosphere of la vie en France.

After some much-needed rest, I was able to run every other day with Gary along some quiet country lanes and through the local forests. It was so peaceful and tranquil — we could hear the birds singing in the trees and the leaves rustling in the breeze. Always up for a challenge, Gary and I rented two canoes one day while the girls went shopping. Gary led the way, shouting and singing his way down the river to give me some audible clues to follow. We made great progress and Gary was impressed with my ability to turn my canoe into a submarine. I don't know what I was doing wrong, but as soon as we got some speed up, the front end of my canoe would slowly but surely start to disappear under the water. What should have been an easy two-hour paddle down the river turned into a four-hour marathon. Still, it was an enjoyable afternoon and a welcome distraction from missing out on the world champs.

Soon after we got back from France, I got a call from the GDBA to let me know they had a guide dog replacement for Quando. My faithful friend was now 11 years old and he had earned his retirement. It was the end of an era. Quando had been an exceptional guide dog. He was as happy when he was in his harness guiding me as he was when he was let loose for a run, and he did both at break-neck speed. On our last official journey together as a unit, I was almost in tears. Quando had been by my side for the last ten years and it was sad to think that he wouldn't be with me any more on my daily trips. When he retired, Quando became Kath's dog, and with the replacement we now had two dogs at home.

Barely three months after Quando retired, he was in the garden one morning when Kath noticed he was limping. Over the next couple of hours he found it increasingly difficult to walk. A week, and two different vets, later, an orthopaedic veterinary surgeon diagnosed and operated on a trapped nerve in his neck. Quando made a remarkable and quick recovery, progressing from a robotic shuffle to an ungainly run within six weeks. Despite never quite walking the same again, this procedure prolonged his life considerably. I still occasionally took him for a walk around the block. His ability to guide and his speed were still there — he just rocked a little bit more than he used to.

My new dog's name was Jemma, and she was an 18-month-old German shepherd. It was very difficult not to compare the two dogs. Quando and I had been partners for a decade, and we knew and understood each other so well. Quando and Jemma had very different personalities. Jemma walked along the pavement serenely, where Quando drove into his harness. Jemma would slow right down before reaching a curb, where Quando would roar right up to a curb before stopping dead. I knew Jemma was a good dog and we would learn to work well together, but apart from the fact that she wasn't Quando, she had one other significant fault. She suffered from excitable urination and had to sleep in the kitchen at night as there was usually a puddle to clean up in the morning.

When Jemma's episodes of excitable urination still hadn't ceased six months later, we had to make the really difficult decision, together with the GDBA, to retire her on medical grounds. This was really hard, as Jemma was a lovely dog. We were starting to get used to one another, and Kath and I had become extremely attached to her. It wasn't easy to say goodbye to her.

Jemma's replacement was Watson, a three-year-old black labrador who had already spent some time working with another guide dog owner, which hadn't worked out. He was a nice lad, but the main problem was his incessant whining when he was left alone for any length of time. For instance, at the gym when I had to leave him behind the reception desk while I worked out, he would get quite vociferous, even when he could see me. It was very embarrassing and not what I or the public expected from a highly trained guide dog. Much later, I learned the whining was partly responsible for him being returned to the GDBA the first time around.

Naturally our partnership wasn't perfect — few are in the very early stages — but you would at least hope for a steady, marked improvement. Three months into our time together, however, I realised that no matter how hard I worked with Watson, his concentration wasn't always there. One morning we were going to the local shop and we had to turn around because I was too nervous to go any further with him. He had already bumped me seven or eight times. I really didn't want to give up on him as that would have been too easy, so I persevered.

In November 2002 I travelled down to London to attend the eight-month diploma course at the London School of Sports

Massage (LSSM). Ever since I'd finished the first massage course ten years before, I had wanted to do the advanced sports massage course, and when the opportunity presented itself, I went for it. Watson, however, couldn't cope with the change of surroundings. His whining while I was at the LSSM was hard to handle and unfair on the other students. Although we had been together for ten months, it was clear we weren't suited to each other. Talking matters over with the GDBA, we agreed that it would be best to let Watson go, even though there was no replacement dog available. I was told this would promote me up the priority waiting list, but even so, I had to wait seven months before another guide dog became available.

I had become so used to the freedom that a guide dog gives. I was much faster and more independent with a dog than getting around using the long cane. Somehow I feel less blind with a dog, so it was a hard decision to give up on Watson and go it alone. I went back to the LSSM to attend an additional six-week course. I was lucky that a mate who had been at the previous massage course with me had also enrolled. Derek Lister was a very supportive and invaluable study partner, explaining the origins and insertions of muscles which he'd learned, being able to see the diagrams. Derek was also a great guide around the college and around London at a time when I didn't have a guide dog.

By the end of April 2003, I was growing increasingly concerned when no one at UKA seemed able to let me know what the qualification standards were for the world championships in Quebec that summer, nor the date by which the standards should be achieved.

My phone calls and emails became more desperate, and at last, Wayne Buxton, the endurance coordinator at UKA, rang to say I had until 24 May to set the qualifying standards for both the 5000 m and 10,000 m — this news came through on 1 May 2003.

It was difficult to understand why they hadn't let me know sooner, but I had enough to worry about, having had to retire my guide dog, Jemma, and train with another, plus Kath had developed a mysterious illness which left her tired all the time, so Paul and I resolved just to get on with it and demonstrate that Bob Matthews wasn't finished yet.

I may have been 42 years old and been injured since the Sydney Paralympic Games in 2000, but we knew I was still good enough to win medals for Great Britain. I had been training hard and knew I was fit — the problem was finding races. The first and only opportunity I had to make my mark in either the 5000 m or 10,000 m was at the British Blind Sports (BBS) championships on 24 May. As usual, Paul was my guide, and thanks to him I ran the qualification time in the 10,000 m and, with some very understanding timekeepers who recorded my time at the halfway point, qualified for the 5000 m as well.

Paul couldn't manage the trip to Quebec, but Mike Peters was a very willing and able replacement guide runner, and so I travelled to Canada for the first time. Our trip to Quebec was interesting, to say the least. On our first night, Mike and I were given a key to a room that was nice enough, but we had to share it, and with the temperatures well over 30 degrees and with no air-conditioning, it wasn't a place we wanted to spend much time in. We were forced to leave the window open to try to allow some cooling breeze into the room. That would have been fine if there hadn't been a nightclub next door.

Sleeping seemed unlikely, but nevertheless we must have managed to drift off because we were woken at 2 a.m. by the high-pitched scream of the smoke detector. Mike had just managed to switch it off when there was a knock at the door. Opening it, I found two girls who explained in a sexy French accent that they wanted to come in — things were looking up! However, they said they had only come to sort the alarm out, which they did by simply removing the battery, explaining that the alarm had been triggered by the high humidity. Fortunately we were moved the next day to the cooler, quieter side of the building.

On Monday 6 August, four days after arriving in Quebec, Mike and I were on the start line for the 10,000 m. I was nervous — I hadn't raced enough in the build-up to the championships, so I was nowhere near as positive as usual. It had been a difficult few months, what with Quando's failing health and my concern for Kath's wellbeing. Still, despite my poor preparation, we were having a good race, lying in third place with eight laps still remaining, when the Italian who had clipped Mike's heel several times made a more solid connection, which caused Mike to stumble and strain his hamstring.

He indicated to Rob Dewhurst, who was there as Noel Thatcher's training partner, to take over the guide rope. Rob did a great job, especially considering he'd never run with a blindie before. After stretching his leg, Mike returned and took over the guide rope for the last five laps. Meanwhile, the Italian had pulled away from us, and for only the second time in my career, I finished out of the medals at a major championship.

To add insult to injury, I was disqualified, again for only the second time in my running career. I had changed guide runners twice, and the rules are that the athlete is only permitted to change guide runners once during any track race.

The 5000 m final occurred five days later. Mike put me in a good position before handing over to Rob for the last two laps, and we out-sprinted Carlos from Portugal in the finishing straight to win a silver medal in 16:09.2. I was of course delighted with the silver medal, and had enjoyed running with Mike in Quebec, but I missed Kath not being there. I spoke to her on the phone every night and my concern for her health increased. She told me she had no energy and just didn't feel herself. Thankfully, by the time I got home from Canada, she was starting to feel a bit better.

I was in good shape after the world champs, and I won my

first-ever 10 km road race against sighted runners in a time of 34 minutes 51 seconds. Two weeks later, I set a new British record of 1:15:20 in the Kenilworth half-marathon in a field of over a thousand athletes. The world marathon championships in Athens were a month away and I was feeling good.

Quando was also in top form and was going from strength to strength since his neck operation. He was enjoying his retirement and being out of the harness. However, his good health didn't last long. I was playing with him in the garden one morning when I noticed a lump on his left shoulder. After keeping an eye on it for a few weeks, the vet examined it under general anaesthetic. The biopsy confirmed our worst fears — it was cancer. During the biopsy the vet asked Kath whether he should bring Quando around from the anaesthetic as the bone was already weakened and it would become even more fragile.

I was out running with Paul at the time, and Kath didn't want to make that kind of decision on her own, so she told the vet to wake him up. He wasn't in pain and he was enjoying life, so we felt there was absolutely no reason to put the boy to sleep yet. But after making such a full recovery from his neck operation, to be diagnosed with terminal cancer less than a year later seemed very cruel. Still, Quando coped with it so well. He ran with no fear of fracturing his upper foreleg. Perceptibly though, he was slowing down, becoming less enthusiastic, the leg becoming swollen and tender.

Before I went to Athens for the world marathon championships in November 2003, I told Quando that I'd run it for him. I won a silver medal, so maybe I should have dedicated races to him more often. The weekend after my marathon we went to visit Liz and Derek in Sussex. It was part of Quando's farewell tour. We had already taken him to Buckinghamshire to say goodbye to Jan and Gary where he'd had a short scamper in the park, briefly reminding us all of his behaviour in his younger days. Derek and Gary were two of Quando's favourites, but he loved all of my guide runners and he always made them feel welcome. He used to greet Gary and Derek especially warmly, trotting up to them, 'talking' to them, and then giving them both his paw.

Kath and I had vowed never to be selfish and keep Quando alive if he was suffering at all, or if we felt he was losing any of his dignity. That day arrived on 13 November when we had to do something every guide dog owner and pet lover dreads. We had to say goodbye to Quando, one of the best, most intelligent, charismatic and dynamic friends anyone could dream of having.

When we finally put him to sleep, Kath was in bits. I tried to be strong for her. Little did I know that just 17 days later, Quando's ashes would be resting at her feet as I said goodbye to Kath as well.

Chapter 17 – My darkest days

Kath wasn't a runner before she met me, but soon after we hooked up she was running three times a week to keep fit — she loved it. A few days before her 38th birthday, however, in April 2003, she came home from a run feeling heavy-legged and very tired. She went to her local doctor who diagnosed post-viral fatigue syndrome. Apparently there was something of an epidemic in the area, and Kath was the fourth person he'd diagnosed that week with it.

As a birthday treat for Kath, I had booked a romantic weekend away together in a hotel in Settle in the North Yorkshire Dales. Despite her illness, Kath insisted we went, but unfortunately neither of us realised just how much the drive would take out of her. The morning after we arrived, Kath still felt tired, but was determined to enjoy the weekend. We went for an eight-mile walk, which Kath really enjoyed, saying the exercise and scenery had bucked her up, even though she was enormously tired. By the time we got back home after the weekend, however, she was well and truly wiped out.

She went back to her doctor who prescribed a mild anti-depressant, which helped a little for a short while. When this wore off and subsequent prescriptions had no effect, the doctor advised her that she would have to let the virus 'run its course'. She even stopped taking the contraceptive pill, hoping this might have a positive effect on her body, even though this was taking a chance as we had already decided not to have children who could possibly inherit RP.

Her symptoms were akin to a mild form of ME (myalgic encephalomyelitis). She was very tired and had difficulty concentrating. She had little or no strength, nor energy, and she walked with a shuffle, finding it particularly difficult to walk downhill. Kath had rarely taken a sick day in her life, but by June 2003 she'd been off work for eight weeks. Although still tired, she returned to work four days a week for a few hours in the morning. However, after only three weeks, her symptoms returned worse than before. It was a really frustrating time, and we were both becoming more and more concerned. It didn't help that her doctor couldn't diagnose conclusively what her illness was. He insisted that it was 'fatigue syndrome' and would have to run its course.

Kath's illness forced her to miss the world championships in Quebec, but even if she had been well enough to travel, the dates clashed with her brother Shaun's wedding. She wouldn't have missed Shaun's wedding for anything, but she struggled through the day. I rang her from Canada and she told me she'd nearly fainted at the wedding — she'd tried to blame it on the fact that it was such a warm day.

When I got back from Canada, Kath started to show signs of improvement and was keen to get back to some light exercise. We went to see a physiotherapist to try to identify the cause for her dragging her left foot. She told him she missed going for a run two or three times a week. The physio suggested she could start back doing a little easy running on the treadmill which would strengthen her muscles and reduce the dragging. The effect on Kath's morale was fantastic. At last she felt as though she was getting her life back again after this strange illness had sapped all her energy. It was such an incredible relief for us both, but it turned out to be a false hope.

The weekend after we said goodbye to Quando, we took off to Devon for a couple of nights to get away from it all and try to take our minds off grieving for our mate. We should have been talking about how we felt about our loss and telling stories about the good times with Quando. I think Kath wanted to, but I wasn't ready to face the reality that he was no longer with us. We went on walks along the sea front and around the town and, if anything, I was the one holding us back as my hip was tight and sore after the Athens marathon.

The Rugby World Cup was on, and England had made it through to the last four. We spent a morning in our hotel room, watching England beat France to reach the final. We visited Gary and Jan and, over a couple of pints at Gary's local, I talked about Quando for the first time since his death. Neither Kath nor I had previously brought the subject up, not wishing to upset the other. I suppose I was afraid of upsetting Kath as I thought she was still a little fragile — silly mistake, really.

On Sunday 23 November, we watched England show Australia who was the best team in the world at rugby in the cup final. Gary's wife, Jan, went shopping, but the rest of us were on the edge of our seats when Jonny Wilkinson kicked the drop-goal to win the World Cup for England. It ranked as one of the greatest and most memorable sporting highlights of my life, and I remember with particular fondness how excited Kath was when England won.

Each day Kath was getting stronger and feeling more energetic. She had been working a couple of hours a day, and was now looking forward to increasing her work load as soon as possible. Her boss suggested that she take it easy and only work when she felt up to it, but Kath being Kath, she pushed herself perhaps a little too hard, too soon. She came home from work at the end of her fourth day needing to have a rest, but still pleased to be back at work. As she was feeling better, she even went to a Pilates class that evening which she enjoyed, but she had a sore neck and felt very tired when she got home. I wondered if it had anything to do with my overdoing the spice in the chicken paprika I'd cooked that night.

The next morning, Kath woke up with a throbbing headache, and said she felt sick. She took a couple of anti-inflammatory pills which lessened the symptoms but left her feeling 'spaced out'. We obviously didn't know what the real problem was, and just assumed it was the hangover from her fatigue syndrome. As Cara, her mother, and Shaun, her brother, were having their birthdays, we were due to drive down to Shropshire the next day for a family gathering. Although Kath was feeling rotten with her headache, she was determined to keep her hairdresser's appointment that day as she wanted her family to see she was feeling better and dealing with this odd illness she had been facing for months.

After her hair appointment, she wandered around town, looking for birthday presents, but still feeling spaced out and unable to concentrate, she came home exhausted and empty-handed.

Kath went to bed early that Friday night, feeling absolutely exhausted and with no appetite for the delivery pizza I'd ordered. The next morning, Saturday 29 November, I was up early, working on my computer, and I took Kath a cup of tea just before 9 a.m. It was great to see she felt much better, and she said her headache had lessened. She even finished her tea and ate a couple of biscuits. A good friend from BICA, Joe Argu, phoned to ask how we both were, particularly 'Kathy' as he called her. I told him that Kath was feeling much better and getting fitter, doing more exercise and that it shouldn't be too long before we could jump on the tandem and join the group for a cycle. 'That's grand, thank God,' Joe said. Later, at her mum's house in Wistanstow, Kath spoke to Claire, an aunt in Dublin, and told her that she was feeling better every day.

I have all sorts of mundane memories from that Saturday — it just seemed to be such a normal day. I remember we stopped in nearby Shrewsbury to pick up flowers for Kath's mum, and a luxury yuletide chocolate log to have with a cup of tea. In the evening we'd planned to go out for dinner at a cosy, olde English pub in Hopton Wafers, a small village a 10 mile (16 km) drive away, to celebrate Cara and Shaun's birthdays.

That evening, as we got dressed to go out, Kath said she felt tired again and a little sick. As we walked to the car I couldn't help but feel angry with whatever was wrong with Kath. She had started to shuffle again. We hadn't driven very far before Kath told Shaun to pull over, and she was sick on the side of the road. When this happened again a few minutes later, we turned around and went home, and Kath went straight to bed, feeling worse than ever, with severe nausea and a really painful headache.

Cara, understandably anxious, did what she could to make her daughter comfortable, but Kath asked to be left alone. She felt bad about the cancellation of the birthday celebrations because of her illness. I went up to see her a bit later, and took her up some juice. I felt pretty useless, and all I could do for her was rinse out her sick bowl beside her bed. I was extremely concerned for her, but just assumed she had a virus. She wasn't able to talk as she felt so sick, but just held my hand and squeezed it tightly. I heard her in the bathroom a bit later, and I asked if there was anything I could do. Again she just asked to be left alone. I slept in the spare room that night, thinking Kath was sleeping, and that Cara had crept in to join her and was sleeping beside her on the bed.

During the night, I went to the bathroom and paused outside Kath's door. I heard what I assumed was someone with a cold, snoring, but in hindsight it may have been Kath struggling to breathe. I just don't know. Maybe I should have checked who was making the noise. Maybe I should have called a doctor. Maybe things would have turned out differently if I had. But I didn't. I assumed it was Cara, not Kath, who was making noises in her sleep, and I went back to bed and had the first reasonable night's sleep I'd had for a while.

I awoke at 7.50 a.m. to a lot of commotion in the house. Confused and disoriented, I clambered out of bed, trying to remember where I'd put my clothes the night before. Initially, I had a horrible thought that something had happened to Vicky, who was six months pregnant with her and Shaun's first child. In fact, the commotion that woke me up was Shaun racing downstairs, carrying Kath in his arms. Vicky was on the phone to the emergency services, pleading for an ambulance to come quick. Then Cara opened the door to my room and said, 'Come downstairs — please.'

It was only then that it dawned on me that there was something wrong with Kath. Nothing seemed real. I heard Vicky counting to five, pausing, then counting to five again. Then I realised that she was performing emergency resuscitation (CPR) on Kath. I felt like I was in a nightmare. The next thing I knew there were paramedics tending to Kath, trying desperately to revive her. I felt numb — 'This can't be happening,' I told myself. I do remember thinking I should get properly dressed. I'd only slipped on a pair of shorts. Then I found myself kneeling by my wife's side, willing Kath to breathe for all I was worth. A paramedic instructed me to squeeze a bag that contained some solution or other.

All of this was so unreal. It felt like it was happening somewhere else to somebody else. It felt like hours, but in reality it all happened in the space of a few minutes. Then Shaun put his arm around me and said, 'Kath's gone. I wanted you to hear it from me, not anyone else.'

I didn't understand what he was saying, so he spelled it out: 'Kath's dead.'

Kath was pronounced dead at 8.32 a.m. on Sunday, 30 November 2003. In reality, Kath was probably dead by the time Cara found her. Cara hadn't slept beside Kath that night as I'd presumed — she'd slept in the other spare room, and had gone in to Kath's room in the morning to see how Kath was feeling. Her bed was empty. She checked the bathroom. Empty. Cara went back into Kath's room and found her lying on the floor on the far side of the bed.

The police were called, which is standard procedure whenever there's a sudden death, especially when it is a young person. Kath was only 38 years old. It was a horrible job for the female police officer who had to stay in the room with Kath after the paramedics had packed up and left. I went in first to hold Kath's hand. I kissed her and held her tight, but it was only when I received absolutely no reaction that it began to sink in that I'd lost my lovely wife, my confidante, my best friend. I knelt beside Kath's still-warm body and asked her to forgive me. I apologised for anything and everything. I even told her to haunt me. And then I got a glimpse into the near future and saw how empty my life was going to be. Cara and Shaun and Vicky then came in to hold Kath and say goodbye, and I learned how you can be in a room full of people and still feel so alone.

I know you expect undertakers to be courteous, sympathetic and to make things as easy as possible for the bereaved, but the undertaker who came to take Kath's body to the morgue at Shrewsbury Hospital had little empathy. He gave the impression that he was doing us a great favour, and he seemed to resent the fact that we wouldn't confirm that we'd use him for the funeral there and then.

Around lunchtime we began the incredibly difficult task of informing family and friends. I distinctly recall the enormous empathy I felt for everyone who learned the news of Kath's totally unexpected death over the telephone. I marvelled at how calm Derek seemed, but as he dropped the phone I realised this was just a front. I worried for Ange as she started to hyperventilate when she was told the horrible news. Shaun was brilliant — I don't know what I would have done without him, because I just wasn't able to get the words out. I tried to make a couple of calls, including the one to Ange, but all I could say was, 'Ange, Shaun needs to speak to you.' I wasn't ready to say the words out loud yet — the words which meant my life could never be the same: 'Kath is dead.'

Next morning, whilst speaking with Mike, I was able to say those words for the first time. He made it easy, staying calm and seeming to take the news in his stride which helped greatly. We were on our way to the hospital morgue when Paul Harwood called me from work, struggling to hold onto his emotions. He said he'd come over and, if there was nothing else he could do, he'd take me out for a run and would pick up any kit I needed from home.

It was surreal, looking at Kath lying there in the morgue. Of course I appreciated she had been tired and totally not herself over the last six months, but I still couldn't grasp that what had been diagnosed as a virus had taken my rock, my wife, my Kath, away from me. This wonderful woman, who had been vivacious, full of fun and energy, was left lying here, perfectly still. I looked at the contours of her face — a face I knew so well — but it had already changed from what had once been soft, warm and full of expression to something taut and cool. There was no breath — no words to tell me why she had to go, to tell me that everything would be all right, to tell me that I would be all right. There was no goodbye.

I just couldn't understand it. I could smell her perfume and hold her hand and touch her face, but she wasn't there. I just felt totally numb.

We still didn't have a clue what had caused Kath's sudden and totally unexpected death until after the postmortem, which showed that a blockage in the third ventricle in the brain had caused a build-up of pressure, which in turn had blocked signals from the basal nerve, which tells the heart and lungs to function. Something called a colloid cyst, which can occur anywhere in the body at any time, was the cause of Kath's illness and ultimately her death. Stress can often cause these cysts to develop, and Kath had been through quite a lot over the last year. First of all there was the trouble with my Lottery funding, then the worry over her mum, when Cara had had to go into hospital that January, and lastly Quando's illness and subsequent death.

I really wanted to see my mates first before my family, knowing intuitively that hugging them was what I needed most. On Monday evening, Derek made the four-hour drive up from Sussex. We spent most of the next 24 hours talking about Kath. Derek really helped resolve a number of my dilemmas, such as where Kath would wish to be buried. On Thursday, Paul drove over to Wistanstow to see me. As with Derek, it seemed so natural just to hug one another.

Paul and I ran for six miles (10 km) in misty, cold, invigorating conditions. Naturally, we talked about Kath — the first of hundreds of miles I would spend talking about her. It was the first time I'd run around Wistanstow and I found it cleansing to do something I loved, so close to Kath's beloved home, with someone I could talk to about anything. We could both see and feel her running with us, both then and on many subsequent runs.

Across the lane from Cara's house is a gorgeous, old Anglican church where Kath and Shaun's father, Bill, had been buried 14 years earlier, having passed away at the age of 50. Father Donlan visited us from the Catholic church of Clunn, a village five miles (8 km) away, and he couldn't have been more wonderful at the hardest time of our lives. His advice was sensible and realistic, and his words were comforting. Despite being a Catholic priest, he was able to organise Kath's funeral service in the Anglican church, and he did a perfect job.

Shaun and I were determined to be pallbearers and, if possible, to have a relative and close friend carry Kath as well. Apparently, this isn't too common — a number of undertakers warned us that all sorts of things can go wrong when 'amateurs' are involved in carrying the coffin. Burying someone is a complicated process. We learned that there are only a couple of days in the week when digging a grave is permitted. We had to choose the coffin, select the handles, and decide how many days Kath's body would be on view.

It is a difficult task finding an undertaker who is the right fit and who will listen to what you want for someone you love. It is not something you would ever really think about, especially when your loved one is as young as Kath was. After our initial experience with the pushy undertakers who took Kath to the morgue, Shaun and I were determined to find the right person to look after Kath in her final days before her burial. We were fortunate enough to find Linda Dawson, whose funeral home was only 2 miles (3 km) away in the small town of Craven Arms. She listened to us, made helpful and tactful suggestions and, importantly, she was extremely kind and respectful to Kath.

Kath was dressed really nicely in the clothes she'd worn that last evening, with her own make-up and perfume. This done, Linda made it possible for anyone to see Kath at any time, and always ensured Kath looked her best. I went to the funeral home to see Kath as often as possible, accompanied by Shaun, Ange, Sue or Derek.

During the first weekend in December, Gary and I drove back to Leamington Spa to pick up Quando's ashes, my suit, a photo of our wedding, and some jewellery. Melanie, Steve's wife, came over to help me sort through some of Kath's things. We stayed overnight, went for a couple of runs, and on Sunday morning as I stepped through the front door and pulled it closed behind me, I felt Kath trying to squeeze through the door before it closed. I apologised to her and opened it again to make sure she'd got through.

The vet had placed Quando's ashes in a beautiful casket, and after we got permission from the church and made sure Kath's family didn't mind, I left the casket at Kath's feet, which felt right and appropriate. It was where Quando had usually slept, after all. I also placed our wedding photo on Kath's chest, and in her hand I laid one of my new business cards she'd helped me get printed.

Sue and I got dressed together. She made sure my Sydney Paralympic suit and shoes were straight and spotless, then we waited downstairs for the hearse. Shaun said, 'Let's both stay strong until at least after the service for Kath.'

Standing at the rear of the hearse as the doors were opened and the coffin rolled out was like being at the epicentre of an earthquake. It suddenly dawned on me that this was really happening, that this was my wife, and I was about to bury the most dear and important thing in my life.

The coffin was wheeled into the courtyard of the church where we all stood and waited until it was time for us to lift her to our shoulders. Kath's uncle, Thomas, plus Gary, Shaun and myself were the four pallbearers. We carried Kath into the church as the organist played 'Nimrod' by Elgar — the same anthem that had played on the day I carried my dad into the church for his funeral. I still feel sad and uplifted simultaneously whenever I hear this piece of music.

The church was packed. Many of my guide runners had travelled from all over the country, along with friends from Leamington Spa. There was a minibus full of Irishmen from Birmingham with whom Kath and I had cycled to the west coast of Ireland two years before. There were also a great number of locals who knew Kath's family well, and the village came to a standstill with the mourners' cars parked along the narrow lanes. I felt proud that Kath was the focus of this display of love and respect. Many people commented that it was a really nice service that was obviously organised with a lot of care and thought.

I sat in the front pew with Gary and Derek, who gave the oration, holding one hand each to support me. I felt calm and in control. I don't remember too much about the service, but I do recall wishing it would never end, because when it did, it meant it was all too real. It also meant that I had to start living my life without Kath.

Father Donlan was fantastic and never left Kath's side. He walked around her as he touched and stroked the coffin — he made it a very intimate and personal service. I wanted to pay tribute to Kath, and a friend sent me this verse by David Harkins which seemed so right, and which to me reflected how Kath would want to be remembered. Steve walked the few steps with me to the front of the church, and I could feel Kath's presence as she helped me stay calm and strong as I read the verse:

You can shed tears that she is gone,
Or you can smile because she has lived.
You can close your eyes and pray that she'll come back,
Or you can open your eyes and see all she's left.
Your heart can be empty because you can't see her,
Or you can be full of the love you shared.
You can turn your back on tomorrow and live yesterday,
Or you can be happy for tomorrow, because of yesterday.
You can remember her and only that she's gone,
Or you can cherish her memory and let it live on.
You can cry and close your mind, be empty and turn your back,
Or you can do what she'd want — smile, open your eyes, love, and go on.

Eventually the service came to an end, and we stepped forward to the catafalque to claim the coffin as we hoisted Kath to our shoulders once more. It seemed appropriate to carry Kath from the church with the organist playing 'Swing Low Sweet Chariot'. It was hard to believe that just seven days prior to her death, Kath and I had watched England win the Rugby World Cup together and enjoyed listening to the English fans sing the song in celebration. Today it was a song of mourning. As we stood outside and waited for the rest of the congregation, Gary and I shared a rare moment of light relief with Linda who had heard me mumbling something and thought I was talking to her.

'It's OK,' I smiled. 'I was talking to Kath.'

After the four of us had lowered Kath into the grave, I shook hands with or embraced the many well-wishers who offered their condolences. I still felt calm and strangely detached. It wasn't until we were sitting down to eat that I felt as though my whole world was caving in around me. Somehow, Shaun noticed that I was about to lose it, and took me somewhere private where I could cry on his shoulder, and let go some of my pent-up grief and anger and pain.

As the days and weeks passed, the feeling of shocked bewilderment gradually subsided, but it wasn't until February that I was able to remember Kath as she was. I had the first of many flashbacks of the living Kath — of how she looked and spoke when we were together. The first flashback was of Kath with a towel wrapped around her head after a shower, wiggling her head from side to side, mimicking one of the Indian characters in the British sitcom *It Ain't Half Hot Mum*.

I recognised the delay in being able to visualise Kath was some sort of self-defence — a type of safety valve — that only slowly let memories into my consciousness. Gradually she seemed more and more alive as my memories of her became clearer and I went back to living my life. For example, when I went back to the gym for the first time after Kath's death, it triggered memories of her working out. But it was the common, more mundane memories which hit me hardest. No more would she clean her glasses just before getting into bed; no more would I hear the car pull into the drive around 5.30 every evening. Instead, now there was just silence.

I discovered that some people I'd called friends drifted out of my life quite suddenly. I suppose they weren't able, or didn't know how, to talk to me, which was a little upsetting. Kath had been a big part of many people's lives, and just because she was no longer around, she certainly wasn't out of mind. Most of our friends and acquaintances were good, and a few were really fantastic. I spent many weekends with our friends Gary and Jan and Derek and Liz, who all loved Kath. I shared many dinners with them, and we drank quite a few pints at one pub or another as we shared our memories. Barry and Joy Poultney, who had looked after Quando from time to time when Kath and I were away on holiday, were another couple who helped me through the tough times. Barry, who is a lay preacher, told me how angry he was with God for taking two pairs of eyes from me.

As well as eating and drinking and talking about Kath, I also spent many hours running with Paul and Gary and talking about Kath as we ran. On one particular run in January I experienced what I initially thought was as asthma attack. All of a sudden I could barely breathe as all the muscles in my throat and chest contracted and seized up. After the same thing happened again a few days later, I learned that I was suffering from anxiety attacks brought on by the stress and emotion of losing Kath. This was the first time I realised how strongly emotions can affect you physically. These episodes grew less and less frequent as I learned to deal with Kath's death.

For many months I received fantastic help from Cruse, which is an organisation of bereavement counsellors. Colin, one of their counsellors, was able to coax details from me which greatly helped my healing.

As well as losing Kath, I also had to come to terms with being totally alone in the house without even the solace of a dog's company. Our house, which had always been full of conversation, love and laughter, not to mention the noise and excitement of bounding guide dogs, was a much darker and more silent place.

Getting around without Kath and without a guide dog was tremendously difficult. I had to resort to using the long cane again. With Quando I had been used to walking as fast, if not faster, than any sighted person. Now old ladies in their Zimmer frames passed me by, and obstacles which I hadn't known existed were constantly tripping me up. Ironically, had Kath still been around, she would have been the one giving me refresher lessons with the long cane.

I had to learn how to get to the shops, the bus stop and, once I'd ventured into town, how to find my way around using the long cane. One day, returning from a weekend with Gary and Jan, I thought I could make it from the station to the high street walking through the Pump Room Gardens. Needless to say, I got lost. Nothing was where it should have been. Nothing was as I remembered it. If I let it, these frustrations easily sparked more emotions, laying bare what I'd lost.

I briefly wondered what the point was in my continuing to want to live, and why Kath should have lost her life so tragically early instead of me. I wanted to be with her, but she'd have killed me if I'd joined her deliberately.

Chapter 18 – Life after Kath

Less than a month after Kath died, I spent Christmas with Derek and Liz Jones, whose company made that time a little more bearable. I was still in shock that Kath was dead. This was my first Christmas without her — the first Christmas of the rest of my life without Kath by my side.

As I thought about my lovely wife, the happy memories came flooding back — like the memories of our first Christmas together as a married couple in our new house. I had opened a magnum of champagne, and we were both pretty sozzled by the time we sat down to dinner and listened to the Queen's Christmas message and then snuggled up on the couch to watch a movie. I also remembered Christmas with my family in the West Indies, and the Christmas Kath and I spent with Derek and Liz in Dorset where we'd listened to an entire Harry Potter book on Radio 4 together. We'd spent the evening beside a roaring fire in a pub situated on a small patch of land that becomes an island at high tide. I knew I was lucky to have these and so many other happy memories of my time with Kath, and I tried hard not to think too much about my future without her.

After many months had passed, I felt it was time to pull myself together and get on with my life. It was so hard, however, to get used to life on my own. I missed coming home to a warm house and the aroma of Kath's home cooking, knowing that after dinner we would curl up on the couch with Quando at our feet and watch television. I was lonely, I missed Kath's company, and I missed the closeness of being with another person, a shared cuddle, our good-morning kiss, and our kiss goodnight.

Someone had warned me not to hurry into finding a girlfriend as it was too soon, which was good advice and easy to give, but then they were able to go home in the evening to the arms of their partners. When I had been 15 and still had some useful vision, I would look in the mirror and think, 'God, you're ugly — no wonder you can't get a girlfriend.' Although I knew this was adolescent self-indulgence, I wondered now whether maybe I'd actually had a point back then. Could I have lost whatever had attracted Kath and a handful of others to me?

I was learning to cope with my grief and adjusting to being on my own, but in the process I had lost all confidence in myself as a person. I had become so used to being part of a team that I had forgotten how to be alone. I had also become used to having a pair of eyes to support me, be it Kath's or my guide dog's. Since Kath had passed away, I had also been 10 months without a guide dog, and I was struggling with my cane.

The GDBA were actively trying to find a dog that would suit me, and in August 2004 they introduced me to Joy, a two-year-old German shepherd. We agreed that, as the Paralympic Games were so close, it would be wise to wait until I returned from Athens to train with her. I did walk with Joy a couple of times and found that she certainly liked to get a move on. We seemed to work really well together, and I looked forward to having a guide dog again, not least because of the companionship.

That same month, I decided to go ahead with the extension on my house that Kath and I had planned together. I still needed a room for my sports massage, and the extension would at the very least serve as a good investment. Initially, it was quite exciting as first the garage was knocked down and then the foundations were dug. But after two weeks of the builders' noise, mess and disruption, I was relieved to get away for a month to the Paralympics.

Given the circumstances, I trained as hard and prepared as well as I could for the Athens Games, and training helped me get through those awful first few months following Kath's sudden death. I thought a great deal about Athens and how much it would mean to me to honour Kath by winning a medal, although Gary said later, 'I thought you deserved a medal when you stepped on the track.'

Physically I wasn't in the best shape. For the previous 12 months I had been suffering from a foot problem which was still a little painful. With plenty of treatment, Paul Harwood once again whipped me into shape, putting me through many merciless, punishing and intensive training sessions, ably backed up by Mike and Gary. The hard work was well worthwhile — I qualified to run in the 5000 m and 10,000 m in my seventh Paralympic Games.

I'm used to feeling nervous before races, but in Athens the nerves kicked in a few days before I was even due to race. I worried about how much the 10,000 m would hurt, and whether I'd even be able to handle it, for goodness' sake. Opting not to attend the opening ceremony probably wasn't such a good decision, as the opportunity to walk into the stadium and onto the track for the first time would at least have helped to dissolve some nervous tension.

I received more media attention and interest than ever before, partly because I had lost Kath so recently, but mainly because I was the only athlete competing in his seventh games. Just three days before my first race, I spent three hours giving press interviews to News 24, the BBC, the *Sunday Times* and the *Daily Mail*, amongst others. I spoke freely about how my focus was to run for Kath, and how the Paralympics had helped me get through the initial stages of grieving. I talked about how Kath would have been in Athens with me, if she was still alive, and how she would have wanted me to go and run, and do as well as I could.

By the time we were led into the arena for the 10,000 m, my nerves had vanished. I guess it had been a long day for the stadium announcer, because we weren't introduced to the crowd. The starter just told us to get on our marks and we were away. I felt quite good for the first lap or so, but from then until the finish I seemed to be running on my heels with nothing in the tank.

Every athlete is supposed to have the bell rung to indicate when they have one lap to go. I assume the man with the bell was on a promise — he rang it for the Kenyan, Henry Wanyoike, and then must have gone home. This would have been fine had everyone been on the same lap, but the African had lapped everyone at least once. I finished in fifth position in a time of 34:47.6. Paul was exhausted — not from running, but from shouting at me to get my arse moving!

The support for me in Athens was amazing. Kath's brother, Shaun, was there, while Sue, Guy-Pierre and Ella had travelled all the way from the West Indies. Ange came to see me run for the first time ever; Paul's wife, Zoe, and his daughters, Sally and Lucy, plus Gary and Jan, Derek and Liz, and their daughters, Helen and Laura (with their boyfriends) also made the trip. Despite finishing fifth I still did a lap of honour wearing the 'Team Kath' T-shirt which the whole support team wore throughout the event. I was then asked for an interview for the BBC, but didn't realise the camera was actually rolling until the interviewer asked me to show my T-shirt to the camera.

Five days later, I was aware that the 5000 m could easily be my last-ever track race in the Paralympics. I was much more relaxed and not as nervous, and I even stopped to have a chat with my old mate, Paulo Coelho, about old times. I came sixth in a time of 16:20.4, one second behind the fourth-placed runner; once again Henry Wanyoike from Kenya smashed the world record, along with the opposition.

The curtain had come down on these Paralympic Games for me and, for all I knew, on my Paralympic career. I went out with my friends and family and partied until the early hours, and I felt that Kath was there, celebrating with us, the whole time. For the past ten months I'd used Athens as my focus — my vehicle if you like — to get me through an incredibly difficult and painful time. After my family and friends had gone home, and just before the British team left Athens, I let everything out. The tears flowed, and for the first time in weeks I felt a little better.

I felt better still when I received my third invitation to Buckingham Palace along with the rest of the Great Britain Paralympic team. It wasn't long before the double doors to the room opened, quite close to where Paul and I were chatting, and the Queen began mingling with the crowd. I remember Paul telling me: 'Watch what you're saying, the Queen's standing right behind you.'

'Blimey,' I thought, 'we might even get a chance to talk to her.' The next thing I knew was Phil Lane, the chef de mission from Athens, introducing Paul and me to Her Majesty. It was amazing — for nearly ten minutes we chatted with the Queen. She wanted to know about the bond Paul and I had as running partners. We explained how we ran and how we had to be good mates, having to share the same room for three weeks. We chatted a little about dogs — her corgis and my guide dogs — and then she asked whether I intended to run in London in the 2012 Paralympics.

'Oh, I don't know ma'am,' I replied. 'I'll be 51 by then.'

Smiling, the Queen replied: 'That alone shouldn't stop you, should it?'

Was that a royal decree? It's certainly given me something to think about since then. Perhaps I could be at the 2012 London Games in a different discipline — tandem cycling is a real possibility. It seemed incredible at that time to think I might still be competitive in 2012.

The day after returning from the Greek capital, I was able to get back to some normality and concentrate on training with my new guide dog, Joy. The GDBA was great, allowing me to stay at a hotel in Leamington Spa for the week, which was just as well really because my house was a mess. Looking around it, I was fairly happy with the work the builders had done, but hadn't I said to keep the old bathroom suite? And why was the kitchen taking so long? Granted, Kath and I had decided to have the kitchen extended, which meant the builders had to completely replace the ceiling, but I was informed that they'd just about finished it when the building inspector had told them it had been built incorrectly and they'd had to start again. Of course I had to pay for their poor workmanship. How could that be right? The lesson I learned was never believe a builder's original quote — always double it. In hindsight, going away and leaving the builders to make all the decisions wasn't such a great idea.

Without Kath around, I found it difficult to focus and make decisions, and I often found myself wondering, 'What would Kath do?' Should I put a shower room downstairs, and what about choosing a colour scheme? What should I put on the floor, and where the bloody hell should I put the power points? With the help of some great friends I got there, eventually.

Gary went around the house finding 25 snags — things the builders hadn't finished or needed to put right, such as plasterwork or shoddy tiling — but the outstanding fault was the height of the doorway from the kitchen to the garden which was barely six feet. I had to duck to pass through without banging my head. Backed up by the architect, I convinced them to put it right. That was the second lesson learned — never go with the cheapest quote.

I was inducted into the local BBC Hall of Fame that winter, an honour that I dedicated to Kath. My confidence was returning, I was running better, my house was finished — at last — and Joy had become a great guide dog and companion. My self-confidence was also boosted by managing to woo my first girlfriend after Kath. It was hard to get used to being with another woman, though. I couldn't help feeling guilty in the beginning; it was like I was cheating on Kath.

Since her death, I'd fretted about whether Kath had suffered much at the end, and felt the best way to get answers was to talk to a spiritual medium. I had no idea what to expect, and although

I was somewhat of a sceptic, the medium was amazing. My heart rate increased when she told me Kath liked the fact that I was wearing her wedding ring on a chain around my neck. There is no way the medium could have seen that from what I was wearing. She said that Kath was delighted to be welcomed to the 'other side' by her father, Bill, who had died suddenly, aged only 50 years old. I was overwhelmed at this point.

Then the medium went on to say that Kath was indicating that she'd experienced a terrific headache, like a brain haemorrhage, before she'd died, but that was all and she'd then fallen unconscious. Kath had of course died of a blockage in her brain. What we took for some type of virus was the beginning of the blockage which caused the inflammation in her brain. When the medium then told me, 'Kath says, she's walking her dog,' the tears came to my eyes — Quando had been Kath's dog after his retirement a year earlier, and had died just before Kath.

The medium also told me that I had a positive future and that I would meet someone else. I left feeling thankful that Kath was in a good space, and I felt optimistic about what lay in store for me.

I went speed-dating with a couple of female friends. Blimey, that was hard work! I had just three minutes to get a 'feel' of what the girl on the other side of the table was like, and then put a tick in either the 'yes, I would like to see her again' box or in the 'no, not my type' box before speeding on to meet the next girl at the neighbouring table. Even getting to the tables in that sort of timeframe was a mission in itself for me. After chatting with 16 members of the fairer sex in the same evening, I was absolutely wiped out, and hardly cared whether the girls I'd 'ticked' had reciprocated.

I attended two of these evenings, giving out more ticks than I received, but I was still chuffed that one in three wanted to see me again. Needless to say, these dates didn't really lead to anything long-term.

I made further progress on the road to recovery with a holiday to Malta with Traveleyes, a travel company specifically for visually impaired holiday-makers. We had plenty of opportunity to see as well as feel the sights. One of the highlights of the holiday was my first time on a jet ski. As there was no way I'd be allowed onto the open sea solo, one of the sighted guides gamely agreed to sit on the back while I drove. I was having a brilliant time and I loved the acceleration and the feeling as we bounced over the waves. Maybe my guide didn't quite enjoy it as much; when we were back on dry land, she told me, 'I was just on the excited side of scared.'

The holiday was brought to a marvellous end when I went scuba diving for the first time in 15 years. It was so liberating, finning along, feeling the sandy bottom of the Mediterranean. My dive buddy showed me an anchor, and I realised we must have been swimming beneath the keel of a boat.

As well as dating and travelling, I was also back running — I was determined to get fit. With a lot of help from Paul and Gary, I got back into shape, physically and mentally, and was selected to run in the 5000 m in Helsinki in the European championships. Mum came to visit a couple of days before Paul and I flew to Helsinki, partly to ensure I ate properly, but also so that I wouldn't be alone on 20 August, the date of Kath's and my 11th wedding anniversary. The day itself wasn't too bad, and even though I missed Kath, I was starting to feel more like myself again.

The European championships gave me an opportunity to go for gold at a major championship for the first time since Sydney 2000. There was a strong wind blowing, so it was a very tactical race. Paul really had to be on the ball; he did a brilliant job to keep me in contact but prevent me from colliding with any of the athletes in front of us. Everyone had to concentrate hard, as losing focus could have caused a nasty pile-up. We managed to stay out of trouble, and won gold with a last lap of 65 seconds. The win meant a lot because I wanted to win it for Kath and to prove to myself that I was still at the top as an athlete.

Mum was still at home when I got back. It was wonderful

to have someone waiting for me instead of going home to an empty house. I really appreciated Mum being there (and of course the food was great), but I'd forgotten just how vivacious and garrulous my mum can be, and for a while I felt as though I was under siege. I was knackered from the running and lack of sleep, and I felt punch-drunk as I tried to absorb her bombardment of words. Still, I wouldn't have had it any other way. When she went back home to Yorkshire, the house felt empty again, and I was reminded once again how lonely life was without Kath.

Chapter 19 – Blind date

In December 2005, UKA withdrew my funding as I hadn't won a medal in Athens. It didn't matter that I had won a gold medal in the European championships that year. As far as they were concerned, I hadn't run a fast-enough time to prove I was still capable of winning a medal on the world stage. Naturally I was disappointed, but I was also a little relieved as I realised that now I had the opportunity to do whatever I liked, and my life didn't have to revolve around running. It was a worry to lose my funding, but I was a very competent and confident sports massage therapist by now, so I started seeing more clients and, more importantly, started charging more for my expertise. I'd asked for little more than peanuts before.

I still ran. My approach towards my athletic career had always been professional, so not to train at all was never an option. In any case, I knew I would go potty, just sitting around doing nothing for any length of time, so I set my focus on running the London Marathon in April 2006.

I didn't even need to ease back on my running when I caught up with Sue and her family in the West Indies over the Christmas holidays in 2005, as Gary and Jan came with me, enabling me to train every day. We stayed on to celebrate and ring in the New Year, and on New Year's Day I met Nickie, a Pom, who was on holiday from her home in New Zealand. Her enthusiasm and belief that 'anything's possible' was infectious. She invited me to visit her in New Zealand. Just the thought of seeing and experiencing this beautiful country was exciting. Kath and I had always wanted to visit New Zealand, but my running meant we never got around to it. I couldn't travel anywhere without fit training partners and, in any case, as a funded athlete, I couldn't just skip training and swan off to New Zealand for a holiday because I felt like it. I certainly felt like it now though, and there was nothing to stop me.

The final push I needed to kick-start a new and exciting period in my life came at the end of January, when a very close friend, James Brown, visited from Northern Ireland. Up until that night with James, I hadn't really spoken with anyone regarding my thoughts and feelings after the paramedics had failed to resuscitate Kath. I hadn't shared with anyone how incomprehensible it was to lie beside her, holding and kissing her, and receiving absolutely no reaction. James and I sat on the couch holding each other, both of us crying our hearts out. My tears seemed to come from somewhere very deep inside, and it felt so cleansing and so right.

Next day, life felt good. Out running with Mike, I felt easy. I felt calm. I felt fit and glad to be alive for the first time in over two years. The run seemed to crystallise my thoughts, and I decided 2006 was going to be the year I embraced life again. I decided to take Nickie up on her offer to visit New Zealand. I picked up the phone, booked and paid for my flight, and a week later I was collecting my bags at Auckland airport. I'd arrived in New Zealand!

It is said that life can change in an instant. Mine certainly did when I booked those flights to New Zealand. Nickie introduced me to Mark Allen, who kept me fit by taking me on runs around the rugby fields in Helensville. This beautiful country seemed to open my eyes again; my senses seemed heightened on those early-morning runs. I loved the feel of the sun on my back and the springiness of the grass underfoot — it was impossible not to run fast. On each lap I could hear a line of trees filled with cicadas, the shapes of the trees illuminated by the sound.

I also ran through the countryside with a nice guy called Andrew who, most memorably for me, showed me around his farm. It was great to feed his sheep and to hear the hens pecking around our feet. His herb garden was a truly sensory experience. The aroma of the basil, thyme, rosemary and mint was so strong that my nose didn't know what had hit it.

Amongst the fabulous people I met on my first visit to New Zealand was Inia Taylor, who is probably the most famous tattoo artist in the country. He has tattooed Robbie Williams, Billy Connolly and many of the All Blacks. Inia was also instrumental in designing a Maori emblem for *Earthrace*, a tri-hulled, energy-efficient powerboat which circumnavigated the globe. One day I visited Inia's shop in Grey Lynn. He had just finished tattooing a Frenchman's abdomen, and I was asking lots of questions about the mechanics of tattooing and what Maori symbols looked like. Next thing I knew Inia took my hand and guided me over the man's skin to give me some idea of the symbols as the tattoo was still tactile. He also took me to the Maori pa in the Auckland Museum to show me what a koru looked like, and he described the timber carvings of Maori warriors with their fierce, frightening faces, bulging eyes and projecting tongues.

Through Inia I also learned the truth of the old adage, 'it's a small world'. Crockie worked with Inia and, like me, was born and brought up in the Medway towns in Kent. He was a really interesting character who was covered practically from head to toe with tattoos and body piercings, many of which were his own handiwork. He actually offered to let me tattoo one of the few blank spaces he had left on his body, but I politely declined. I didn't trust myself with a tattooist's needle, but it was kind (or crazy) of Crockie to trust me.

Just days after my arrival in New Zealand I heard the dreadful news about Paul Pearce's death from my mate, Paul Harwood. Pearcey was an incredible guy and we had become friends over the years through running. He was a partially sighted runner and, as such, he was able to run by himself, although he'd often arrive home with cuts and bruises from branches he hadn't seen. Pearcey had been running along a wide road, keeping inside the white line with the traffic speeding past him, when a truck, drifting too far to the side of the road, struck him with its wing mirror. It was a fluke and so unfair.

I was in tears — I couldn't believe it. I felt such empathy for Helena, Pearcey's partner, and could imagine what she was going through. Paul and I discussed the possibility of me returning home early to see Pearcey off, but this would have been a knee-jerk reaction and not what Pearcey would have wanted. I said goodbye to him in my own way — by running on the beaches in Auckland.

Since Kath's death, I'd taken some small steps towards moving on with my life, but the trip to New Zealand was a huge leap. I've never been afraid to dream about doing things that are perceived to be out of my reach. I used to dream of scoring a goal for Chelsea Football Club, or of taking a catch in an important cricket match and accepting the accolades of my team-mates. When I lost my sight, I dreamed of doing well at running and maybe even winning a gold medal. After Kath's death and when I got my confidence back, I dared to dream that I would meet someone else. Then, on Friday, 24 February 2006, I did.

Inia invited Nickie and me to the *Earthrace* launch party. We stopped en route at Soul Bar on the Viaduct in Auckland, where Susie, a friend of Nickie's, was having a drink with some friends, one of whom was called Sarah. 'Hello,' Sarah said, when I was introduced to her. 'Would you like to look at my face?'

It's not every day I get an offer like that! Sarah told me later that it was an instinctive question, partly because she had worked for a blind couple years before and realised how important it was for blind people to see who they are talking to, but also, as she reasoned later: 'I could see your face, and it only seemed fair that you see mine.'

Having established where her voice was coming from, I could tell Sarah was about a foot (30 cm) shorter than me. I moved closer and touched Sarah's cheeks. The first thing that struck me was her beautiful smile. I then followed her hairline, looking at her forehead, her eyebrows, then her ears and drop earrings. I traced her jawline to her chin and managed not to poke her in the eye. This very pleasant close encounter was completed by looking at her cute little nose.

The picture I had was blurred, but clear enough for me to see that she had an attractive, oval-shaped, smiling, bubbly face, and then I saw her hair. Wow, I do love long hair, and Sarah's was not only long, but thick and curly, and she described its colour as red with a blonde or auburn tint.

It was pretty close to love at first touch.

When Sarah told me her eyes were green, my image of her seemed to jump into focus, becoming a vivid, full-colour picture in my mind. I couldn't help myself — I had to ask, 'Are you married? Do you have a partner?'

Laughing, she answered 'no' to both questions and we hardly stopped talking for the next 26 hours. Maybe the fact we're both Geminis helped, but from the word go we communicated really well, talking about anything and everything. Nickie didn't mind leaving us two lovebirds to it, and she headed back to her home in Helensville.

I soon learned that Sarah had lived a rich and varied life, and experienced many different things. She'd attained a degree in anthropology and Egyptology, and worked in London for four years in marketing, including one project with Richard Branson. She had travelled widely, both on business and for pleasure, and had seen much more of the world than I had been able to see on my travels abroad, especially as most of my trips were for international athletics meets where I saw little more than the airport, the stadium and the hotel. In 2001, Sarah had started her own interior design company which was now extremely successful.

She told me how from 2002 she had presented an interior design programme called *Changing Rooms* on New Zealand television for two years. She also spoke about the design column she wrote for a magazine and her regular speaking engagements to talk about design trends.

During that first evening together, Sarah slipped in the fact that she was a little nervous about her first triathlon on Sunday, the day after next, having started training the previous November. Blimey, I thought, she's also sporty! Partly as a way of getting to know her better, I asked her, 'How would you feel about guiding me on your bike while I run beside you?'

'I'd love to give it a try, but don't know whether I'll be fast enough,' she answered.

That was good enough for me; at least I had a pretext for contacting her after our first meeting, and perhaps someone else to train with. As things turned out I needn't have worried. At the end of an amazing evening, I went back to Sarah's house and we talked through the night before grabbing a couple of hours' sleep around dawn. It was incredible how we had sparked from the moment we met.

Around 9 a.m. we went together to register and rack her bike for Sunday's triathlon. I was a little apprehensive about meeting a couple of Sarah's closest friends, who in turn were intrigued about Sarah's new friend.

Sarah also had a two-hour talkback radio show on Radio Live, called 'Design and Build', on Saturday afternoons where she and 'Stan the builder' answered queries from callers about interior design or building work. The programme had nothing to do with sport or running, but Sarah insisted on having me as a guest on the show to talk about my achievements. She made a tenuous connection to interior design by talking briefly about the renovation of my home in England. Sarah found it fascinating that I had chosen the colour scheme for the house without any guidance.

Sarah may have fooled some of her listeners, but she didn't fool

237

her mum. After the show, Sarah got a call from her mum: 'Who was that guy you were flirting with on air?'

Although it hadn't even been 48 hours since we'd first met, Sarah and I were already pretty certain we wanted to spend the rest of our lives together — I was convinced I'd found my soulmate — so not surprisingly I was a little anxious when Sarah told me we were invited for Sunday dinner at the family home. I wanted to impress upon Sarah's family that I was worthy of their daughter's love and affection, and I hoped my being blind wouldn't be a problem.

I couldn't help but feel nervous about the visit. I didn't want to trip over anything, or make a mess while eating my food — I'm usually a very good eater and quite good at finding my mouth. Sarah assured me that everything would be fine, and I had a quiet word with myself to calm my nerves. I am so glad that once again I didn't take the easy option, which would have been to excuse myself and meet the Kerr clan at Sarah's house, which I felt was more familiar.

The family were out at the christening of Sarah's niece that afternoon, the daughter of her brother, Damian, and his wife, Tessa, but Sarah came back early to familiarise me with her parents' house before the clan arrived. We'd just finished the tour of the house and were in the garden when they joined us. I'd only just said hello to Sarah's parents, Sharron and Bruce Kerr, before Sharron showed me around her pride and joy, two and a half acres of gorgeous gardens, pointing out this plant or that tree and their buds and fruits; it was fantastic. Sarah joined us with a glass of vino which I managed to sip now and again. When we got back to the house, I met two of Sarah's nieces, Imogen, nine, and Isabella, two, and then she introduced me to Veronica, her sister, and her brother-in-law, Will, who owns Dale Carnegie in New Zealand and happens to be a motivational speaker.

It seemed to me that every second person I met in New Zealand had their own business; I later learned that this country is a land of entrepreneurs. Sarah's entire family are all entrepreneurs, owning their own businesses in insurance, sales, and of course interior design. It was helpful chatting with Will; I told him of my plans to join the circuit of motivational and after-dinner speakers in New Zealand, having enjoyed speaking in the UK, and he was able to give me some useful tips. Motivated, I got my speaking business up and running soon after emigrating, and have since spoken to corporations and groups across the country. However, I have barely scratched the surface and am really looking forward to speaking to many more businesses and individuals across New Zealand and Australia, as well as the UK.

After lunch, Sarah showed the video of me winning gold in Sydney to her family. I was actually a little emotional as well as proud of my achievement that day, mainly because Sarah and her family were watching it with me. I instantly loved Sarah's family — they were incredibly easy to get along with, and couldn't have been more welcoming or friendly. Sarah told me later that they thought I was a great guy and that we were perfect together.

Sarah and I were so sure of our future, and yet we'd only spent 11 days together, before the time came for me to leave New Zealand to return to the UK to run in the London Marathon. I had not been in full training for a month and I had been away from my regular guide runners, so it took some hard work to get up to speed. Paul Harwood and I prepared well and enjoyed a pretty good pre-marathon dinner of pasta and pizza, a good sleep and then a breakfast of croissants, cereal and toast — similar to the breakfast Haile Gebrselassie (the world record holder for the marathon) was having on the next table to ours at our hotel. Another important ingredient was having a few phone conversations with our wife and girlfriend respectively.

Paul and I were in a team of runners raising public awareness of the charity British Blind Sport (BBS), for which we wore bright-yellow singlets. The BBC's *Lifeline* programme wanted to film our preparation immediately before, as well as getting some footage during, the race. This was my fourth 'big city' marathon, Paul's twelfth, but you never quite get used to the size of the running crowd. There were nearly 40,000 runners gathered on Blackheath Common, all hoping to complete the 26.2 miles (42.1 km) to Westminster. It took a while to weave through the crowd and force our way through the thousands of runners to get to the front of the field and the start line. Paul and I shook hands with Gordon Ramsay (the celebrity chef), and wished each other a good run, and then the crowd were counting down the last 10 seconds to the start.

Paul did a great job of keeping me out of trouble and away from runners' heels which meant swerving from the road onto the grass and back, but thankfully after half a mile we had cleared the pack, and running became easier and more relaxed.

Having travelled up to London many times as a child with fairly good sight, I was able to visualise the landmarks as we approached them. Through my eyes as an eight-year-old, I could see the masts and rigging of the iconic tea-clipper, the *Cutty Sark*, at Greenwich around the 7 mile (11 km) mark, from when we toured the 19th century sailing ship as a family.

Close to the halfway point we crossed over Tower Bridge which I'd run over many times with Jim on lunchtime runs when I worked in London. I could clearly visualise both supporting pillars on either bank, the bridge spanning the Thames, and the two sections raised to allow passage for tall ships.

With each water station on Paul's side, the right, it was easy for him to pick up two bottles and pass one to me, until the water station at 16 miles which was on my side, the left. Paul had to drop the guide rope, letting me run free, come around behind me and pass me the water, then come back to pick up his end of the rope. Drinking water was the only time I became breathless and a little tense. Experience helped here; Paul told me to relax and regroup. I was surprised my mile times remained constant.

We were running really well, faster than I'd expected, and passed through the first 10 km in 37:40 and the half-marathon in just over 81 minutes. I was feeling strong and confident. However, from 18 miles (29 km) I really needed to work hard, concentrating on getting through each mile positively with no negative thoughts. I'd expected to be able to push on over the last mile, especially the last 400 m, but somehow I'd swapped my running shoes for diving boots (well, that's what it felt like) and I just couldn't move my legs any faster.

By this time, Paul and I had realised that the British record (2 hours 47 minutes, which I'd set in the Sydney Paralympics) wasn't possible, but with Paul helping to keep me focused, I was delighted to come home in 2 hours 49 minutes.

I'd begun to think that I would never run for Great Britain again — it would just be too hard — but then I received an email saying that I'd been selected for the marathon at the world championships for the disabled in the Netherlands in September 2006. I was delighted! The email went on to say that should I do well there, then there was a chance I would get my funding back, which strangely enough I wasn't sure I wanted.

At that stage I had just turned 45, and being a Lottery-funded athlete came with a lot of demands — I had to account for every mile I ran. Besides, I was looking forward to an exciting new life with Sarah in a new country. This said, the lure of continuing to compete internationally was irresistible. I was still ambitious and hungry to compete, and in no doubt that I was still capable of winning a medal.

The problem was that my heart was in New Zealand, but my guides and the races in which I needed to compete were in the UK and Europe. Sarah and I spoke for an hour a day, racking up enormous bills on the telephone, and she agreed to visit me in

England only 12 weeks after I had left her in New Zealand.

On 13 May, my regular taxi driver, Tom, took me to Heathrow to meet Sarah. Despite all the hours we'd spent on the phone, I was excited but also apprehensive as I waited for her to come through the gates. We'd only been together for 11 days in New Zealand, and three months had gone by since we'd last seen each other. Would she even remember what I looked like? It was important to me that I could impress her in my own environment by showing her I could walk around as easily as though I were sighted, and that I could cook for her.

In Auckland, I had been restricted to short walks with the long cane, unless I was being guided, as I didn't know the area and wasn't sure of finding my way home. In Leamington Spa, I had Joy and I knew the routes so well that I could go anywhere I wanted and at speed. Whilst the phone had enabled us to get to know each other better, would we feel the same way about each other once face to face again? I briefly wondered whether the two-week romantic holiday on a Greek island and in Turkey I'd planned might not be the best time or place to propose to Sarah.

What was I thinking? Sarah appeared through the arrival gates, came straight up to me, and kissed me — it was like we had never been apart. On the journey home, I felt sorry for Tom — I don't think he knew where to look, with all the snogging that was going on in the back seat. He didn't get much in the way of conversation! He was probably a little embarrassed at his fare behaving like a couple of love-struck teenagers.

That night I wowed Sarah with my spaghetti bolognese (which I had spent most of the previous evening cooking). The next day she got to see me race for the first time with Paul Harwood at the Warwick county championships, and then she met some of my mates in a pub that evening. Mike Peters took me to one side and said: 'How did an ugly bugger like you get a looker like her?'

My family had thought the world of Kath and were devastated by her death, so it was very important to me that they could see why I had fallen in love with Sarah. The next day, Sarah met Ange and my niece, Jade, in London, and they got on well from the start. While we were in London, I took her to St Paul's Cathedral. I told her that as a Member of the British Empire (MBE) I was entitled to marry there. She didn't seem too keen on the venue as it hadn't been too lucky for Charles and Diana, but at least she didn't seemed scared off by the implication.

Derek and Liz Jones, two of my closest friends, were next on the list, so off we went down to Sussex to see them. They are more like family to me than anything else, and were very close to Kath, so I really wanted them to love Sarah and see how happy we were together. I needn't have worried — Sarah swept them off their feet, and if they needed any further convincing of what an amazing and supportive partner Sarah was, her performance in Accident and Emergency later that day 'sewed' things up.

We had decided to go for a swim at the local health club. I came out of the changing room before the girls, and a guy who worked at the club guided me to the pool steps. I told him I wanted to jump in, but unfortunately I don't think he understood and guided me to the wrong place. The next thing I knew there was nothing under my left foot and I fell in, catching my left foot on a chipped, tiled step. I had to get out as my foot was painful. I was sat on the edge of the pool, holding my foot, when Sarah arrived; she asked what was wrong, then she saw the blood. A&E, X-rays, four local anaesthetic injections and three stitches later, I left the hospital, complete with crutch and a heavily bandaged foot. Sarah was brilliant and didn't complain once about her 'bloody boyfriend'.

With close family and friends introduced to Sarah, we were ready for our romantic holiday on a Greek island. I can't say it was the proudest moment of my life, getting a lift on a 'golf buggy' at Gatwick airport to the departure gate with the blue-rinse brigade. It was certainly an unwanted but unavoidable test of Sarah's patience, guiding me through airports, the Greek islands and Turkey with me not able to walk very far or very fast, but she took it all in her stride, even coping with climbing the steep cliffs of Pammukale in Turkey with me hobbling beside her.

I had planned to propose to Sarah at the right time during the holiday. After a couple of false starts I plucked up the courage on her birthday, 22 May. Getting down on one knee by the picturesque harbour of Symi, I popped the question. She didn't even hesitate, saying 'yes' straight away. We bought a bottle of Moet to celebrate and were dying to tell someone our good news, but it was too late to phone overseas, so we told the hotel owner that we had just got engaged, completely forgetting that I had booked the best room, saying we were on our honeymoon! Needless to say, we didn't quite get the reaction we were hoping for.

Four days later we had moved onto Bodrum in Turkey for the last few days of our holiday. There were a few 'must do's' while we were there. The first was seeing the beautiful Turkish rugs being made by hand. It was fascinating, seeing the framework the rugs were weaved on and learning something of each carpet's history. We bought a long carpet for a hallway we didn't yet have, but Sarah couldn't resist it. The next 'must do' for me was going to a barber shop to have a cut-throat shave — it certainly was a close shave, if not a little hair-raising at times. The most memorable part of the barber's treatment was when he set fire to my ear and nose hair without telling me what he was doing. I called out to Sarah who was having her nails done on the other side of the room to ask her what the hell was going on, as I felt a flame close to my ears. I think she was just as shocked as I was. The smell of burning hair was awful, but it was effective — the rogue hairs evaporated.

My birthday is four days after Sarah's, on 26 May. Sarah stunned and delighted me by giving me a white-gold antique Braille fob watch, complete with its chain, while we were at an incredibly romantic dinner overlooking a floodlit Turkish castle. Opening the lid, I instantly saw the face was Brailled. Sarah then told me the story of how she'd been inexplicably drawn to a fob watch four days before we met when looking for some pieces for a bar she was designing. Asking to see the watch, but not knowing why she was drawn to it, the shopkeeper told Sarah it had been made in Switzerland, so was of excellent quality, in the 1920s. He also told her that he had never had another fob like it, and when she opened the face, she saw that it was a Braille fob watch. She knew she wanted to buy it, but had no idea why. Call it serendipity or destiny — we both found it amazing.

We both knew that there was no way we would be apart from now on. Sarah's business was booming, and I really liked the idea of moving to New Zealand. There was no reason not to go.

Chapter 20 – Bright future

On our way home to New Zealand together, Sarah and I stopped off in Sydney. We took the train to Olympic Park where I hoped she would get a sense of the fantastic atmosphere I had experienced during the Paralympic Games. I had heard that medal winners from the games had their names recorded on bricks laid in Olympic Park, close by the stadium, so I was particularly keen to see that for myself.

Stepping on the double-decker train, I was taken back to the time immediately after I won gold in Sydney, when the whole carriage stood to applaud me. Once at Olympic Park, we found the bricks which had been set into a mosaic of gold, silver and bronze, depicting the rays of the sun. The bricks were laid out beneath what had once been the cauldron where the Olympic and Paralympic flames had burned. The Australians had tastefully and rather ingeniously converted it into a fountain.

With a squeal Sarah let me know she'd found the first brick with my name on it, recognising my silver medal in the 5000 m. She soon found the gold and other silver. There I was, 'Bob Matthews, Great Britain', and the bricks were clearly printed with raised letters so I could read them for myself. Blimey, those Aussies think of everything! It was emotional for us to see my name recorded in Olympic Park for eternity. It was a hot day, so we danced in the fountain to celebrate, oblivious of onlookers.

Moving to New Zealand was a huge step, not just for me, but also for Joy, my guide dog. Booking her a space in the cabin on our flight was the easy bit. Two months before the flight, we made the first of many visits to the vet, as Joy needed a series of tests to make sure she didn't bring any nasty diseases into New Zealand. Finally, armed with her pet passport complete with her photograph, Joy was ready to move to her new home in New Zealand. I knew Joy would take the journey in her stride. However, my main concern was whether she would be able to hold on for the toilet for the ten-plus hours to LA, and then another 12 hours to New Zealand. She was fine, though, and kept her paws crossed until we could speed her outside for a toilet stop.

It was refreshing to step outside Auckland airport into the fresh air, and I know Joy was glad we'd arrived. After the cobwebs were blown away, I realised Sarah hadn't been kidding about it being winter in New Zealand. It was 15 degrees, raining hard, and it was windy enough for a few trees to have been toppled, causing an electricity blackout across much of the city. Luckily, power was restored by nightfall, otherwise light-dependents wouldn't have known how to handle the dark.

Having slept the journey away, Joy showed no signs of jet lag. Our first few days back in Auckland were spent with Sharron and Bruce at their 2.5 acre farm. Joy loved it, spending every moment outside, investigating and chasing her ball like a puppy. I too was having a ball — Bruce even let me drive his ride-on lawn mower, and with his shouted directions I managed to avoid defoliating Sharron's beautiful flower beds.

Sharron and Bruce lived in a beautiful country home made cosy and warm by a very effective wood burner. When we moved into Sarah's fairly modern apartment in Ponsonby, which she shared with her girlfriend Susie, it came as a surprise just how chilly it can feel in Auckland. Certainly the North Island is considered to be subtropical, and so radiators and double-glazing aren't considered to be essential throughout the house as they are in England.

I received some great help and advice from the the Royal New Zealand Foundation of the Blind (RNZFB) who invited me to a selection of computer courses. Never did I think it possible for me to shop at a supermarket online or design my own web page.

Unfortunately I haven't yet mastered checking my bank, phone or power statements online, but I'd always been able to do this reading the statements in Braille. I was really surprised to learn that service providers do not offer this facility in New Zealand.

Joy and I had already found and become regulars at a really good café around the corner from our Ponsonby home, soon discovering how much better the coffee is in New Zealand than back home in England where it's difficult to get coffee any better than average. The RNZFB's Guide Dog Services (GDS) gave me fantastic assistance, accompanying Joy and me around the Ponsonby area, showing us safe places for crossing roads, or pointing out pedestrian crossings, teaching Joy to find the buttons which activate the lights and audible signal. I do this by showing her the box with the button, making a big fuss of her initially, and from then on I just need to say: 'Find the button' and she takes me right up to it. With help from GDS, we learned the route from Ponsonby to Sarah's work in Grey Lynn, 3 km away, which involved 23 road crossings.

Ponsonby was great, but it was soon obvious that an extra person and a large German shepherd weren't ideal in Sarah's apartment, which didn't have a garden, so we rented a house in Kohimarama in the waterfront bays area of Auckland. This was a great location for me. Within a ten-minute walk I could get a coffee or beer, or stroll on the beach. I loved it. The community of shops had everything we needed, and I could do the shopping, and so things were sorted for dinner when Sarah returned home in the evening. I really loved this part of Auckland.

We made the most of being so close to the beach, where Joy loved chasing toys and swimming. It was marvellous to be able to listen to the waves rolling onto the sand and smell the tang of the salty air as I walked along the beach or on the footpath. Just as good for me was being able to run along Tamaki Drive, the coastal road which twists and turns around the eastern bays for over 6 miles (10 km) from the city to St Heliers. I still love running here, with the sound of the sea close by, and can visualise

Rangitoto Island, the volcano that dominates the sea view from Auckland 3 miles (4.6 km) out in the harbour.

As soon as I'd arrived in New Zealand, I had looked for athletic clubs in order to find guide runners. I'd also joined the Les Mills gym where Gaz Brown, a personal fitness instructor, guided me around the friendly but rather noisy and cluttered-feeling gym twice per week. I'd have been a danger to myself and others had I attempted to do this on my own. The breakthrough came when I joined the YMCA marathon club in July; suddenly I had access to a number of potential guide runners. Andy Harper was my first guide, and he introduced me to Dave and Brent, but it was Cam Watts who became my most regular guide runner.

It was good to get back running again after sustaining my foot injury which had prevented me from training for six weeks. However, I was now obviously concerned about my ability to put in a good performance in the world championships for the disabled in Assen in the Netherlands, given that I only had 10 weeks to prepare for the marathon.

Cam quickly became confident at negotiating obstacles, and found the best way of guiding me over the tricky curbs around Auckland. These curbs are unlike any curbs I have seen around the world — the best way I can describe them is being akin to deep, ankle-turning gutters. When you are running at speed and can't see where you are going, there is a real risk of injury at any road crossing. For this reason, I do find it hard to relax on inner-city runs; given the choice, I much prefer training in the countryside, along the coastal road or on the running track.

Although Cam was a very good runner in his own right, he was soon calling me the 'run Nazi' as I insisted we should run through, not slow down before, the finishing line on all efforts. I was so used to hard training with more experienced track runners, such as Paul Harwood, who had agreed to be my guide runner in Assen.

Although I felt confident at the start of the marathon at the world champs, I was feeling the pressure after only 6.25 miles (10 km) when I realised just how short I was of speed endurance — I was having to work far too hard just to keep in touch with the leaders. The wheels finally fell off just after halfway when, for the first time in my life, I had to walk in a race. Not being able to train because of my foot injury had really taken its toll. However, I didn't regret taking this opportunity to run in Great Britain colours, as it turned out for the last time, and whereas fourth place was frustrating, it was also satisfying in so much as it showed what could have been achieved with a better build-up.

It was with Cam that I ran the Auckland Marathon in October 2006, my third marathon in fewer than seven months. The television cameras followed us most of the way from the start at Devonport. Similar to the Sydney Paralympic marathon six years earlier, the course took us over the harbour bridge. Unlike Sydney, however, there's a rather unfriendly 1 km climb to the apex of the bridge. It was great running around the familiar bays with the wind mostly behind us, until we turned back on ourselves and had a head wind for most of the last 7 miles (12 km). By concentrating on just one kilometre at a time, that last leg was just about manageable; even so, the last 2.5 miles (4 km) were done on memory. Seeing Sarah and Sharron as well as Bruce (who passed me water on the run) did help. Cam and I finished in 3:06, but blimey, I was a mess when I saw Sarah at the end. Fortunately, all the camera saw was me kissing her, not her propping me up and helping me dress. When we were home, I could do little more than vegetate — such a marked contrast to my experience at the London Marathon earlier that year.

Those first six months in New Zealand were exciting and very busy. I was back running regularly, writing my book, and starting my speaking career on the New Zealand circuit. I thoroughly enjoy being a motivational speaker, interacting with the audience and sharing my story.

Sarah and I were also planning and making the arrangements for our wedding, which was really exciting and just a little stressful. I was really disappointed, but understood that most of my family and close friends wouldn't be able to make the journey down under, but I was delighted that Derek and Liz Jones and Paul Rowe had said they would be able to join us. Mike and Zara Peters had also committed to fly out for the wedding. We found the perfect venue — Mantells in Mt Eden — and booked it for 18 March.

My sister, Sue, had already told me she wouldn't be able to make the wedding, and she didn't know when she and her family would be able to make it to New Zealand to visit us. It wouldn't have felt right for me to marry Sarah without Sue meeting her future sister-in-law first, so Sarah and I spent that Christmas before our New Zealand wedding holding a pre-wedding celebration in St Maarten, and were lucky enough to have both nieces there to enjoy the night. We also had further celebrations with Mum back in England.

By this time, my house in Leamington Spa had been on the market for some time with little serious interest. That changed big-time now that I had a professional interior designer on my side. Sarah was the perfect person to make the difference for prospective buyers. She chose new curtains, carpet and a colour scheme, and totally transformed the house. The proceeds from the sale arrived four months later.

It wasn't until we were sorting through my possessions accumulated throughout 40-odd years that it really hit me that I was leaving the country that I will always call home. It was hard to watch as my things were sorted into piles for the skip, car boot sales or the packing crate. I had to leave it to Sarah to make the decision of what stayed and what went. At first she involved me in the decision-making process, but as the time was short and the items plentiful after years of hoarding, she just had to be ruthless.

I still remind her she threw certain things out when I realise I don't have something. Eventually we boiled my worthwhile belongings down to a couple of cubic metres of 'stuff' to be shipped, including the mahogany coffee table I'd made at school, and my treadmill.

Twenty-two years before moving to New Zealand, when I had my last appointment at Moorfields Eye Hospital in London, I started accepting that it was unlikely I would ever see again. Wanting to find out more about the hereditary factor of RP, Sarah and I went to see an eye specialist, Dr Andrea Vincent, in Auckland. She was able to update us on the research underway around the world to halt and possibly reverse some eye conditions such as RP. She confirmed my form of RP was 'dominant' and the chances of passing it on were 50/50.

During the examination she noted that my cataracts were cloudy and that I could benefit from a simple procedure which would reduce the glare I've always struggled with in bright sunshine — for this reason, I always wear sunglasses outdoors. She likened my discomfort to being similar to the low sun hitting dust on the car windscreen and dazzling a sighted person. Although she made no promises of improved vision, she did say that it should make things more comfortable, even without sunglasses. I was delighted after the operation, finding it had made a difference. I didn't need to squint as much, and my face was much more relaxed.

Initially some people find it difficult to understand how sunglasses would help a blind person. I remember once overhearing a runner say after a race, 'That blind guy can obviously see — he's wearing sunglasses.' I found his short-sightedness amusing — perhaps his problem was that this blind bloke had soundly beaten him in the race.

Sarah and I found a perfect house to become our new family home. From the moment I walked into the house, it had a good feel about it. It was airy, and I could see daylight which seemed to be everywhere in this sunny open-plan home.

Only three weeks before our wedding, we were delighted when Ange gave us the brilliant news that she would be able to make it to New Zealand for our wedding. As adults, we have become much closer, and it was great to spend quality time together and for Sarah to get to know her sister-in-law better. We had no qualms about only taking a three-day honeymoon as it meant we'd have more time with Ange before she flew home. It felt so right to have at least one member of my immediate family at our wedding. My close mate, Paul Harwood, had tried hard to make it, but unfortunately it wasn't possible for him.

Andy Harper, who'd started me running in New Zealand, and Bruce, my father-in-law-to-be, jointly organised my stag do and booked a boat to go fishing one evening. Seventeen of us had gone fewer than 500 m when the captain cut the engine, anchored, and told us that he had heard the fish had been biting in this area earlier that morning. We were a little sceptical, but the first hook had hardly broken the surface when the first snapper gave himself up. It was amazing — no sooner were the hooks baited and lowered to the ocean floor than another fish was being reeled in. At first it seemed as though I attracted the clever fish that were able to nibble the bait off my hook. I moved to the stern and changed my bait, and in 15 minutes had brought in six big snapper ranging from 31 cm to 41 cm in length. In an hour we'd reeled in 45 big snapper. It was the first time I'd held a rod since I was six on Rochester Pier. It was a marvellous evening.

With the fish safely on ice, we visited a couple of bars before going to the Ice Bar on Auckland's Princes Wharf, where you need to dress in a fur coat and gloves. The bar is carved out of ice, and it's maintained at a chilly five degrees below freezing. There were sculptures all around the room which I had great fun investigating. However, there was still some drinking to be done, and in the Ice Bar the drinks are all vodka-based as it doesn't freeze. They are served in glasses also made out of ice, and go down the drain when you have finished with them. The whole evening was great fun — I loved being able to share it with some great mates, including Damian, Sarah's brother, and Will, her brother-in-law.

The night before our wedding, Sarah spent the night with her parents, Bruce and Sharron — her last night as a single girl. She needed some space as our house was filled with the English mafia. The next time I saw my bride was a few hours before our wedding when I got to have a good look at her in her wedding dress on the balcony of our hotel overlooking the Pacific Ocean. Sarah looked so beautiful I could hardly credit the fact that this woman would be my wife very soon.

We arrived at Mantells in a 1950s Silver Shadow Rolls Royce. I didn't want to miss an opportunity like this to ride in such a magnificent car. I was dropped off while Sarah, Sharron and Bruce drove around the block. The first person I saw was Paul Rowe dressed in his ancestors' tartan. I'd never had the opportunity to look at a scotsman's kilt and sporran, and it was fascinating. When I'd given him the once-over he carried the rings around for everyone to give their blessing before the ceremony started. Sarah's two best friends since infant school were involved in the wedding. Rachel was the official photographer and Annie read a verse, as did Mike.

Apart from the bride's entry, one of the highlights of the wedding was the performance by Sarah's sister, Veronica, who sang beautifully. Sarah was in tears and I don't think she was the only one. Will was the MC. He comes across as a quiet, thoughtful chap, but as MC he was transformed into a witty, entertaining performer — he was absolutely perfect for the job. All of the speeches went down well; in fact someone commented it was like listening to a string of professional speakers. During his speech, Bruce shared the family rules with the guests:

- Do not expect 45 snapper on every fishing trip.
- Do not anticipate any male member of the family — namely Damian, Will or myself — will be your guide runner. At your pace, you are on your own, buddy.
- And again from the males — in our company, do please always keep your shirt on in public.
- Health and safety warning — always allow ample room when jiving on the dance floor with Sarah.
- Do not mortgage your house on winning the duet section of *NZ Idol* with your new wife.
- Do explain some time how you are able to deal the cards without reading the Braille numbers.
- Don't expect us to begin following your beloved football — unless of course New Zealand makes the World Cup again.
- You can expect us to support England — whenever they are playing Australia.
- This one, you are already on to — when the females of the family are gathered, do not expect to be able to finish a sentence, or to get a word in edgeways.
- And finally, you can expect our total and full support in your married life with your Sarah.

One of the things I love about Sarah's family and our friends is the fact that they don't treat me like I am blind. I'm just Rob, a son-in-law, a brother-in-law and a mate. They are just so natural and they look me straight in the eye when we're talking. It's often something I'm aware of because you can hear when someone you are talking to is looking away from you. People that really know me don't watch what they say and will naturally say, 'Rob, did you see the cricket?' or 'Rob, have a look at this.' Sarah often says she forgets I can't see, and so do our friends and family.

This means a lot to me. Treating me differently makes me feel blind. I have a strong visual memory because I didn't lose all my useful vision until I was 20. I clearly remember colours, scenery and what things look like, so I am no different from anyone else when I say 'I watched the game'. Sometimes, I think sighted people might think this is a bit strange, but it's just normal for me to visualise whatever I am 'watching' on the television. I feel like I am just like anyone else.

I really have been on what seems like a very long and difficult journey. I have come from a very dark, lonely and traumatic place, when Kath died so suddenly, to meeting Sarah and moving to New Zealand. I am so happy with this space I'm in, and am looking forward to spending the rest of my life with this wonderful, gifted and beautiful woman. I am so grateful that Sarah came into my life. I really can't believe what a lucky bloke I am and that she should have chosen to spend the rest of her life with me. She is not only gorgeous, but gifted, funny and kind.

If I thought things were perfect before, I was wrong — they got even better two weeks after the wedding when Sarah discovered she was pregnant! 'Blimey, it's official. I am super sperm,' I thought. We were absolutely delighted as I was 45 years old and didn't think I would ever be a father. We knew the risk of our baby inheriting RP was a 50/50 chance, but this baby would be absolutely loved, and we would cross that bridge if we needed to. All tests to date show that Thomas is not affected by the gene.

Just after midnight on Wednesday 24 October, Neil Buddicom, our obstetrician, made the decision to deliver Thomas by C-section, as 18 hours of labour were enough for mother and baby. The decision made, things happened incredibly quickly. Bruce and Veronica, who had been with us the whole time at the hospital, waited outside while Sharron acted as my eyes and went with me into the operating theatre. While we changed into surgical cap and gown, rather bizarrely I found myself chatting about running with the South African anaesthetist. We talked briefly about our running careers and he told me that his cousin was also a Paralympian.

I was sitting beside Sarah, dreading what Neil was about to do to my beautiful wife, when moments later Neil was lifting up my son, Thomas, and we heard the magical sound of him crying for the first time. The procedure from beginning to end took seven minutes; Thomas was born at 12.50 a.m. We were so impressed with how professionally Neil and his team had handled everything. Quickly the nurses checked Thomas over, and then I cut the umbilical cord. He was weighed and measured — a healthy 8 pounds 11 ounces (3.94 kg) — and then, while he was still wet, I had my first chance to hold my son. He was very annoyed at having been removed from his warm home into this strange, brightly lit place, and my overriding image of him was how large his feet seemed.

Nothing can prepare you for holding your son in your arms for the first time. This tiny perfect bundle with tiny hands, ears and nose seemed so vulnerable — feelings of love and connection washed over me. I was so proud of Sarah bringing our healthy little boy into our life, and I felt so proud to be a daddy. Blimey, after all these years, I was a daddy! We left a happy, knackered Sarah and a sleeping Thomas at the hospital, hearing the birds twittering as dawn broke.

If proof of my feelings for this latest addition to our life were needed, Thomas was just 18 hours old when I had to take him for an X-ray as it was feared his intestines might be blocked. He'd brought up some greenish bile which sometimes indicates a blockage. I stood by impotently as the radiologists inserted a tube up his nose into his stomach and pumped some dye into him which would help highlight any abnormality, all the time Thomas crying his eyes out. I was one relieved dad when they told me he was fine, but it was one of the hardest things I've ever had to endure.

When Thomas was only six weeks old, Sarah and I took him to my eye specialist to try to determine whether he had inherited my RP. It was a horrible experience for the three of us. He was unhappy about the specialist shining a bright light in his eyes, but when she needed to clamp each eye open to get a clear view of the retinas, I needed to hold him firmly while tears flowed down his beautiful little face. This was my gorgeous son and I felt dreadful putting him through this ordeal; I felt responsible for him being here.

Talking it over beforehand, Sarah and I agreed that, should he inherit RP, he would understand from my example, as I had from my dad, that doors would remain open to him, and that with enough determination and drive, anything would be achievable. However, when it came down to it, I was really nervous. How would I feel if she told us he had RP? Might his early life mirror mine, going from one specialist to another? As Thomas screamed, Sarah sat in the room, crying and scared. The procedure only took two minutes, but seemed to last for ever.

We breathed a sigh of relief when the specialist told us that his retinas appeared to be perfect. What a relief — we were delighted! However, with her next breath she brought us down to earth, saying there was no indication of 'early onset' RP. So in effect, we'd put him through all that discomfort to learn that at this stage he showed no sign of having RP. We left the hospital feeling positive about his eyesight; the specialist had said they were perfect, and it was what we wanted to hear.

When we took Thomas back, aged one, the specialist looked into his eyes, and she again noted that his eyes were perfectly normal and the retinas were healthy. At least this time he was old enough for her to be able to distract him with toy cars, which he loved, as he sat quietly on my knee while she looked at the back of his eyes.

We were asked if we would like a blood test to be done to compare Thomas's genes with mine; this would provide us with one hundred per cent certainty whether my son had the RP gene or not. My blood had already been taken and sent to Estonia, of all places, where the records of faulty RP genes are kept and identified. However, Sarah and I decided not to have this test performed, as what would it prove? Would we treat him differently, or would it be better to treat our son as a fully sighted little boy (which he is, and hopefully always will be)?

When Mum made the journey from England to see her first grandson, her comments greatly assured us: 'Thomas is much more confident in uncertain light than you were, Rob,' she said.

Nothing can be done right now to prevent RP, but we are keeping tabs on any medical advances. Current research results are hopeful — perhaps in the not too distant future, gene therapy will halt its progression so any child born with the rogue gene could retain the vision they were born with. Who knows? Perhaps one day I too may be able to see again.

Having gone through this with Thomas, Sarah and I decided that, should we have another child, we would opt for a procedure called Pre-Genetic Determination (PGD). PGD involves going through IVF and then the embryos are tested to see whether they have the RP gene. If the embryo doesn't appear to show signs of RP, it will be implanted in the uterus. There remains a chance the gene may slip through, but it's only a 5 per cent chance, which is infinitely better than the current 50/50 risk. We have been accepted as PGD candidates and are currently going through the process of tests.

Being a parent has really changed the way I look at life. I can't believe how much my son changes every day — from his first smiles to copying my actions and blowing raspberries back at me. He melted my heart when his first word was 'Dadda'. Thomas has inherited Sarah's lovely smile and infectious laughter, and is developing into quite a chatterer. He has developed his own hilarious language — who knows what 'goggie gog' means, but he says it a lot.

I'm in the enviable position of being able to spend much of my time with Thomas, and I try to be an active dad, showering or bathing him, dressing him, and teaching him things. When he was very little, we established a routine in the morning where I would take him downstairs and, while he was drinking his bottle, we would watch the football from England; of course he always clapped for Chelsea.

By the time Thomas was eight months old, he had learned to roll around the floor and was starting to crawl. I clearly remember bringing him downstairs one morning and leaving him in the middle of the rug as usual for a moment while I fixed his bottle. When I went back to pick him up, I could only find empty space. The thought flashed through my mind, 'Bloody hell, I've lost our son,' then I looked under the coffee table, and there he was, making his escape. Since he was three months old, I've been able to put him in a baby-carrying backpack and we go for walks with Joy. I'm used to people telling me what a great-looking dog I have, and then they see the cute baby on my back — honestly, I feel like a spare sometimes.

The day before his first birthday, he was up and walking, and from then on he was off and literally running. I might find my running machine a means to an end, but from 14 months Thomas would trot up to it, climb on and run on the spot until I turned it on for him, and then he'd be away. He's now so fast that I have had to put bells around his ankle so I can keep up with him when he's on the move. It certainly looks as though I have a guide runner in the making. I love the idea of running with my son, and he gives me the incentive to stay young and fit to be a part of his future.

Sarah and I have learned such a lot from Thomas about not taking things for granted. For instance, when he was 19 months old, we learned never to step outside, even for five seconds, unless we had a house key. I was out running early one morning, and Sarah was home with Thomas. She popped out to put some rubbish in the bin, only to find Thomas had bolted the door. Dressed only in a dressing gown, she had to go to the neighbours to phone her dad who had a spare key, then watch helplessly as Thomas pulled down and unwrapped his cousin's birthday present. At least Joy stayed close to him, ensuring he came to no harm.

I try to be as good a dad to Thomas as my dad was to us — loving and kind, firm but fair, giving advice, not thrusting it upon him. Hopefully we'll develop our relationship into best mates, like Dad and I did. It really is an amazing feeling to be loved unconditionally by your son. Thomas doesn't know that I am blind, and he doesn't care. It isn't a big deal. And why should it be? It wasn't a big deal for my dad, or my mum and sisters, and it wasn't a big deal for me.

Joy has coped incredibly well with this strange squawking bundle of energy foisted upon her. She is remarkably tolerant of him following her around and grabbing at her, often coming away with little handfuls of hair. He is, however, learning to be more gentle and appreciate her more with gentle pats instead of treating her as though she were a drum, leaning on her rather than sitting on her, and even jumping on her and trying to catch a ride. She's withstood this with incredible patience, with never so much as a growl, let alone a nip. Thomas doesn't know how lucky he is. Obviously we'll teach him to be much more circumspect with other dogs.

I had a dream of carrying Thomas around on a lap of honour following a Paralympic success, but in order to do this, I first had to get fit, and then be good enough to be selected to run for my country again. The first thing I needed to sort out was my New Zealand residency. I had set the ball rolling to gain residency as soon as I arrived, and had employed the services of an immigration lawyer. It was necessary for me to use a lawyer as, being blind, I would have to have jumped through all sorts of hoops, with no guarantee of success at the end.

The lawyer made the case that our relationship was a genuine love story, not a marriage of convenience. He also emphasised the fact that I would be self-employed in careers which didn't require vision, such as speaking, sports massage and as an author. As such, I wasn't just coming into New Zealand looking for a free meal ticket on tax payers' money. My permanent residency for New Zealand came through in July 2007.

I really wanted to support and embrace my new country, and I let my heart rule my head — I made the decision to run for New Zealand in Beijing in what would have been my final Paralympics. I signed over my rights to run for Great Britain to run for my new country.

With the benefit of hindsight, switching countries was a mistake. I discovered in March that I had to run a medal-winning time of 4:15 for the 1500 m to qualify for the New Zealand Paralympic team. This was 7 seconds faster than the Great Britain qualifying time. You'd have thought I might have discovered this before burning my bridges, but I'd just assumed New Zealand would have similar qualification times to those of Great Britain. Anyway, I knew I could do this time — I held the world record at 4:05, for goodness' sake, but I was starting to worry. Did I still have the ability to get up to that sort of speed in the short timeframe, given I had only trained for the longer distances since the Sydney Games in 2000?

The Beijing Paralympic Games in 2008 surely had to be my final games. As I had been a 1500 m runner at the beginning of my athletics career, I felt my best chance of winning a medal would be at the shorter distance. The other reason I chose the 1500 m was that the organisers, in an effort to abbreviate the programme, had decided to combine some of the events; the T11 totally blind athletes (my category) would be competing against the T12 and T13 partially sighted athletes in the 10,000 m and the marathon. As a result of this, the qualifying standards went through the ceiling for the blind athletes. For example, my personal best for the marathon is 2:47 and I believe I'm capable of improving my time by 8 minutes, but running against the partially sighted athletes, I would need to improve my personal best by at least 13 minutes to 2:34 to stand a chance of winning a medal.

The 1500 m was familiar territory, and I felt that the 4:15 qualifying time was achievable, but my issue was that I needed faster guides to train with — and I needed them quickly. I had been looking for good-quality 1500 m runners for months, and in March I struck gold when Nick Buck and Greg Thompson offered to run with me. I also met Graham Sims, an ex-All Black, who coached and supported me. All three became good friends and helped my preparations for Beijing. I made the pre-qualifying standard with Nick of 4:34.9 in April for the 1500 m which was also a new New Zealand record. Paralympics New Zealand granted me another six weeks to knock the other 20 seconds off, but it was the end of the racing season in the Southern Hemisphere, and the only option for me was to race in England. I knew my best chance stood in going back home to train with Paul Harwood who knew how to whip me into shape.

All of this was fine, but this decision meant spending two months away from Sarah and Thomas, who was then six months old. He was changing every day and I would miss so much of his development during the next few weeks.

Back in the UK, Paul and I trained hard — so hard I usually had a headache from the lactic acid which accumulates during intense sessions on the track. I got my time down to 4:27 when I won the Warwickshire county track championships age group category against fully sighted runners. After only 10 weeks of specific training, it was a good result, but time had run out. It seems the older you get, the harder you have to train for smaller gains — certainly I'd never trained so hard to run so slow, but Paul and I felt things were falling into place and knew the times would have come very soon.

This wasn't good enough to qualify me for the NZ Paralympic team. Ironically, had I stayed with Great Britain, I would have only been 5 seconds away from their qualifying time, and it is likely that I would have run in Beijing in my eighth Paralympic Games. What made things even more frustrating was that I knew that I was capable of running sub-4:15 that September, which would have won a medal in the Paralympic Games.

It was incredibly disappointing. Not only did I have to accept that my international athletics career was most likely over, but it was over without my having had the opportunity to really give it my best shot. Had I found faster guides to train with earlier, things could well have been different.

But then, maybe eight Paralympic Games would have been a little greedy. I've achieved so much and have so many fantastic memories from the 25 years of my international athletic career, and I have nothing more to prove. I've been very successful: I improved the 800 m world record from 2:15 to 1:59.9, the 1500 m from 4:31 to 4:05.11, and the 5000 m from 18:13 to 15:43.4. I was credited with being the most successful totally blind athlete throughout the 1980s and 1990s by the International Blind Sports Association (IBSA), and my achievements were recognised with an MBE after my first three Paralympic gold medals, as well as the two honorary MA degrees more recently. It would be fantastic were the MBE upgraded to an OBE for my services to sport for the disabled, having won five Paralympic gold medals and set eight world records subsequent to my investiture in 1987. Who knows? It could yet happen.

However, retiring from international athletics left me with something of a void in my life. Being a runner and a Paralympian was so much a part of who I was, and for the four years leading up to each Paralympic Games, they were my focus — they were what drove me. Sarah really helped me look towards the future. She reminded me that I could still run competitively and encouraged me to tell my story as a motivational speaker. I knew I was fit and ambitious, and I just needed to find other sporting goals on which I could focus my energy.

A friend suggested the open-water swim from Rangitoto Island across the approaches to Auckland's Waitemata Harbour to St Heliers beach, a distance of 2.88 miles (4.6 km). To give me extra motivation I announced my intention to do the swim during an interview on national television, so I couldn't back out! Greg Thompson turned from guide runner to guide swimmer in November 2008 and introduced me to the water. The first thing we had to do was figure out how to swim together. We agreed that synchronising our legs would be much simpler than trying to synchronise our arms, and we fashioned the inner tube of a bicycle into a guide rope by looping one end around my knee and the other around Greg's ankle so that he'd be half a body length ahead of me, making clashing of arms less likely.

With some practice we soon got the hang of it, but the person who really brought my swimming on in leaps and bounds was Spencer Vickers who is a very good triathlete and swim coach. Coaching and training me for the Rangitoto swim certainly challenged him, but gradually I went from a slow-moving agitator of the water into something resembling a swimmer.

I'm a runner, and to me, running seems so simple — you just put one foot in front of the other and cover the ground as quickly as you can. However, I'm not a natural swimmer — it's so technical! In the water you can't breathe when you want to. I've learned how important it is to be aware of where your body is in the water — as Spencer kept reminding me, I had to 'lift my arse'. Not being able to swim in a straight line has been something of a disadvantage, not least because anyone else in my lane in the swimming pool is taken out as I veer across it. Alone in the lane I'm quite good at inflicting damage upon myself, either by catching the lane rope with elbow and fingers or smacking my elbow against the wall.

The day of the swim arrived — 1 March 2009 — and we stepped

off the boat onto Rangitoto Island to find it was a beautiful day with a flat, calm sea. 'There is a god,' I thought. It had been a different story 24 hours earlier, when there had been 3 m swells and the race was on the point of being cancelled. This race had a deep-water start, so Spencer and I jumped in and waited for it to begin. It was marvellous, floating around with the sunshine reflecting off the sea near the start line, and hearing the other 450 swimmers jumping into the sea around me like so many penguins leaving their colony. With the sound of the claxon, we were off. I had a quick word with myself and remembered to relax and not to panic in those first 200 m or so, but once I got into my stroke I really enjoyed the crossing, feeling the improvement I'd made, 'grabbing' the water and pulling myself along.

Along with my poor technique, the most difficult aspect of swimming for me is the loss of hearing and spatial awareness. I asked Spencer twice how long we'd been swimming, but mainly I depended on counting my strokes. I reckoned a stroke equated to a metre, which helped me figure out roughly how far I had swum, although counting out 4600 strokes, I did lose count a few times. I had almost touched St Heliers beach when, through the water, I could hear Sarah, Sharron and Veronica, ably backed up by Bruce, Will, the kids and some of my massage clients who were waiting on the sand, supporting me. It was the first time I've ever really entered an event with the aim of just getting to the finish line, but even so, I managed to swim the 4.6 km in 1 hour 45 minutes which was 15 minutes faster than expected. I was chuffed!

The 'King of the Bays' swim six weeks later emphasised the extremes of open-water swimming. This was a shorter distance — 1.75 miles (2.8 km) — than the Rangitoto swim, along Auckland's North Shore from Milford to Takapuna beach, but the conditions were horrible. A strong onshore wind was blowing the waves onto the beach, and from the moment we ran into the sea I had water up my nose. I was starting to panic and wondering whether the prudent thing to do was pull out, but I didn't. I'm so pleased to say that I pushed on and finished the race in 1 hour 20 minutes.

The training and discipline required for these swims has been great, and really helped me maintain my fitness for my next sporting challenge. I am training hard to keep improving my swimming and cycling as well as running because I have been selected to compete for New Zealand in the World Paralympic Triathlon Championships in Australia in September 2009. You never know — I might take the Queen's advice and aim at the London 2012 Paralympic Games, this time in the tandem cycling discipline.

Sarah blinked and her mouth dropped open when I told her of my desire to compete in the Polar Challenge which is a 650 km ski race where teams of three pull their own equipment from Canada to the North Pole in fewer than four weeks. Having closed her mouth, Sarah laughed and said, 'Well, I didn't fall in love with just any ordinary bloke, did I?' Alongside raising enough sponsorship, the toughest aspect of this challenge will be leaving Sarah and Thomas behind in New Zealand.

If my life's journey has taught me one thing, it is not to give up. I could have easily taken blindness as my lot in life, and used my lack of vision as an excuse to have a less than extraordinary life. I am so pleased that my positive attitude to my blindness has dictated the direction my life has taken.

I have had a successful running career, and I'm so grateful to athletics in general, which has been my life, and to my guide runners in particular, for giving me the opportunity to find myself. Running has allowed me to dream. It's given me confidence and self-esteem, and enabled me to see that I'm inferior to no one. It's convinced me that anything is possible.

I've met some terrific people, travelled around the world, and visited some amazing places. Athletics has given me all of this, but most of all, athletics has given me friendship. Running over 100,000 miles (160,000 km) with over 100 guide runners on the other end of a piece of rope forms an incredible bond, and builds mutual trust in one another. Even though I've lost touch with some, I'm proud to call many of them close friends.

And of course, athletics has also given me something to write about.

Yes, I've had an extraordinary life. I've been fortunate to know the love of two incredible women, and to experience the immense love for my own son. I have had the support and love of family, friends and guide runners who have enabled me, with their descriptions, to see through their eyes.

I know that my future will be bright, but most of all, I know that it won't be ordinary.

Appendix

ROB MATTHEWS MBE, MA (Hons)

AWARDS PRESENTED

Year	Award
1983	Runner-up for the ITV World of Sport Courage Award
1984	Named one of the 12 Access 'Men of the Year' for outstanding contribution to athletics
1984	Named the Sports Writers' Association Disabled Sports Personality of the Year
1984	Runner-up for the ITV World of Sport Courage Award
1987	Made a Member of the Order of the British Empire (MBE) by Her Majesty the Queen
1988	Radio Kent Sports Personality of the Year
1989	Received the Evian Health and Fitness Award for Outstanding Achievements in Sport
1991	Hereford Disabled Sports Personality of the Year
1991	Hereford Men's Sports Personality of the Year
1992	Hereford Men's Sports Personality of the Year
1996	Royal Mail award for the Paralympian Who Best Embodied the Paralympic Spirit
2001	Honorary Master of Arts degree, University of Warwick
2004	Inducted into the BBC Hall of Fame (Midlands)
2006	Honorary Master of Arts degree, University of Worcester

BEST PERFORMANCES

Status	Event	Event time	Date	Location
World record	800 m	1:59.90	July 1986	Brighton
World best	1000 m	2:38.00	August 1986	Medway
World record	1500 m	4:05.11	June 1989	Crystal Palace
World best	1 mile	4:33.40	August 1986	Birmingham

Status	Event	Event time	Date	Location
World best	3000 m	8:55.00	August 1989	Sutton Coldfield
European record	5000 m	15:43.40	May 1989	Crystal Palace
European best	5 miles	26:36.00	April 1992	Weston-super-Mare
World best	10 km road	32:42.00	January 1992	Hereford
British record	10,000 m	34:33.50	July 2004	Leamington Spa, Warwickshire
World best	10 miles	55:03.00	January 1988	Canterbury
British best	Half-marathon	75:20.00	September 2003	Kenilworth, Warwickshire
British best	Marathon	2:47:38	October 2000	Sydney, Australia
New Zealand best	1500 m	4:27.01	May 2008	Nottingham

PARALYMPIC GAMES

Date	City	Country	Event	Result
1984	Long Island, New York	USA	800 m 1500 m 5000 m	Gold Gold Gold
1988	Seoul	South Korea	800 m 1500 m 5000 m	Gold Gold Gold
1992	Barcelona	Spain	800 m 1500 m 5000 m	Silver Bronze Gold
1996	Atlanta	USA	1500 m	Silver
2000	Sydney	Australia	5000 m 10,000 m Marathon	Silver Gold Silver
2004	Athens	Greece	5000 m 10,000 m	6th place 5th place

WORLD CHAMPIONSHIPS

Date	City	Country	Event	Result
1986	Gothenburg	Sweden	800 m 1500 m 5000 m	Gold Gold Gold
1990	Assen	Netherlands	4 x 400 m 1500 m 5000 m	Gold Gold Gold
1994	Berlin	Germany	1500 m 10,000 m	Silver Bronze
2003	Quebec	Canada	5000 m 10,000 m	Silver 4th place
2004	Athens	Greece	5000 m 10,000 m	6th place 5th place
2006	Assen	Netherlands	Marathon	4th place

INTERNATIONAL EVENTS

Date	City	Country	Event	Result
1990	Melbourne	Australia	800 m 1500 m 5000 m	Gold Gold Gold
2000	London	England	Marathon	2:53:18
2006	London	England	Marathon	2:49:25
2006	Auckland	New Zealand	Marathon	3:06:00
2008	Nottingham	England	1500 m	NZ national record

EUROPEAN CHAMPIONSHIPS

Date	City	Country	Event	Result
1983	Varna	Bulgaria	800 m 1500 m 5000 m	Gold Gold Gold
1987	Moscow	USSR	800 m 1500 m 5000 m	Gold Gold Gold
1989	Zurich	Switzerland	800 m 1500 m 5000 m	Gold Gold Gold
1991	Caen	France	4 x 100 m 4 x 400 m 800 m 1500 m 5000 m	Bronze Gold Bronze Gold Gold
1999	Lisbon	Portugal	1500 m 5000 m	Gold Gold
2005	Helsinki	Finland	5000 m	Gold